RICE IN MALAYA

RICE
IN MALAYA

A Study in
Historical Geography

R.D. HILL

KUALA LUMPUR
OXFORD UNIVERSITY PRESS
OXFORD NEW YORK MELBOURNE
1977

Oxford University Press
OXFORD LONDON GLASGOW
NEW YORK TORONTO MELBOURNE WELLINGTON
IBADAN NAIROBI DAR ES SALAAM LUSAKA CAPE TOWN
KUALA LUMPUR SINGAPORE JAKARTA HONG KONG TOKYO
DELHI BOMBAY CALCUTTA MADRAS KARACHI
© *Oxford University Press 1977*
ISBN 0 19 580335 3

Printed by Wan Fung Printing Co.
Published by Oxford University Press, 3, Jalan 13/3, Petaling Jaya,
Selangor, Malaysia

For Foon

Acknowledgements

To my wife go thanks for her forbearance with the inevitable stresses generated by my major preoccupation over a long period. My periodical absences in the field and whilst doing archival research cannot have made things easy. She was also a cheerful companion during travels in Sabah, Thailand, central Luzon and many parts of Malaya. In addition she assisted in the location of the innumerable place-names mentioned in the sources and finally brought her editorial expertise to bear on successive drafts of the manuscript.

It is my pleasure to acknowledge the very material aid of the following who helped me obtain sometimes exceedingly obscure materials: the Director of the National Archives, Kuala Lumpur, and his staff; Datin Patricia Lim, Librarian, Institute of Southeast Asian Studies; Miss Manijeh Namazie, Reference Librarian, University of Singapore Library and her staff; Mrs. Yoke-Lan Wicks, Deputy-Director, National Library, Singapore, and her staff. The Commissioner of Lands, Penang, kindly allowed access to records in George Town.

A host of others helped me more than they know: Haji Ani b. Arope and Dr. Peter Goethals in Trengganu, Agricultural Officers and District Officers throughout Malaya, my former colleagues of the University of Singapore, especially Dr. Tham Seong Chee, Dr. Zahri Azhari, Dr. Geoffrey Benjamin, Dr. Hsuan Keng, Dr. Sharom Ahmat and above all, Professor Ooi Jin Bee who not only went through the final draft of the manuscript in detail but also provided a number of valuable suggestions. Professor Paul Wheatley of the University of Chicago and Professor Wilhelm G. Solheim II of the University of Hawaii kindly commented at length on the earlier chapters. The fact that I have not always followed their suggestions in no way diminishes my gratitude for those that I have accepted. Drs. E.S. Simpson and C.M. Turnbull very kindly commented upon the final draft.

On the technical side, it is my pleasure to acknowledge the aid of Miss Julie Yeo, Mrs. Lim Kim Leng, Mr. Poon Puay Kee, Mr. Wong Weng Kong and especially Mr. Dominic Wong, all of the Geography Department, University of Singapore, and Mr. Charlie Ng, photographer of the University of Singapore Library.

Miss Meimei Wong, assisted by Miss Betty Chun Kar Yee, both of the Department of Geography and Geology, University of Hong Kong, very efficiently typed the final drafts of the manuscript.

Department of Geography and Geology   R.D. HILL
University of Hong Kong
July 1975

Contents

Tables

Figures

Abbreviations

Ag	Acting
AR	Annual Report
BPDO	Batang Padang District Office
BR	British Resident
CLR	Commissioner of Land Revenue
CO	Colonial Office
Col. Sec.	Colonial Secretary
DM	District Magistrate
DO	District Officer
EIC	[British] East India Company
encl.	enclosure
FMS	Federated Malay States
FMSAR	*Federated Malay States Annual Report*
GGPWISM	*Government Gazette, Prince of Wales Island, Singapore, Malacca*
HC	High Commissioner
IOL	India Office Library
JMBRAS	*Journal of the Malayan Branch, Royal Asiatic Society*
JP	*Jawi Peranakan*
JSBRAS	*Journal of the Straits Branch, Royal Asiatic Society*
K.	*Kuala* (river-mouth)
KDO	Kuantan District Office
Kg.	*Kampong* (village)
KLO	Kinta Land Office
MJLB	Maharajah of Johore, Letter Book
.MR	Monthly Report
NSSS	Negri Sembilan State Secretariat
perm.	*permatang*
PG	*Pinang Gazette*
PGG	*Perak Government Gazette*
PP	*Parliamentary Paper*, Great Britain
PRM	*Penang Register and Miscellany*
PWI	Prince of Wales Island (Pulau Pinang)
PWIGG	*Prince of Wales Island Government Gazette*
RDM	Resident's Diary, Malacca
S.	*sungei, sungai* (river)
SCCR	*Singapore Chronicle and Commercial Register*
SDT	*Singapore Daily Times*
SFP	*Singapore Free Press*

SFPW	*Singapore Free Press Weekly*
SS	Straits Settlements
SSAR	*Straits Settlements Annual Report*
SSGG	*Straits Settlements Government Gazette*
SSS	Selangor State Secretariat
ST	*Straits Times*
TDO	Temerloh District Office
VNL	Vajiranana National Library

Preface

THE importance of rice in the life of the great majority of Asians needs no emphasis. For most, rice is literally 'food' and other comestibles are something to be eaten with food. Thus for Malays, *nasi* is food in general as well as cooked rice in particular. Moreover, the great majority of Asians not only eat rice as the staple food, but most of them, except in the north-west of the Indian sub-continent and in northern China, also grow it. In this the peoples of Malaya, now Peninsular Malaysia, are exceptional in that the descendants of the Chinese and Indian immigrant communities, neither now nor in the past, have taken a significant part in rice-growing. Even amongst Malays, the growing of rice plays a much smaller role than it does, for instance, amongst Javanese, Khmers or Vietnamese.

It was not always thus. In pre-colonial and early colonial times in Malaya rice was of overwhelming importance as a crop, except amongst some aboriginal shifting-cultivators. Occupied land was largely rice land. Permanently-developed land was rice land and land development meant development for the growing of rice. As the Malay states successively came under imperial control these generalizations became increasingly less true with the notable exception of the north-west where, especially during the last quarter of the nineteenth century, production on the Kedah plain expanded enormously under the influence of the Penang market and at the direction of enlightened rulers.

It is with the nineteenth and early twentieth centuries that this book is primarily concerned since it is for this period that adequate source materials exist. Nevertheless, one question in all historical studies is, how did this situation arise? Thus, partly because it has not been attempted elsewhere, and partly because of plain curiosity, an attempt has been made to draw together what little is known or can be reasonably conjectured about earlier periods. In this, the Peninsula has been viewed in its broader regional context since to do otherwise would have not only drastically curtailed discussion but would also have left much unexplained. Since the number of sources increases with time in something approaching a geometrical progression, a broad view has been adopted at the outset, followed by a narrower and more detailed region-by-region focus towards the end of the period under study.

The choice of the end of the first decade of this century as a terminator requires some justification. At that time government interest in rice-growing was minimal. Official attention was directed largely towards the modern sector of the agricultural economy, as is evidenced by the overwhelming attention devoted to commercial crops in the *Agricultural*

Bulletin of the Malay States and the Straits Settlements. Except for brief spasms of official interest first during the First World War, when rice imports were vulnerable to enemy action and again in the 1930s when rubber smallholders suffered severely from the effects of the world-wide economic depression, rice-growers were left largely to their own devices. It was only after Independence in 1957 that a number of the development schemes proposed in the 1930s were actually implemented along with further major works aimed at making the country substantially independent of rice imports. But these are modern developments worthy of full treatment in themselves. Moreover, since 1910 the Malay rural economy, while remaining peasant in orientation, has nevertheless changed very markedly. Furthermore, although virgin lands have been developed for rice since 1910, that year roughly marks the end of colonization activities by individual entrepreneurs whose function later came to be largely replaced by formal governmental agencies.

In studying the development of rice agriculture in Malaya, several problems arise. The major one is an imbalance of sources both in space and in time. Thus the main sources for the three most important rice-growing states in the north of the country, Kedah, Perlis and Kelantan, are official reports published at the very end of the period. The Kedah State Archives contain much of interest in other contexts but, according to Dr. Sharom Ahmat, little relating to rice. Duplicates of land grants formerly held in the Kelantan Land Office are of considerable potential value, but are in too poor a state of preservation to be used. There may also be useful materials in the Thai Royal Museum archives, but despite a journey to Bangkok for the purpose, it proved impossible to gain access to them.

For the rest of Malaya there is a large corpus of governmental documents available locally, much of it housed in the National Archives, Kuala Lumpur. This includes published reports, some, the monthly District Officers' reports, being exceedingly detailed. Two major sources are the Negri Sembilan and Selangor State Secretariat files, neither of which was catalogued during my period of research. Regrettably, Selangor was not an important rice-growing state, whilst two important series of local administration files, for Kuantan (Pahang) and Batang Padang (Perak), are from essentially non-agricultural areas. Nevertheless all these contain useful materials. After about 1900 these manuscript sources become exceedingly voluminous, five to ten shelf-feet per year, and being uncatalogued, were not further researched. The Taiping Land Office records, dating from 1889, lack land-use data and refer to an area in which padi cultivation is not important. These records were not used. The Penang Land Office holds duplicates of grants made in the 1830s in Province Wellesley, and these provided useful statistical data. For Perak, in British eyes a 'model state', the *Perak Government Gazette* contains much information, a good deal of it extremely detailed.

Most British officials give consistent and often penetrating accounts. Paternalists such as Swettenham, Clifford, Martin Lister and D.H. Wise are in this class, but their never-ending, Eurocentric cry of 'Malays are incurably lazy', must be discounted. So far as agriculture and the preservation of Malay life were concerned, their attitudes might be characterized as 'imperialistic paternalism' rather than the 'colonialistic exploitation' of the later civil servants, and thus their writings in the agricultural field are probably reliable for the most part.

Standard sources for Malayan historiography are the records of the Colonial Office (mainly CO 273) and the India Office in London. Of these, the whole of the CO 273 series was inspected with but slim pickings, but of the India Office material only those parts available on microfilm in Singapore have been consulted. The latter contained so little relevant material that further search was abandoned. Little of this has been catalogued. The various series of the Straits Settlements Government records are held on microfilm in Singapore but much is excessively difficult to read and is uncatalogued. Like the India Office material, the Straits Settlements Government records consulted contained so little relevant information that an extensive search was not made.[1]

Newspaper publication began in Penang in 1806 and newspapers have continued to be published without major sequential gaps. These contain a good deal of material of interest to the historical geographer but only a little is relevant to the present study (Hill, 1971).

In addition to these documentary sources, valuable background data have been gathered in the field during the course of successive journeys to every state in Malaysia except Sarawak, to India (mainly Bengal and Tamil Nadu), Burma, Thailand, Cambodia, the former Cochinchina, and Luzon (central plain, Bontoc and Banaue).

---

[1] A comprehensive bibliography of writings in English for the period 1786–1867 is given in Turnbull, 1966. Another useful bibliography is Tregonning, 1962.

A Preliminary Note

THROUGHOUT the work the term 'Malaya' has been used to denote that portion of the Malay Peninsula south of the Isthmus of Kra, and especially that region comprising the former British Malay states, together with Penang, Malacca and Singapore which made up the Straits Settlements. 'Malaya' does not therefore carry any political connotation.

In the text, nineteenth-century spellings have been retained both for place-names and other Malay terms. Anglicized plurals have been given to many Malay terms. All translations from French, Dutch and romanized Malay are by the writer.

1

Rice in the Prehistoric Cultures of South-East Asia

Documentation of the spread of wet padi through South-east Asia must be regarded as a priority in historical research in that region....

Paul Wheatley, 1964, 74.

It is a measure of the scattered nature of archaeological and 'proto-historical' research that few generalizations can be made concerning the place of rice in the economies of South-East Asia, which in early times must be extended to include South China on grounds of ecological and cultural similarity. The most that can be claimed is that rice culture spread relatively slowly, that its displacement of the older tuber- and seed-based cultures proceeded most unevenly in both space and time, that this process was not complete until the present century, that rice was just one of many crops grown and that the spread of rice-growing was not necessarily associated with the spread of peoples. Nor was the development of civilization an inevitable concomitant of rice-growing. Rather, the elaboration of rice-growing techniques was a consequence and a part of evolving and elaborating civilization. The lines of evolution from simple rice cultivation systems to successively more elaborate systems, doubtless with halts and regressions on the way, can be modelled on the basis that complex succeeded simple and that some combinations of techniques are mutually exclusive (see Chapter 9). But in reality supporting evidence is often lacking. Before considering the evidences for rice cultivation in the early cultures of South-East Asia in general and Malaya in particular, it is well to indicate the main cultural periods following Solheim's schema (Solheim, 1970; 1972b):

1. Lithic: ending perhaps 40,000 years B.C., chipped and flaked stone tools, collecting.
2. Lignic: roughly 40,000 to 20,000 B.C., stone, wood and bamboo tools, collecting, early Hoabinhian.
3. Crystallic: roughly 20,000 to 8000 B.C., ground and polished stone tools, plant collection, protection and, by about 10,000 B.C., some domestication, middle to late Hoabinhian.
4. Extensionistic: 8000 B.C. to A.D. 1, though beginning at different times in different places; rectangular adzes, slate knives, cord-marked

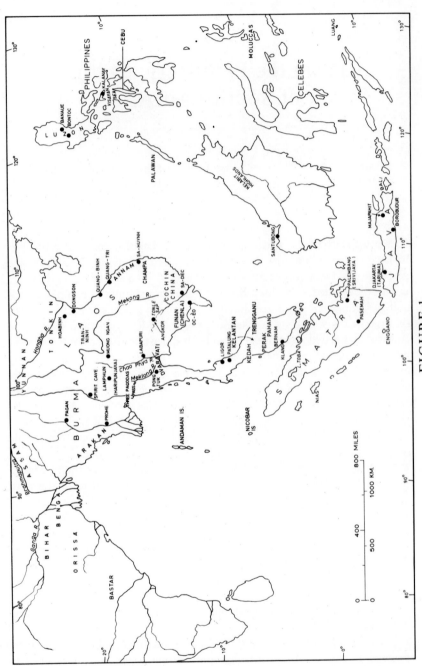

FIGURE 1

PLACES MENTIONED IN THE TEXT

pottery; agriculture (probably including rice) becoming dominant; late Hoabinhian and many local cultures, some quite widespread.

5. Conflicting Empires: roughly from the time of Christ, civilization; centralized, agriculturally-based states, Chinese-influenced in Tonkin and Annam, Indian-influenced elsewhere.

RICE IN HOABINHIAN AND RELATED CULTURES

The major culture of late Pleistocene and early Recent times in South-East Asia is known as the Hoabinhian and is thus named from a type-site in what is now north Vietnam. Its earliest phase may date from about 40,000 years ago and as a recognizable, though varied culture, it lasted in some places until perhaps 2500 B.C. (Solheim, 1972a, 38). The culture was widespread in both mainland and insular South-East Asia, including Malaya (see map in Gorman, 1971, 302). The evidence relating to the economy of Hoabinhian peoples shows that they were hunters, fishers and collectors, exploiting a wide range of animals and plants. The details of economic patterns vary from place to place, though in part variation is more apparent than real because of deficiencies in the techniques at some of the earlier excavations (Chang, 1964, 369).

By about 3500 B.C., there is clear evidence of village-based farming in the region. The Non Nok Tha site in north-east Thailand and the Ban Kao site, near the Three Pagodas Pass, are post-Hoabinhian. At the former site rice was present as one of many types of plant remains, though the question of whether or not it was actually cultivated is not yet settled (Solheim, 1970, 151, 155; Gorman, 1971, 315).

Equally unsettled is the question of whether or not late Hoabinhian peoples saw the transition from hunting and collecting, through plant protection to actual cultivation. The evidences now to be examined are far from conclusive. In the Peninsula, the Hoabinhian is represented by a number of limestone cave sites in Pahang, Perak, Kedah and Kelantan. In these nothing has been found pointing conclusively to any form of agriculture (Tweedie, 1936, 22; Sieveking, 1954–5a, 93–101). The occurrence of 'mealing stones', grinding slabs, mullers, mortars and pestles in a number of sites could be interpreted as suggesting the use of grain, although in some cases, the existence of red ochre on the slabs points to the use of cosmetics, a practice clearly indicated for Sumatra and the Peninsula though not Indochina (Wray, 1894, 7–14; Collings, 1936, 9; van Stein Callenfels, 1936, 42; McCarthy, 1940, 34). Certainly the existence of late Hoabinhian pestles may suggest some rudimentary form of agriculture or seed collection (Coedès, 1966, 14). Colani (1940, 196), in modifying her earlier view that the Hoabinhians were not agriculturalists (Colani, 1930, 317), has pointed out that a number of Indochinese sites contained only a few bones of hunted animals, implying a largely vegetable diet, and asked if the Hoabinhian short axe ('hache courte') were not in fact a harvesting knife and the Hoabinhians rice cultivators. Solheim too (1972a, 41) has pointed to the similarity of slate knives found in the upper levels of the

Spirit Cave site in north-west Thailand to those used today to harvest rice in many parts of Indonesia and Malaysia. Evidence from Gua Cha in Kelantan shows an abrupt decrease in faunal remains about 4,800 years ago (Gorman, 1971, 313). This decrease could be diagnostic of a change to agriculture.

On balance therefore, it would seem unlikely that Hoabinhian groups in the zone of wild rices were unacquainted with the rice plant. This surmise is strengthened by indications of plant domestication, though not specifically of rice, from the Spirit Cave site in north-west Thailand. These evidences date from about 7000 B.C. and are associated with specifically Hoabinhian artifacts (Gorman, 1969, 672). Nevertheless, as Gorman (1971, 305) suggests, the shift from Hoabinhian exploitative patterns to those associated with early cereal agriculture remains one of the least documented problems of South-East Asian prehistory.

RICE IN THE CULTURES OF THE EXTENSIONISTIC PHASE

The extensionistic phase of South-East Asian prehistory partly corresponds with the neolithic of the older terminology and is characterized by the development of several distinct ceramic traditions, notably the Lungshan, the Sa-huỳnh Kalanay and the somewhat later 'Bau-Malay' tradition (Solheim, 1964, 383). At the same time there was a considerable effluxion of both peoples and ideas. The directions of movement were various and their origins, in so far as these can be interpreted, were likewise varied.

The older view is that the spread of rice into the Archipelago was linked with the spread of peoples speaking Malayo-Polynesian languages. The earliest Malayo-Polynesians spread widely both in the Archipelago and beyond into the Pacific. These groups are known to have had ceramics but may not have had rice. The evidence for this is indirect. In historical times it is known that a number of marginally-located peoples were probably not rice growers. These include some Naga groups of the Assam-Burma border, the islanders off the west coast of Sumatra, the Kelabits of Borneo and possibly the Bontocs of Luzon. These may be remnants of an early cultural substrate over which later, more complex, but still Malayo-Polynesian cultures intruded (Heine-Geldern, 1935, 307; Loeb, 1935, 16; Benedict, 1942, 599).

The specific linkages between the possession and the growing of rice on the one hand, and ceramic traditions on the other, have mostly yet to be demonstrated. Chang has fairly convincingly shown that the possessors of the widespread Lungshan ceramic tradition also grew rice, though probably not, as he suggests, on artificial terraces or under irrigation (Chang, 1959, 81, 87; 1963, 92, 126; 1964, 369, 372–3). Solheim, in a personal communication, has modified his earlier view that the Sa-huỳnh Kalanay ceramic tradition is derived from the Lungshan (Solheim, 1964, 383) and now suggests that they both probably had a common origin and that basically Hoabinhian. It has been argued above that the Hoabinhians of the mainland wild-rice core-area were not unacquainted with rice, and since Lungshan peoples would seem to have been rice growers, it would seem reasonable to conclude that at least some bearers of the Sa-huỳnh Kalanay tradition were also rice growers. Yet this may not have been the case since Sa-huỳnh Kalanay sites known thus far do not contain remains of rice (Groslier, 1962, 28). Ceramics of this tradition occur in southern New Guinea, New Caledonia and Fiji where *taro* (*Colocasia* spp.), possibly irrigated, not rice, was almost certainly the basic crop (Barrau, 1965a).

Concerning the timing of Lungshan and Sa-huỳnh Kalanay traditions there is some agreement. The beginnings of the former tradition have not been dated but are broadly post-Hoabinhian while its latest date is around the middle of the second millenium B.C. (Chang, 1964, 369). The time and region of origin of the Sa-huỳnh tradition is unknown though it could well be that it developed as a recognizable tradition somewhere in the eastern islands of the region. The earliest pottery in Palawan may date from before 2000 B.C. (Solheim, pers. comm.) though this may be before a clear Sa-huỳnh Kalanay tradition had evolved. Pottery finds indicate a wide spread, to Tonkin by 500 B.C., to the Visayan islands, Borneo, Java, India and ultimately Madagascar by A.D. 500 (Solheim, 1964, 383).

A second major Malayo-Polynesian ceramic tradition, the 'Bau-Malay', was probably derived from the 'Geometric' tradition of south-east China. The 'Geometric' peoples undoubtedly grew rice, fruits and possessed domestic animals including pigs, dogs and cattle (Chang, 1959, 83). At a later stage they may also have possessed a stone-tipped plough (Chang, 1963, 257). By c.1500 B.C. the 'Bau-Malay' tradition was clearly established, but it was probably not until peoples making this pottery came under pressure from the Han Chinese in Ch'in and Han times that they began to move out. Some may have moved north into Japan taking wet rice cultivation with them but most seem to have moved south and west into Palawan, Borneo, Sumatra, Malaya, Thailand, Vietnam and Cambodia. Solheim (1964, 384) suggests that they reached Palawan c.200 B.C., the Santubong area of Sarawak by A.D. 500,[1] southern Malaya not before A.D. 1000 and further north not until well into historical times from the twelfth to fifteenth centuries. These people may have possessed the wet-field form of rice cultivation.

But of direct evidence that Malayan post-Hoabinhian peoples cultivated rice there is none. As Tweedie has observed (1953, 61),

It is...not impossible that the Malayan neolithic people cultivated rice....We have abundant evidence that the Malayan neolithic people were accomplished potters. It can be assumed with confidence that they were also...cultivators. No purely hunting and food-gathering people could have the leisure, continuity of tradition and resulting opportunity for specialised employment implied by the variety and quantity of artifacts....

[1]For a brief discussion of the Santubong area see Cheng (1969). Harrisson and O'Connor (1969) give a full report on these important sites.

Sieveking's categorical assertion (1954, 123) that the Malayan neolithic was the product of a migration of agriculturalists from south China cannot yet be supported and the matter remains open.

LATER EVIDENCES OF RICE

The conventional interpretation of a range of traits, including the building of megaliths and the working of bronze and iron, is that these mark distinct and widespread cultural traditions, one element of which was the growing of rice. Thus the finding of remarkable bronze drums in Laos, Annam and Burma as well as in both the Peninsula and the Archipelago has been held to be evidence of a widespread culture dating from 400–600 B.C. centred upon Dongson, the type-site in Tonkin (Heine-Geldern, 1935, 315; 1937, 194; Karlgren, 1942, 6, 25). Similarly, the even more widespread occurrence of megalithic remains, including stone-work irrigation systems, dry-stone bridges, causeways and staircases, menhirs, stone seats and cist graves, has been interpreted as being evidence of one or several related cultures (Heine-Geldern, 1935, 329; 1937, 178; 1945, 141; Wales, 1961, 60–5, 81–6; Coedès, 1964, 20–3). Whether or not this interpretation is correct is a matter for professional judgement by practising prehistorians. Nevertheless, various artifacts, dating possibly from the middle of the first millenium B.C. down into proto-historical times perhaps a thousand years later, give some indications of agricultural activities. Upon these evidences modern ethnography throws additional light.

Amongst these artifacts, handsome bronze drums of the type termed Dongson are of importance, though they are found and were made, possibly by itinerant craftsmen, in regions far removed from Dongson in Tonkin. Their decorative motifs include certain figures which give fairly firm evidence for rice cultivation, as distinct from rice possession. These may be briefly listed.

1. Muong drum (tympanum): two long-haired figures of indeterminate sex pounding into a knee-high box, or trough mortar, employing pestles which are about as long as the figures are tall (Karlgren, 1942, Pl. 1, 2).

2. Ngoc-lu' drum (tympanum): (a) two figures similar to those on the Muong drum; (b) four figures on a band below which is a set of drums. Figures striking the earth with dibbles; (c) directly opposite (d) and similar to it (described by Parmentier, 1918, 17, and also figured by Goloubew 1929, Pl. 2).

3. Hoang-ha drum (tympanum): two pregnant women 'pounding rice' (Goloubew, 1940, Pl. 26). Goloubew's figures 4 and 66 clearly show husking while his figures 6d and 7d seem to show preparatory clearing of the ground (see Fig. 2).

Documentary evidence from the first or second century of our era confirms the archaeology. In the time of the prefect Jen Yen (任 延), recorded the *Hou-Han Shu* (Goloubew, 1931, 112),

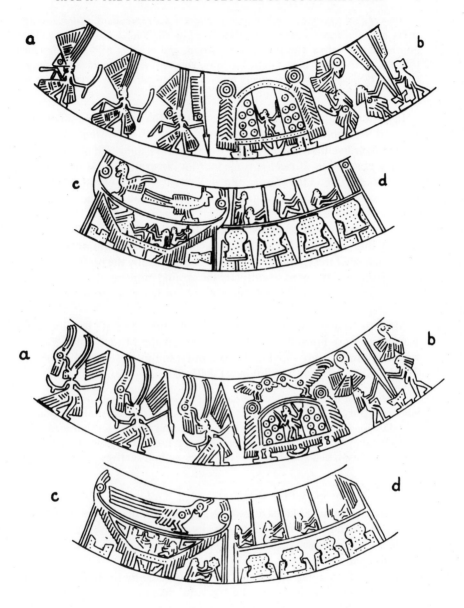

FIGURE 2
PANELS ON DONGSON DRUMS SHOWING CEREAL-HUSKING AND
PLANTING OR POSSIBLY WEEDING (AFTER GOLOUBEW, 1940)

...the entire territory was only marsh and forest where elephant, rhinoceros and tigers multiplied and where the natives lived by the hunt and by fishing. They nourished themselves with the flesh of pythons and of other wild animals which they killed with their bone-pointed arrows, and to these they added the meagre crops of ricefields which they made by burning a corner of the forest before the rainy season, neither turning the soil nor irrigating....

In commenting upon the chronicle of the Han general Ma Yüan who invaded the Tonkin delta *c*.43 A.D., Janse (1958, 19) shows that the natives earned their livelihood chiefly from hunting and fishing and also practised shifting cultivation of rice. It is clear from illustrations and maps of the area that shifting cultivation could just possibly have been practised on the adjacent hills which form the Dongson water-gap, but the lithosols of the hill slopes are excessively thin and it is much more likely that shifting cultivation was practised on the flood-plain and terraces of the Song-ma. It is likely that subsequently, around the centres of administration and under the influence of the Chinese governors, and especially the prefect Jen Yen, these people commenced to cultivate the ground more regularly, following the example of the Tonkinese colonists whom Jen Yen had brought in.

Modern ethnographical evidence confirms the views of Goloubew and Karlgren. Janse himself was present amongst the Muongs of Ngoc-Lac whose ceremonies provided tableaux similar to those preserved on bronze drums (Janse, 1936, 44). Goloubew (1940, 387) adds that

The scenes [on drums] analysed by us indicate clearly the primitive population whose funerary rites, the custom of mingling in a sort of orchestral ensemble the sound of gongs and bronze drums with a regular and continuous cadence such as is produced by the husking of rice. This custom is produced by the Muongs of the present in Thanh-hoa and the province of Hoa-binh. It survives equally amongst the Dayaks.

Other Dongson artifacts include what Goloubew (1929, 19) has suggested are plough blades but which appear to be hoe blades, and 'vases' which the same author suggests are, by analogy with Moi and Dayak models, containers for padi. More likely they are mortars, being very like those figured on drums.

The use of a digging stick or dibble is suggested by the figure of a man striking the ground shown on the Ngoc-lu' drum in the Hanoi museum. This cannot be a figuring of a pestle and mortar since no mortar is shown (Goloubew, 1932a, Pl. IIIa).

Dongson bronzes have been found in a number of places in the Peninsula and Archipelago. In the Peninsula there have been finds at Klang and Tembeling (Linehan, 1951, 1), which have been contextually dated at 200–100 B.C., and more recently a find of pottery, drums and wood at Kampung Sungai Lang, Kuala Langat district, Selangor, and Batu Burok, near Kuala Trengganu (Peacock, 1965, 253; 1966, 198). Wood from the former site was dated (by C^{14}) at *c*.485 B.C. Sherds from the latter site were tempered with what may have been straw or husk. But these bronzes cannot be indigenous since Malaya is virtually devoid of copper ores (Löwenstein, 1956, 6). Moreover, the Klang and Tembeling finds do not bear human figures and are therefore of a fairly late type, later drums invariably lacking figures (Karlgren, 1942). Wheatley's speculation that 'Dongson farmers' possibly 'entered the southern tracts of the Peninsula from Sumatra by way of the west coast rivers' (Wheatley, 1961, xxx) is no more than that. Furthermore the Batu Burok find negates a hypothesis of a solely western entry. Finds of Dongson drums are therefore not diagnostic of rice cultivation in the Peninsula because they are not of local manufacture and the question of the provision of an economic surplus to support craftsmen does not arise. What would be really diagnostic of rice-growing would be grain impressions on pots and it would seem likely that these will ultimately come to light, hopefully in association with datable material.

In the Archipelago, bronze drums have been found at Pasemah (Sumatra), in Java, in Bali and on the island of Luang, east of Timor (Goloubew, 1932b, 137–50; van der Hoop, 1932; van Heerkeren, 1958, 30). Rouffaer (in van der Hoop, 1932, 87) concluded that the drums were introduced into Java and the eastern islands of the Archipelago between 100 and 600 A.D. Van Heerkeren (1958, 30) noted that some Luang islanders assert that the drum was brought from the west together with the rice plant, but this event is undated and may very well have been as late as the eighteenth century since Rumpf did not report rice east of the Celebes (Rumpf, 1741–50).

From the foregoing discussion it must be concluded that although Dongson drums and other bronze relics have been found in the rice-growing regions of Tonkin as well as in the Peninsula and Archipelago, there is no evidence of a corresponding spread of rice cultivation from one region to the other.

Much the same is true of those remains which may be termed 'megalithic'. If it is held that megalithic remains indicate a more or less uniform and widespread culture, then it could be argued that having established a linkage between rice-growing and megalith-building in one place, it would be a reasonable assumption that this linkage was also present wherever megalithic assemblages are to be found. There is, however, no sound basis for such a proceeding, though taken on their own, individual groups of remains are certainly suggestive of rice-growing, though scarcely conclusively so.

Evidence for irrigation by a megalithic Malayo-Polynesian people is well preserved in the massif of Gio-linh in Quang-tri province, Annam. Here are numerous mortar-less stonework irrigation systems each of which consists of an upper terrace with a holding tank below it to store mountain run-off. This feeds a small reservoir or spout which the Vietnamese now use for domestic water and this in turn feeds a tank from which flows water for irrigating the rice fields (Wales, 1953, 98; Wheatley, 1965, 135–9; Coedès, 1966, 19). Colani (1935, 169) has suggested that similar megaliths at Tranninh are no earlier than the first century A.D. and may well be later.

It is generally held that such integrated stonework irrigation systems, together with dry-stone bridges, causeways and staircases, and cult objects such as menhirs, stone seats, earthen pyramids and circular mounds are all integral parts of a cult system (Wheatley, 1965, 136). That this cult system was widespread in the region seems probable, but it is certain that not everywhere did terracing and irrigation accompany it. It may even be questioned if rice was in fact the crop being irrigated.

Barrau (1965a, 342) follows Kolb (1953, 526–7) and supports Keesing (1962, 319) in suggesting that for the Philippines at least, irrigated fields and terraces may have been first used for taro-growing and much later for rice. This would accord with the Bontoc custom of a symbolic planting of tubers along with rice which suggests a rather later adoption of rice (or a remarkably persistent custom). In a more speculative vein is the reminder that Polynesian megalith-builders never had rice. Similar systems, as yet undated, are found in Assam, Java, Bali and Nias.

A link between the builders of the Gio-linh irrigation works and the builders of irrigated terraces in the Banaue and Bontoc uplands of Luzon cannot yet be established although one authority, Beyer (1947, 2), suggests that the terrace-builders were Bronze/Iron age immigrants. In a review of the irrigated rice terrace question, Keesing (1962, 318–24) inclined to the view of an independent origin of the Luzon rice terraces possibly initially for taro-growing. In support of a very late origin for irrigated rice terracing, Keesing (1962, 322) noted the lack of references, though no lack of observers, to rice terracing prior to the nineteenth century.[1] Against this must be placed the fairly conclusive evidence of three carbon-14 dates from Ifugao of around 1000 B.C., about 700 years ago and about 200 years ago (Solheim, pers. comm.). Thus the terraces cannot be late though growing rice in them may be.

In Sumatra and Malaya elaborate dry-stone irrigation works are lacking and megaliths are represented by dolmens, cist-graves and iron tools and in Sumatra only, by stone troughs and mortars and occasional stone sculptures as well. The mortars, known in Malay as *lesong batu*, are always found in close association with other megalithic artifacts and have been assumed by van Heerkeren (1958, 18–19) to have been used for the husking of cereals. The same author describes stone sculptures representing buffaloes from a number of Sumatran and east Java sites (van Heerkeren, 1958, 77–8). A number of megalithic burials also contained the remains of domestic cattle together with iron sickle-shaped knives (van Heerkeren, 1958, 50). Taken together these remains suggest a cereal, presumably rice-growing system of farming, not substantially different from that of the present time.

---

[1] I have been unable to assess the validity of Keesing's view for lack of sources. DeMorga (1867, 284), speaking of the close of the sixteenth century, stated that the region had not yet been penetrated. De Comyn in 1810 stated merely that the inhabitants came down from the hills to trade, while as late as the 1850s it was stated that their only husbandry was sweet potatoes and sugarcane (La Gironière, 1962, 80).

In Malaya, iron sickle-shaped tools (*tulang mawas*, 'apes bones') have been found in cist-graves in the Bernam valley but these are of unknown date, although Löwenstein (1956, 62) dates them tenth to fourteenth centuries by analogy with Javanese finds. Linehan (1951) is certainly in error both in suggesting a much earlier date and an agricultural use.

RICE IN PREHISTORIC TIMES: SOME CONCLUSIONS

Bearing in mind that 'prehistorical' means different periods in different places, it is appropriate to pause and summarize the argument thus far. It is clear that many of the assumptions made by workers who carried out most of their field research prior to World War II are untenable. To give only one example: there is in fact not a shred of evidence that late neolithic Malayo-Polynesian-speaking peoples entered the Peninsula between 2000 and 1500 B.C. bringing with them rice cultivation, domesticated cattle or buffaloes and the custom of erecting megalithic monuments (Heine-Geldern, 1935, 307).

The pertinent major arguments are as follows: the first is that the late Hoabinhians of Indochina and Thailand may well have possessed rice since they lived in a region of wild rices. Rice figures in the post-Hoabinhian archaeological record and they or later groups may have domesticated it. Alternatively, following Ho (1969) there were wild rices in South China and the Lungshan farmers domesticated local wild rices. The second point is that there is no evidence that the Hoabinhian of Malaya included rice unless stone mortars and pestles (unnecessarily harsh tools) are accepted as being used for husking and mealing as well as for preparing cosmetics. Early Malayan agricultural peoples lived outside the zone of wild progenitors of rice and they could not therefore have domesticated it. There are few satisfactorily demonstrable linkages between surviving artifacts and rice-growing. In the third place, if it can be shown that Sa-huỳnh Kalanay peoples were rice growers, then rice-growing was widely spread by them. The fourth point is that the presence of clear evidence of cereal, presumably rice-growing, on certain Dongson drums does not lend itself to the conclusion that there was a South-East Asia-wide Dongson culture of which rice-growing was a trait, though in the region of Dongson there was such a culture and drums are widespread. Finally, the 'Bau-Malay' peoples were probably rice growers and may have brought rice-growing to Sarawak by A.D. 500.

If, for the sake of argument, it is assumed that rice was nowhere of more than marginal interest, that it was merely one crop amongst many in the early agricultural communities of the mainland, the explanation of a number of facts becomes possible. This assumption is by no means unsoundly based. The existence of irrigated terrace taro cultivation in New Caledonia and Hawaii (Keesing, 1962, 319–20) and irrigated taro cultivation in Tahiti serves as a reminder that there is no essential connexion between rice and irrigation or terracing. Such an assumption would explain the continuance of the custom of ceremonial planting of tubers in irrigated rice terraces by the Bontoc and kindred groups. It would help to explain why, according to Keesing (1962, 322) pre-nineteenth century travellers in Luzon nowhere mention rice on irrigated terraces and why nineteenth and even twentieth century observers in India, Nagaland and the west coastal islands of Sumatra report a relatively recent incursion of rice-growing amongst several marginal peoples. For example, von Fürer-Haimendorf (1938, 203) noted that '...taro is as important a part of the diet as rice and some Konyak [Naga] villages grow no rice but live exclusively on taro and a small amount of millet. The choice of crops is by no means climatically or geographically determined....' Hutton, a major authority on the Nagas, commented that, 'Rice came in as wet cultivation and is now cultivated dry. I think it probably came in with the terrace cultivation [by the Angami Nagas]....' (von Fürer-Haimendorf, 1938, 219). Von Fürer-Haimendorf (1945, 81–2) also noted that in India the Bondos of Orissa and the Hill Marias in Bastar similarly favour millet and taro rather than rice.

On the islands of Nias and Enggano, off the west coast of Sumatra, rice is of recent introduction. Furthermore, there is the suggestion that the *lesong batu* were not used for husking rice but for some other purpose, sacred or profane. Rice certainly could have been husked in wooden mortars as at present, so this line of evidence on its own is inconclusive (van der Hoop, 1932, 102, 166–7; 1934, 43). The same authority perceptively noted (1932, 194) that, 'Whether the cultivation of rice on irrigated fields, still common in South Sumatra, was inherited from the megalith builders still remains to be proved.' That it has been so inherited has been generally assumed but the arguments advanced here are sufficiently strong to throw strong doubt upon this assumption.

A further evidence of the recency of rice in some parts of the region is the agriculture of the Kelabits in Sarawak. Barbara Harrisson (1964, 198) has suggested that the origins of their present system of agriculture are not necessarily embedded in rice. Elsewhere, Tom Harrisson (1963–4, 189) has concluded that

...rice is a relatively recent introduction in Borneo...certainly in the interior; and some of the rather curious features of rice irrigation in the Borneo uplands are only intelligible if one thinks of it as being carried over from the previous cultivation of other crops, with which I happen to be familiar from having spent two years in the New Hebrides; where there is elaborate irrigation of taro....

In Malaya the use of rice amongst upland-dwelling peoples seems to be a fairly recent phenomenon. The Temiar (Benjamin, pers. comm.), for example, have a story of the millet king who, after a great struggle, was displaced by the rice king. Moreover, amongst those uplanders who still grow significant amounts of tubers (nowadays mostly manioc), the tubers provide as much as two-thirds or more of basic carbohydrate requirements yet occupy perhaps one-third of the land and only require that or a lesser proportion of the labour.

Since carbohydrate needs can be filled much more easily by tubers than by rice it is not to be wondered that rice took an exceedingly long time to take over this role. This take-over may have been finally consummated only when the sources of fat and protein earlier supplied by game, and less often by domestic animals, became so attenuated that a satisfactorily balanced diet was no longer being obtained. Furthermore, the growing of a cereal would supply superior raw materials for the brewing of alcoholic beverages, neither taro nor yam (*Dioscorea* spp.) yielding anything remotely palatable in this line. This is one reason why many present-day groups of upland Borneo grow rice.

While not conclusive, the arguments and evidence adduced thus far throw considerable doubt upon the very general assumption that rice-growing, as distinct from mere possession of rice, in the Peninsula and Archipelago especially, has a long history. Underlying this assumption is the notion that societies which were technically advanced to the extent of producing fine ceramics, of using bronze and iron in sophisticated ways, must necessarily have grown rice which alone could supply the surplus requisite to the support of specialization of labour necessary for such relatively advanced technologies. This idea would seem to be of dubious validity. For an example of an advanced tuber-based culture in the tropics one need look no further than Incan civilization or within the region to Champa where wet rice seems to have been marginal to the agricultural economy. As to whether the place of rice in the economies of prehistoric peoples was considerable or not there is as yet insufficient evidence to reach a definite conclusion. But an inconsiderable role for rice, at least down to the period of Funan, would accord with what little is known or can be reasonably conjectured.

2

Rice in Early Historical Times

[There was] a change from tribal chief to god-king, from gerontocracy to
sultanism, from consensus to hereditary charismatic authority inherent in
manifest divinity, from *pawang* to 'brahman', from head-hunter to *ksatriya*,
from primitive tribesman to peasant, from kampong to *nagara*, from spirit
house to temple, from reciprocity to redistribution, in short from culture to
civilisation.

Paul Wheatley, 1964, 43.

FROM around the second century B.C. in northern Indochina and several
centuries later its southern portions and in the Peninsula and Archipelago,
there was a major social and economic transition marking the beginning
of the period of conflicting states. In Tonkin, then Annam, then in the
Mekong delta, later again in the Chao Phya delta, and on a smaller scale in
the Peninsula and Archipelago, this change seems to have been accompanied by an increasing sophistication in agriculture and importantly, by
the beginnings of large-scale colonization of deltas. The relationships
between the Peninsula and surrounding regions are obscure and the most
that can be attempted is to indicate possible links, many of which remain
based on no more than spatial proximity.

TONKIN AND NORTHERN ANNAM

In northern Indochina, in Tonkin and northern Annam, Han Chinese
influence was clearly marked by the first century B.C. and Sinicized Vietnamese and later, Han Chinese farmers had begun to displace the Malayo-
Polynesians. The indigenous *Lac* peoples of the Delta had been absorbed
into a Chinese protectorate by 111 B.C. They were doubtless peasant
rice farmers, who, as Wheatley notes, had reclaimed the deltaic terrain at
the initiative of Chinese authority. Although a considerable corpus of
hydraulic technology must have been involved, there is no evidence of
irrigation as distinct from drainage (Wheatley, 1965, 126–8).

It is possible that the traction plough was beginning to come into use
at about the same period. Although the animal-drawn plough was in use
in much of India by the middle of the first millennium B.C., it did not come
into use in China proper until the second half of the fourth century B.C.,

having been preceded there by the foot-plough (Bishop, 1936, 277–8). It is not known if the foot-plough preceded the traction plough in Tonkin but the latter may have reached Indochina by about the beginning of the Christian era (Bishop, 1936, 280). Janse (1931, 131–7) noted the affinities of bronze plough-shares from Tonkin with those of Mongolia but suggested that three bronze shares from a late Dongson site, synchronous with Han, may equally be hoe blades. The figures (in Janse, 1931, 135) do not permit a decision one way or the other. Whatever tools were in use in either Tonkin or North Annam, it must be agreed with Wheatley (1965, 131), that neither documentary nor archaeological sources point to a technically advanced agriculture already a millennium old.

In northern Annam a number of important archaeological finds suggest that a form of syncretism had developed between the immigrant 'Chinese' culture (*sensu lato*) and the pre-existing culture (Janse, 1951, 50, 181). But this syncretic agriculture must have been spatially limited by the adversities of environment, although wet (irrigated?) fields existed in Annam by the fourth century A.D. (Wheatley, 1965, 132). Indeed it is just this sort of environment in which irrigation makes sense rather than in the heavy clay soils of Tonkin in which the water-table usually lies at no great depth and periodically rises above the surface. But direct evidence of links between the Dai-Viet of Tonkin and northern Annam and the Peninsular Malay states is lacking.

THE MEKONG: FUNAN, CHAMPA AND CAMBODIA

Whereas the events leading to the Sinicization of the north-east of the Indochinese peninsula are well documented, this is less true for the Indianized states to the south-west. All that can be said is that no archaeological remains showing Indian influence date from earlier than the second century A.D. and that culture contact between Funan, Champa, then Cambodia, and India was intense and long-continued. To what extent the 'conquest of the mud' by Funanese rice growers or the development of Khmer irrigation systems owed anything to Indian influence is unknown. Equally, it is not possible to assess the effects of contacts with established lowland rice-cultivating groups to the north in Annam and Tonkin. But Funan exercised sovereignty over the northern Peninsular and Isthmian states and may equally have been responsible for developments in agriculture and for this reason agriculture in Funan merits a detailed examination.

FUNAN

It is clear from Chinese dynastic histories that the kingdom now popularly referred to as Funan was a large and prosperous state with a developed Sanscritic orthography, centres of learning and wide-ranging commerce, specialized handcraft industries, all of which were supported by lowland rice cultivation (Malleret, 1951, 78; 1962, 419). By the Chin dynasty (A.D. 265–419), Funan was reported as having 'walled villages, palaces and houses' but agriculture was still relatively unsophisticated (Pelliot, 1903, 254). Although there is abundant evidence of ancient canals it does not follow that these were used for irrigation. Malleret (1962, 324; 1963, 131) has referred to these hydraulic works as systems of drainage and navigation, not of irrigation. Indeed, as in Tonkin, drainage was essential but irrigation superfluous. The canals in the vicinity of Oc-Èo, the type-site for Funan, probably date from the second half of the fifth and the early sixth centuries. They were results of agricultural colonization motivated at least in part by the desire to extend the lands belonging to various divinities (Malleret, 1962, 313). Divinely 'owned' estates seem to have been common. An inscription from Sa-dec province, dated A.D. 639, for example, enumerates the donors of lands given to the god Sri Viregvara. The lands were mostly rice fields, though some were in fruit trees, probably much on the modern pattern of rice in the lower lands and fruits on the levées and other drier soils (Malleret, 1963, 132).

But it would be an error to suggest that all the rice fields were as yet regularly cultivated or perhaps even to suggest that rice was incontrovertibly the major staple. The earliest documentary reference to agriculture comes from the *History of the Chin Dynasty* in which it is stated that the people 歲 種 literally, 'one time plant, three times harvest'. This statement has been misinterpreted by several writers. Pelliot (1903, 254) translates it, 'They sow in one year and harvest during three'. Braddell (1939, 187) has, 'They sow one year and leave fallow for three', but this is clearly an erroneous translation from the French of Pelliot, not from the original Chinese. Malleret (1962, 419) repeats Pelliot's mistranslation and in a curious *non sequitur* concludes that 'harvest during three years, is an index of an exceptional [soil] fertility which permits [us] to admit a culture of floating rice'.

The use of the graph 種 , 'plant', instead of 播 , 'sow', may or may not be significant. The phrase could be taken to refer to some crop (a tuber, not a cereal, since a tuber is planted, not sown) planted in one year and harvested at the end of three years. Although this interpetation is possible, it is unlikely that anything other than rice is meant. The *History of the Southern Ch'i* (A.D. 479–501) refers to the 'five cereals' (one of which is rice)[1] in the holy mandate by which King Jayavarman reigned (Pelliot, 1903, 257). To clinch the matter, blackened rice grains were found at Oc-Èo at a depth of 2.30 m (Malleret, 1960, 88). The *T'ai-p'ing yü-lan* confirms these evidences with a note that rice was used in ceremonies designed to reveal the identity of petty pilferers in the household (Pelliot, 1903, 280; Braddell, 1939, 196).

Nor is there a basis here for Malleret's supposition that the phrase

[1]Hsüan Keng, Department of Botany, University of Singapore, in a personal communication has suggested that in the original sense the following were the five cereals (五穀): 粱 *Oryza sativa*, 粟 *Sorghum vulgare*, 麥 *Setaria italica*, 黍 *Hordeum vulgare*, 稷 *Panicum miliaceum*. Of these, *Hordeum* could not possibly have been grown in the climate of Funan. However, Wheatley, in a personal communication, has pointed out that in other texts from other ecological environments, other grains are listed. Moreover in many texts, 'five cereals' is simply a metonymical expression for agriculture.

points to floating rice, although the existence of floating rice is attested by Chou Ta-kuan in the twelfth century (Malleret, 1960, 87–8). It is perfectly possible that *Oryza perennis* or a near-relative was referred to by the Chinese observer, but equally *O. sativa* could have been the object of his description, since even modern rices produce a 'ratoon' crop after the first harvest. It is to the harvest of successive ratoon crops that the writer of the *History of the Chin Dynasty* probably referred. After the third harvest the field was presumably too weedy and the yields too low to continue ratooning and the field was then cultivated once more. Wheatley, in a personal communication, suggests that *chung* 種 must be understood to imply cultivation in a broad sense, in which case the text could well refer to cultivation in which a cleared patch of land was cropped for three years and then abandoned.

There is therefore no evidence of annually-sown irrigated crops at that time but merely of either a one-year-in-three rain-fed system of rice cultivation with what may be termed a 'self-fallow' and collection of ratoon crops or, alternatively, of three years' cropping of clearings. The manner of tilling the soil cannot be established, for although the Indians possessed the animal-drawn plough, there is no evidence that the peasants of Funan did. If they did so the plough must have been drawn by cattle or zebu and not by buffaloes since buffaloes are neither mentioned in the Chinese texts nor do their bones figure amongst archaeological finds (Malleret, 1962, 345–8).

Thus while Malleret (1962, 324) is undoubtedly correct in suggesting that at Oc-Èo the remains of a large planned town associated with an extensive canal system point to a rich and powerful central authority, the agricultural basis for that authority had scarcely begun to resemble that of classical Khmer times. On the other hand its craft, commercial and artistic bases were well on the way to elaborate and sophisticated development when Funan fell to Chen-la in the seventh century. Funan thus provides little support for the suggestion of Coedès (1966, 1–2) that, 'The only way of ensuring a supply of cereals abundant enough to provide the staple diet of an expanding population is to practise irrigated rice cultivation'.

CHAMPA AND CAMBODIA

The kingdom of Champa abutted upon the northern portion of coastal Funan. Founded perhaps in the second century, it was strong enough by A.D. 248 to carry out raids in Tonkin (Majumdar, 1955, 26–7). The sources do not permit a reconstruction of agriculture at this early period and the small extent of lowland would suggest a limited role for wet rice. By the early thirteenth century, the *Chu fan chih* recorded rice, grown in fields ploughed by a pair of cattle, and a wide range of garden crops, including haricots, peas, aubergines, cucumbers, millet, sesame, hemp, sugarcane, pepper, bananas, coconuts and areca (Maspéro, 1928, 3, 33). But although the Chams were a Malayo-Polynesian people, it would be dangerous to suggest that the northern Peninsular peoples gained their knowledge of rice agriculture from this source. They may have done, but evidence is lacking.

To the north-west of Champa, Cambodia was already a significant power by the sixth century. Rice must have been cultivated in fair quantity but whether by shifting cultivation, by entrapped rainfall and natural rise of the water-table or by controlled irrigation or, as is more likely, by all or at least the two former methods there is no telling. The simple two-storeyed structure of the forests in the region of Angkor would suggest long-continued shifting cultivation possibly combined with cattle-rearing since cattle-keepers appear in fair numbers in the epigraphic lists of donations to religious foundations (Coedès, 1937–66; Wheatley, 1965). These suggest that buffaloes were less common than cattle or perhaps, were of such economic importance that they were retained by their owners. By 1186, the Ta Prohm inscription shows that food surpluses were being produced. In the kingdom of Jayavarman VII, 66,625 people were employed in temples and hospitals. The annual donation of rice was 117,200 *kharikas*, each kharika being equivalent to about 38 kg using Indian standard measures (Majumdar, 1955, 70). But as in the case of Champa there is not the slightest evidence that the sophisticated cultivation methods of Cambodia actually spread to the Peninsula.

THE PIEDMONT KINGDOMS

Scholarship has yet to elucidate the details of the early history of the piedmont zone which extends from the region of the Burma-Assam border through Thailand and Laos into south China, a region once partly inhabited by Mon peoples. For the study of the spread of rice this region is crucial, containing as it does a zone of abundant wild rices. All that can be attempted here is to indicate briefly what little evidence of rice-growing there is.

Concerning the Mon kingdom of Haripunjaya, centred on Lamphun, two texts, the *Jinakalamalini* and *Camadevivamsa*, give little information concerning economic life. The foundation myth of the kingdom refers to cattle while the king of Hamsavati, who took in refugees from Haripunjaya *c.*1050 is recorded as having given them rice and padi (Coedès, 1925, 104). Certainly by the thirteenth century Haripunjaya was using irrigation. During the reign of King Mengrai (1258–1317), irrigation laws were promulgated and in 1281 a major canal was dug by corvée labour (Bruneau, 1968, 163–4).

Of the west, the *History of the T'ang Dynasty* (618–905) reported that in the region of Prome, 'The land is suited to pulse, rice, and the millet-like grains' (Harvey, 1925, 13). On the fall of Prome early in the ninth century, the people migrated to Pagan, a singularly arid spot where today the soil could not feed the population of any considerable city. Inscriptions dedicating rice fields at Pagan still exist and the account of the reign of King Nyang-u Law-rahan (931–64) mentions rice-offerings (Harvey, 1925, 15–17). But whether these slight evidences should be interpreted as showing the existence of irrigation, presumably an essential in this low-rainfall zone, or should be interpreted as showing that rice was a rather special, rare crop whereas the main cereal was millet, is a matter for conjecture.

The Gupta-influenced kingdom of Dvaravati may have been a rice-growing state but an inscription from Sal Sun (Labapuri) in very archaic Mon merely records a gift to the pagoda of slaves and cattle. A Khmer stele of 1022 from the same site mentions doves, buffaloes, pigs, goats, chickens and ducks but not a single crop. Only in the eleventh century does a stele from this site mention rice (Coedès n.d., 9, 12, 18). Despite its paucity however, the evidence points tentatively in the direction of some irrigated rice cultivation by the Mon.

SIAM

The irruption of the Thai into the Mon areas began late in the thirteenth century and there can be little doubt that the Thai took over going agri-cultural concerns. But the great Thai achievement, colonization of the Chao Phya valley and delta, does not seem to have been accompanied by a corresponding development of agricultural techniques. As late as the period of European contact the picture is of a remarkably primitive system of cultivation. The Thai seem not to have practised irrigation whereas the Mon had some skill in this field, perhaps extending even to the use of irrigated rice terraces, as in the Muong Ngan area of the north-east (McCarthy, 1902, 190).

The earliest European account to give a satisfactory picture of Thai agriculture is that of Nicholas Gervaise (1688, 7) who recognized three kinds of rice.

One grows wild and does not require damp, marshy soil. . . . That kind is cheap and not very good. The other two kinds must be sown by man; one is called Ponlo . . . it grows on the hills and, consequently, it is lighter and drier, and, also so dear to buy that only the rich and great lords eat it. . . .

The final type (not mentioned) was presumably wet rice. Floating rice was reported in 1693 by de la Loubère who also noted the practice of bunding and transplanting. Both buffaloes and cattle were put to the plough (de la Loubère, 1693, 18, 19) and used for threshing (Turpin, 1771, 212), the latter a common enough practice in Siam and formerly in Kedah though today it is unknown in Malaya. But rice had not yet completely displaced millet (Gervaise, 1688, 7; de la Loubère, 1693, 17) and older methods of cultivation such as the preparation of the soil by the trampling of buffaloes, and broadcast sowing of the seed remained common until the end of the nineteenth century (Bowring, 1857, 1, 201; Smyth, 1898, 2, 278; Carter, 1904, 156).

To de la Loubère, as to Sir John Bowring a century and a half later, advanced Thai husbandry was of Chinese origin. According to the former, rice-growing techniques spread from China through Tonkin to Siam along with the custom of the monarch ploughing the first furrow of the season (de la Loubère, 1693, 20). Bowring (1857, 1, 201) likewise implied that improved husbandry in the form of ploughing, rather than trampling, and transplanting, rather than broadcast seeding, was of Chinese introduction.

Certainly the Thai, at least in the Chao Phya valley and the delta, were not irrigators, their obvious skill as drainage and transportation engineers notwithstanding. As late as 1844, an unsuccessful attempt was made to block up the river to provide irrigation water during a severe drought (*SFPW* 22.4.1844). Canals existed for transportation only and even in the early years of this century it was noted that no system existed for raising the water of innumerable canals onto the fields (McCarthy, 1888, 118; Grindrod, 1895, 23, *Encyclopaedia Britannica*, 1910–11, 5, 25).

In view of these considerations it is vain to suggest that the origins of Malayan rice-growing owe anything significant to the Thai in the Chao Phya valley. However, Smyth's review of Peninsular Siam noted 'garden' i.e. lowland transplanted wet rice, which was grown using irrigated seedling nurseries in the Maung Talung and Patalung provinces. In Lakorn, cattle-rearing was extensive and the province then grew more rice than any other province of Siam, even though broadcast sowing was usually employed by the Malays there (Smyth, 1898, 2, 117–29, 278). It is perhaps significant that not so far away in the foothill zone and the Meklong valley was the possibly sixth century Mon (Dvaravati) site of Pong Tuk (Coedès, 1928, 202). Do we thus see a link in a chain of Mon and Malay states practising the cultivation of wet, broadcast-seeded rice perhaps employing irrigation and making use of animals but possibly not ploughs, in soil preparation?

THE ARCHIPELAGO

Before proceeding to a discussion of the Peninsula in early times it is appropriate that at this point attention be directed to the island regions surrounding it. For Sumatra evidence is exiguous in the extreme. It may be presumed that the capital of Sri Vijaya had an agricultural base and that base was rice. The *Malay Annals* clearly refer to the region of Palembang in the story of Wan Empak and Wan Malini who had planted (dry) padi on Bukit Si-Guntang (Brown, 1952, 24). In the sixteenth century the Sumatrans' diet included millet, rice, seeds and wild fruits (Lach, 1965, 1, 575). By the end of the eighteenth century the common pattern of dry rice in the uplands and swamp rice in the lowlands had emerged (Marsden, 1811, 66–77), though the western islanders probably still lacked rice. In the Minangkabau areas, not described by Marsden, irrigation was by ditch and the current-driven water-wheel (Malay: *kinchir ayer*), was almost certainly long since established, the water-wheel possibly being ultimately of Mon origin.[1]

In Java, rice cultivation has been said to have been begun by Indian

[1]For comments concerning the current-driven water-wheel see Hill, 1973, 88n.

colonists in the second century (Nagai, 1959, 579). An undated inscription (A.D. *c.*400) from the vicinity of Jakarta refers to the King of Taruma at whose command a canal seven miles long was built in twenty-one days but Vlekke (1959, 22) considers this to be more fiction than fact. The earliest directly relevant epigraphical record, the Changgal inscription from Borobudur, dated A.D. 732, is also somewhat equivocal. Braddell (1941, 41) quotes four differing translations from the Sanscrit, only one of which mentions rice, the others referring only to grain.

There can be little doubt that the Sanscritic name *Yavadvipa*, 'millet island', refers to a large island in the Archipelago (Schegel, 1903, 238n). Wheatley (1966) suggests that this island was probably not Sumatra, nor necessarily Java. Could it be Borneo, which would accord with a late date for rice there on other grounds? Nevertheless, in Java Merrill (1954, 364) has noted that at Borobudur rice is nowhere figured, whereas *Setaria italica* is, leading him to conclude that millet was then the leading cereal. The same authority further noted that the word *daua*, widely used in the Malaysian plant realm and in the Philippines for *Setaria*, is an unmodified Sanscrit term and is probably the word from which *yava* was derived (Merrill, 1954, 364).[1]

How long millet remained dominant is not known. It may have been the staple of the kingdom of the Brantas valley, but by the end of the thirteenth century, Majapahit certainly had rice since it figures amongst the gifts that the people were required to present to the monarch. The uncle of King Vijaya exhorted the district headman to neglect nothing that the rice fields may flourish, that the dikes of the *sawahs* be maintained so that the water does not run off and the people have to leave for better homes. At this time horses, elephants and oxen were noted but not buffaloes (Vlekke, 1959, 75, 77–8).

Although it might be suggested that rice fields together with their Javanese name, sawah, may have spread to the Peninsular peoples from Majapahit, this could be true only of the south where sawah is nowadays used to the exclusion of *bendang*, which term is confined to northern Malaya.

Having thus considered the possible sources of rice and rice-knowledge in adjoining regions, it is appropriate to go back in time to the point at which the northern kingdoms were subject to Funan and to treat of the evidences for rice agriculture in the Peninsula down to the latter part of the seventeenth century.

THE MALAY PENINSULA

The authority of Funan extended into the Peninsula where a number of Indianized states were tributary to it. But whereas the evidence for rice cultivation in Funan itself is textual, epigraphical and archaeological, that

[1]It may also be significant that the Javanese term *segu* or *sega* is used in central and east Java to signify cooked rice (Malay: *nasi*). Segu would seem to be related to the standard Malay *sagu*, the English sago, which is made from the palm *Metroxylon*.

for its Peninsular tributaries and their successor-states is almost exclusively textual and moreover is burdened with problems of identification. The evidence is brought together in Wheatley's *Golden Khersonese* upon which subsequent discussion largely relies.

One such country was Tun-sun, a commercial centre probably in the Isthmus (Wheatley, 1964, 45). Another was Chin-lin, somewhere on the shores of the Bight of Bangkok, but like Ch'u-tu-k'un and Chiu-chih, also Isthmian states, nothing is known of their agricultural practices (Wheatley, 1961, 288). They presumably gained a good deal of their wealth from trans-peninsular trade and the supply of jungle products. Prudent rulers would likely have taken some steps to secure a local supply of the staple crop. But that such prudence may well have been largely lacking is shown in the case of Malacca which, according to the *Ying-yai Sheng-lan*, produced little rice as late as the fifteenth century (Groeneveldt, 1887, 243).

With the fall of Funan to Chen-la, continental control over the Peninsular states lapsed. In the period of Chen-la (A.D. *c*.550–800) some half-dozen states are recorded in the Peninsula. Chih-tu, a wealthy Buddhistic state located in north-east Malaya, was reported as '. . .constantly warm in winter and summer. Rainy days are numerous, fine days few, and there is no special season for planting [conditions] allow [the cultivation of] padi, panicled millet, white beans and black hemp. . . .' (Wheatley, 1961, 29, 32–6). Chih-tu was thus unquestionably an agricultural state. The lack of a season for planting does not necessarily betoken a climate without seasons but may suggest merely that the cultivators did not bother to follow the march of the seasons.

Tan-tan, possibly in the region of Besut or Trengganu, possessed a highly diversified system of mixed farming in which rice was the only cereal amongst a list of crops far more diverse than those of today. Of livestock, goats, pigs, fowl, geese and deer were recorded (Wheatley, 1961, 52). The lack of cattle and buffaloes indicates the lack of the plough. In the same region was Pan-pan, which had the same products as Tan-tan.

Ko-lo, ancient Chinese Ka-la, the Arabic Kalah, which Wheatley (1961, 59, 270) locates in the region of Mergui, was a state of considerable size, centred on a stone-walled city (Groeneveldt, 1887, 241; Wheatley, 1961, 217). In addition to being a major centre for tin and for trade in forest products, according to the *New History of the Tang Dynasty* (618–906) it possessed many cattle but whether they were used for draught or not is unknown (Wheatley, 1961, 56). Abu Dulaf (Wheatley, 1961, 217) reported numerous gardens and suggested that the basic cereal was wheat, though this could have been millet which it resembles much more closely than rice, though rice is possible. Ibn Muhalhal (*c*.941) supported this picture of Kalah, referring to it as 'a great city with high walls and gardens and canals' (Winstedt, 1920, 29). But these canals, like those of long-defunct Funan, were not necessarily used for irrigation. Similarly the mention of a tank in the Ptolemaic Takola emporion (now Takuapa) is not evidence of irrigation (Coedès n.d., 34; Lamb, 1964, 78).

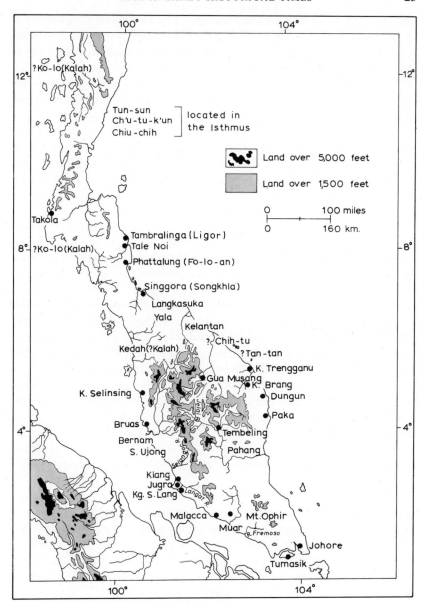

FIGURE 3
PLACES IN THE MALAY PENINSULA MENTIONED IN THE TEXT

Another northern kingdom was Langkasuka which seems to have existed in the vicinity of Singgora (Songkla) from the second century until the early sixteenth century (Wheatley, 1964, 49). Its products were similar to those of Funan. It seems unlikely that city-states surrounded by walls with double gates, towers and pavilions (Wheatley, 1961, 254) would have been supported by trade alone, yet Chinese texts of the twelfth and thirteenth centuries clearly list rice amongst the imports of both Lang-

kasuka and Tan-ma-ling (Tambralinga=Ligor), a sister dependency of
Sri Vijaya (Wheatley, 1961, 67–8). Wang Ta-yuan, in the mid-fourteenth
century, noted that the soil of Langkasuka was of inferior quality but by
this time Tambralinga produced more grain than it consumed (Wheatley,
1964, 64–5). Langkasuka grew glutinous rice for brewing whilst Tambralinga used millet for this purpose (Wheatley, 1961, 70, 77). These cereals
were presumably also eaten.

Amongst this proliferation of northern Peninsular kingdoms, the only
one whose name comes down to the present is Kedah, the Chinese Chieh-
chah, which reached its apogée under Sri Vijaya (Wheatley, 1957). The
location of Kedah was certainly the south flank of Gunong Jerai (Kedah
Peak) to which access from seaward was by the Merbok estuary. Excavations by Evans, Wales, Lamb and others have revealed evidences of a
strongly Indianized trading community but little that permits definite
conclusions concerning its agricultural base. All the authorities agree in
suggesting that this base was rice, though there is not the slightest evidence,
as Khan (1958, 35) claims, that wet rice planting had already existed on
the alluvial plains of Kedah since the first century A.D.

A model plough and yoke in silver found in a bronze reliquary would
suggest that plough agriculture may have reached Kedah by the eighth
or ninth century (Lamb, 1960, 107; 1961, 81). This is the earliest evidence
for the plough in both the Peninsula and the Archipelago and it is clear
that the plough was of Indian inspiration if not of actual origin. This is
supported by the fact that the Malay word for plough, *tenggala*, has close
kin in both Sanscrit and Pali. But whether the term applied to ploughs in
general or only to an imported type, perhaps a shared plough, is not
known. Yet the fact that the model was merely a ritual object of an unknown place of manufacture, plus the lack of animal bones, would suggest
that real ploughs did not yet exist. Wales (1940, 2) implies irrigation, but
of this there is no evidence.

Wales (1940, 1) also makes the important point that the earlier colonists
would have had to ensure their food supply because piracy would prevent
a small colony from ensuring regular imports, but in Kedah it seems very
likely that rice-growing occupied no more than the immediate vicinity of
the town's defences and it was designed to provide only an absolutely
essential portion of total requirements. By the mid-fifteenth century in
Kedah, this was possibly no longer true. Khan (1958, 35), without
providing documentation, suggests that north Kedah was kept by the
Siamese as a granary for their army besieging Malacca. For this purpose
Siamese farmers were brought in from Langawan, Chaya, Karahi and
Tambralinga. Elsewhere, in times of peace, the *rakyat* presumably spread
their settlements along the rivers.

Trengganu is another northern state in which rice was grown. A Malay
inscription dated 1303 throws light upon the economy (Paterson, 1924,
253–7). The inscription reads in part,

Kelima derma barang orang . . . [mer]deka jangan megambil tugal buat . . . emas-
nya jika ia ambil hilangkan emas.

Fifth Law: whatever person...[a freeman?] must not take the dibble for making ...money if he takes [he] loses money.

This somewhat obscure statement certainly indicates the existence, continued to the present, of the use of the dibble (*tugal*), hence grain, almost certainly rice, cultivation. The law also hints that production of the staple was a government monopoly.

In general, the techniques by which rice was grown in the north were rather primitive, Kedah alone showing the slightest evidence of the plough, while at Kuala Brang the dibble was still important as late as the beginning of the fourteenth century. Since trade was much more profitable than rice-growing, then as now, and various sources, especially Chinese, suggest strongly hierarchical societies, it may be presumed that rice-growing was largely, if not exclusively, in the hands of a subordinate or slave class. And in this may lie the reason for the apparent long continuance of simple methods of cultivation.

If the picture of the north Malayan and Isthmian kingdoms is shadowy, that of the more southerly regions is positively ghost-like. Perak seems to have existed perhaps by the sixth century since Gupta-style figures have been found there. The important trading centre at Kuala Selinsing may also have existed between the sixth and twelfth centuries (Wheatley, 1961, 193, 197) though there is nothing in the Kuala Selinsing finds indicative of an agricultural community.

Pahang, in the form P'eng-K'eng,[1] does not appear until the thirties and forties of the fourteenth century. The *Tao-i Chih lueh* noted that the soil was fertile and fairly good for cereals (Wheatley, 1961, 78). For the rest of the east coast of Malaya southwards of Kuala Trengganu there remains only a list of toponyms, 'Trengganu, Nasor, Paka, Muara Dungun' and at the southernmost extremity of the Peninsula, 'Tumasik' (Wheatley, 1961, 302). Of these, 'Nasor' remains unidentified and the remainder seem not to have been agricultural centres of any significance. The *Hsin-Ch'a Sheng-lan* compiled in 1436 noted that the crops of Tumasik were 'very poor' and moreover the people were daring pirates (Wheatley, 1961, 91, 305).

Across on the west coast, tiny settlements that can be recognized, but merely as toponyms, were Sungei Ujong and Klang. Johore may have existed at this time and indeed possibly much earlier as the Ptolemaic 'Palanda' (Wheatley, 1961, 157) but Johore does not appear in the 1365 *Nagarakrtagama* list noted above. The *Malay Annals*, however, refer to a (Malay) rice planter of 'Seluang', the last place that is visited by voyagers up the Johore river and also to the export of sugarcane, bananas, yams and aroids but significantly, not rice, to Singapore (Winstedt, 1932, 4).

Malacca was founded probably before the end of the fourteenth century but throughout its history it was a 'city that was made for merchandise'. Nearby Muar may have contained a small community of rice growers and fishermen since it was there that the founder of Malacca, Parameswara,

[1]For a note on the identification of this toponym see Hill, 1973, 97.

had earlier had occasion to seek refuge. But well known as Malacca itself was to Arab and Chinese master mariners, the hinterland remained little known and little exploited. The swamps backing the sand ridges and low hills of the town-site were used for sago not rice, the bulk of that grain being imported, while the hills were occupied by orchards (Wheatley, 1961, 312). Ma-huan's description of 1451 confirmed that of Fei-hsin of 1436 and noted that the soils were sandy and saline and that the infertile fields yielded little rice (Wheatley 1961, 321, 324; Mills, 1970, 47).

Pires's account (1512–15) gives further details of Malacca and other west coast settlements. In the reign of Muhammed Iskander Shah, that monarch begged his Siamese overlord always to help him with foodstuffs (Cortesão, 1944, 2, 238), indicating some lack of locally-produced staples. Iskander's successor took up land on the river 'Fremoso', i.e. the Batu Pahat, '...on which river there is a little rice, meats and fish' (Cortesão, 1944, 2, 244). Muar was self-sufficient in rice. Malacca was not self-sufficient, being 'not very fertile', yet according to Varthema (Jones, 1863, 225) some grain was produced and there were many elephants, horses, sheep, cows and buffaloes. Not mentioned by Pires were settlements of Sumatran Minangkabau peoples who seem to have begun to settle the modern Negri Sembilan, perhaps by the end of the fifteenth century since their migration was already in progress when noted by Albuquerque in 1512 (Shamsul, 1964, 13).

Northwards, Pires mentions settlements at the mouth of the Jugra,[1] at Klang, Bernam, 'Mimjam' (?=Dindings), Perak and Bruas, concerning which place he noted that 'This Bruas[2] has plenty of rice' (Cortesão, 1944, 2, 261). Northwards again was Kedah, now '...a very small kingdom, with few people and few houses...[but] rice in quantities and pepper' (Cortesão, 1944, 1, 106–7).

In the time of Pires, Malaya was thus largely under forest, a green blanket scorched here and there, along the major river valleys, with the yellow of ripening padi. This was produced in sufficient quantity in Kedah for there to be an export along with an 'abundance of fine pepper' (Dames, 1921, 2, 165). For the rest it must be presumed, for lack of evidence to the contrary, that the peasantry produced little more than enough for their own and their master's needs. The populace in the immediate vicinity of Malacca town used imported rice. The fishermen of the coasts and the shrimpers, the crabbers and the shell-fish gatherers of the sea beaches and estuaries may have been a small group who bought rice from the inlanders in return for the protein-rich products of the sea. In inland Pahang, Perak and around Mount Ophir, inland from Malacca, small groups of specialist miners and smelters may have existed, but both mining and the collection of jungle produce were likely to have been no more than off-season

[1]Pires has 'Cinyojum' which Cortesão (1944, 2, 260) located at the mouth of the S. Jugra, a river not to be found on modern topographical maps. The southern mouth of the S. Langat, near Bukit Jugra, the traditional seat of Selangor royalty, is clearly meant.
[2]The 'Bruas' of Pires lay near the modern Bruas, at that time probably on the Perak river which has since changed its course. See Hill, 1973, 99n.

occupations undertaken at the behest of authority whose economic position would be strengthened thereby.

Nevertheless, by the early sixteenth century several rice-growing traditions may be dimly discerned. The most recent and most skilled was that of the migrant Minangkabau, growers of rice in hillside dry fields, in valley-floor fields flooded by water entrapped on the surface, in fields irrigated by water-wheel on the river-terraces. To the north, around the Merbok estuary in Kedah and also in the Kedah plain proper was another tradition. This was probably partly of Indian origin to the extent of using the plough, *tenggala*. This tradition is also distinguishable by a constellation of regional terms for various aspects of rice-growing but to be reliable, etymological studies would have to show that the proportion of Kedah dialect words relating to rice was greater than the proportion of Kedah dialect words in Malay as a whole. This is not yet possible. Was this tradition, as Malays in the north have it, in fact derived from Songkla and Patani, in turn the successors of as yet hardly-known Mon states? Elsewhere in the lowlands little beyond the fact that rice was grown can be stated with certainty. In Kelantan and Trengganu the characteristic implements were the dibble and the short hoe (*keri*). Transplanting was not universal, if indeed it was practised at all, since even today it is not universal (Hill and Arope, 1969). Had the plough extended beyond Kedah and its immediate environs it would surely have been noticed. In the uplands non-Malay peoples were probably still growing tubers and millet (*Setaria* or *Coix*) but to European observers clinging to a maritime life-line, the hills were mere physiographic expressions.

During the following centuries to the beginning of the colonial era little more comes to light. Nevertheless sufficient evidence exists to dismiss as needlessly speculative the views of those who would suggest that rice-growing was introduced by Indians from Sumatra (Bird, 1883, 262) or claim Siamese models for non-existent irrigation systems (Ong, 1958, iii).

3

Towards a Colonial Economy:
The Peninsula North and South
to *c*.1800

Patani is a place which of itself yields little.

George Ball, 1618, VNL, 1915, 1, 87.

Queda is [*sic*] a good marshy Soil...
In former Times the Country was well peopled, and abounded with all sorts of
Provisions, especially Rice and Cattle...

Commodore Beaulieu, 1619–22[1]

Malacca—The countrie yields not any fruit, but some little corne in certain
places.

Mathew Lownes and John Bill, 1615, 184.

ON the whole the irruption of Western powers into the waters of South-
East Asia did little to influence the production of staples. Although country traders occasionally engaged in the rice trade and the supply of rice
to essentially non-producing areas such as Patani, Johore and Malacca
(at that time not a production area) was a matter of strategic importance,
there is only indirect evidence that ships' victualling and the needs of
trading centres promoted the production of rice. A major exception was
Siam, an exporter by the seventeenth century (Tachard, 1686, 199). Both
Arakan and Java were rice-exporting regions in the same century (*Dagh-
Register 1641–2*, 177; van Leur, 1955, 128), and in the Peninsula, Kedah
had a small but steady export except for several periods when it was
ravaged by war. For the rest of the region, subsistence production with
some local trade must be assumed though not until the end of the eighteenth century, following the widespread imposition of partial imperial
control, do the sources permit a comprehensive account.

By the early years of the sixteenth century, rice culture was widespread
in the Archipelago, except in the south-east, in marginal areas such as
Enggano, the Andamans and Nicobars and in the upland preserves of
aboriginal peoples. But older crops had by no means been completely

[1]Harris, 1764, 739.

displaced by rice. In the Moluccas, Barros reported that millet and rice were available in small quantities but the basic diet of the islanders was sago. In Cebu rice and millet were in use and in Palawan rice and rice wine were consumed by the inhabitants. A number of Portuguese sources confirm that the Sumatrans' usual diet included millet, rice, seeds and wild fruits (Lach, 1965, 1, Bk. 2, 575, 605, 636–7). Much later several sources note the growing of millet or 'wheat', clearly millet, in Siam (Gervaise, 1688, 7; de la Loubère, 1693, 17). There is no direct evidence that rice was more than one of a range of staple food crops in the Peninsula. That rice was probably one crop of several is supported by evidence from earlier times (Chapter 2) and by the evidence from the circumjacent areas just enumerated.

THE NORTHERN REGION

In the north, the main centres of settlement were Patani, Singgora (now Songkla), Ligor and finally Kedah, which was linked with these by overland trade routes. Of these only Kedah was unequivocally an important centre of rice production whilst Perak on the west, and Kelantan and Trengganu on the east were little known.

PATANI, SINGGORA, LIGOR

Early in the seventeenth century, East India Company factors at Patani consistently reported that Patani, like Malacca, itself produced but little rice, requiring to import it from Siam (VNL 1915, 1, 87, 103, 138, 166). Towards the end of the same century, the *Hikayat Patani* reported the digging of a canal on the S. Tambangan in order to freshen the water supply of the town, and, according to the editors of the *Hikayat*, to prevent further damage to rice fields (Teeuw and Wyatt, 1970, 177, 245).

Nearby Ligor produced pepper and possibly rice early in the century since a report of the blockade of Pahang by the Queen of Patani mentions junks laden with rice from Ligor (VNL 1915, 1, 109; Moreland, 1934, 72). However, later in the century the Java Factory Records reported the sending of a factor to Ligor to sell rice (VNL 1915, 1, 167). The earlier Batavia *Dagh-Register* records do little to clearly establish whether the north-eastern states produced rice. In 1624 and 1625 ships from Patani and Singgora arrived with cargoes of rice, but rice is not listed subsequently.

It must be concluded therefore that these states were at best self-sufficient in rice and at times were importers of the staple. Yet towards the close of the following century, Patani was said to abound with grains and fruits (Middleton, 1779, Chapter 12, Sec. 3).[1] Accepting the accuracy of this observation, it is clear that the north-eastern states were not to be classed with Kedah as rice-producers and that their development as rice-producing centres in the era of Western contacts post-dates, not antedates, that of Kedah.

[1]A century after the Middleton report, McCarthy (1898, 10–12) noted large areas of rice land in the Patani and Yala areas.

KEDAH

Kedah early in the sixteenth century was a place of little consequence and although Pires noted the production of rice in quantity (Cortesão, 1944, 1, 106–7) his contemporary Barros failed to mention it. But where was Pires's Kedah? The chronicles noted only that it was up-river. The fact that pepper was locally produced points to the traditional centre of settlement on the southern flank of Gunong Jerai (Kedah Peak). Rice was thus presumably grown in the narrow valleys of the massif and on the higher side of the Merbok valley, the lower levels of which must have been, then as now, under mangrove vegetation.

In the 1580s, Linschoten noted the existence of pepper (not necessarily pepper-growing) but not rice (Burnell and Tiele, 1885, 1, 103). Nevertheless, until its sack by Acheh, Kedah possessed a flourishing agriculture based upon cattle, rice and pepper. Trade links extended westwards to Bengal, Surat and Coromandel (Beaulieu[1] in Harris, 1764, 1, 739; *Dagh-Register 1641–2*, 93). Thomas Bowrey, in the 1670s, noted of Kedah that, 'Rice they have in great plenty...' (Temple, 1905, 279). Schouten, 1663, confirmed this description (Temple, 1905, 260n) and there must have been a surplus to support the fortress-building activities of the young Raja twenty years earlier (VNL 1915, 2, 6).

By the second half of the succeeding century, Kedah was a recognized provisioning point for vessels of the East India Company (Bassett, 1964, 122). The state also had a regular system of written titles to land (Kedah AR 1909, 14). The flat country resembled Bengal and the population was increasing (Forrest, 1784). Forrest continued, 'At *Queda* there is great plenty of rice, bullocks, buffaloes, and poultry.... *Queda* is a flat country, favourable for the cultivation of rice....' Pires noted the production of pepper as well as rice whereas Bowrey, Beaulieu and later Forrest do not report pepper-growing on the mainland. Since for ecological reasons pepper cannot have been grown on the Kedah plain, it seems likely that 'Old Kedah' at the foot of Gunong Jerai had greatly declined and may have been abandoned during the first half of the seventeenth century. The focus of rice production was subsequently centred around the capital, variously located at or near Alor Star, but the state remained of small account as a rice-producer until the following century (Foster, 1930, 1, 39).

PERAK

Perak was above all the source of tin. Still, it must be presumed that rice production was at least sufficient for local requirements. The Batavia *Dagh-Register* has an occasional note of the arrival of vessels from Perak which included rice in their cargoes, although the quantity was possibly little more than ships' stores (*Dagh-Register 1643–4*, 24). Nor is there a single account of Perak importing rice. As in Kedah (*c.* 1663), 'The soil...

[1]Beaulieu visited Langkawi and Kedah in the period 1619 to 1622. Whether his 'large river' of Kedah was indeed the present Kedah or in fact 'Old Kedah' on the Merbok is not known. Hulsius (1601, frontispiece) and Bowrey (Temple, 1905, 262, 284) mention both settlements.

would be very productive, but, as there are a great many woods, wild districts, mountains and swamps...those who would like to devote themselves to agriculture dare not undertake it. For this reason, very fertile tracts remain uncultivated' (Schouten in Temple, 1905, 260n.).

Both lowland wet rice and hill padi were being grown although the evidence is exiguous. A Perak Minangkabau legal digest c. 1700–28 mentioned wet rice fields (bendang) and permitted headmen to give out fields abandoned for three years to others who wished to take them up (Winstedt, 1953, 8). Whether local Perak Malays, as distinct from immigrant Minangkabau, also cultivated bendangs is unknown. In the reign of Sultan Mozafar Shah, one Raja Khalim was ordered out of the capital, Kuala Kangsar, and ultimately went to Tanjong Putus where he planted hill rice (Maxwell, 1882b, 259).

In Forrest's day (1783) Perak was considered 'favourable for the cultivation of rice', and it was presumably produced in some quantity, especially around the capital, then at Rantau Panjang (Forrest, 1792, 27).

KELANTAN AND TRENGGANU

Records of these two states between the time of the Trengganu stone and the nineteenth century are rather scanty but of the two, Trengganu was much the more important. Alexander Hamilton's picture is idyllic.

Trangano is a very pleasant and healthful country...the hills are low and covered with evergreen trees, that accommodate the Inhabitants with Variety of delicious Fruits....And in the Vallies, Corn, Pulse, and Sugar-canes. The ground is cultivated by the *Chinese*, for the lazy *Malayas* [*sic*] cannot take that Trouble.
Foster, 1930, 2, 83.

The presence of Chinese agriculturalists in those parts was confirmed by Hsieh Ch'ing-Kao, who visited Kelantan in 1785–95 (Wang, 1960, 34) but Chinese may well have already been in this region for a millenium (Chen, 1923). Concerning the Kelantan Malays, Hsieh suggested that most were fishermen, though those living in the hills either cultivated land or gathered wood (Wang, 1960, 33–4). Hamilton's report of Chinese in Trengganu is further confirmed by Pallegoix (1854, 23) who estimated that they comprised almost one-fifth of the total population. This raises the tantalizing possibility that it was the Chinese who introduced advanced techniques such as ploughing, bunding of fields and transplanting. If so, and the matter is open, then bunding and transplanting would seem not to have been taken up by the populace in general, since Hugh Clifford (1897, 31) reported that only 10 per cent of the rice was from bunded and transplanted fields.

THE SOUTHERN REGION

The west coast of the Peninsula, from Perak to Linggi, seems to have been the haunt of peoples best described as 'strand-loopers'. The inland regions were but sparsely and sporadically inhabited by tin-miners, the outlets for whose produce were the Perak river, Larut, Klang, 'Porselar' i.e. Jugra, Bernam and Linggi (Meilink-Roelofsz, 1962, 29). Concerning agriculture nothing is known. The same can be said for the whole of the east coast south of Trengganu, with the exception of parts of Pahang. The major focus in the south was of course Malacca, concerning which observers were unanimous in denying major agricultural importance. The remainder of the west coast and the area along the Johore river seem to have had but little agriculture and little rice. Pahang at this time, as earlier, is something of an enigma. Minangkabau migrants had moved east as far as the vicinity of Temerloh, but upstream, mining, not agriculture, was important and Pahang, like Johore, imported most of its rice requirements.

MALACCA AND THE MINANGKABAU STATES

Rice cultivation in the Malacca region seems to be of fairly late origin, as of course was Malacca itself. Initially rice production was minimal, the people being occupied mainly with fishing and washing tin (Groeneveldt, 1887, 246, 253) but by 1586 'Portuguese' Christian settlers had moved inland along the Malacca valley where they had made orchards and gardens (Chardon, 1940, 110).

One reasonably comprehensive account of the agriculture of Malacca is that of Eredia in 1613 (Janssen, 1882; Mills, 1930). People living in the suburbs of the town were not agriculturalists, some deriving their income from fishing and occasional work in the forests of the interior, and some by tapping *nipah* and other palms. In the outlying parishes along the Malacca river large cattle and farmyard animals were raised. Only in the interior were food-crops grown.

The land is extremely fertile there and very suitable to the culture of food-crops: it produces all types of rice and grain. . . . The foodstuffs of the natives include a great variety of tubers and yams which the low-lying terrain produces in great quantity besides rice and grain. It is rice above all which is the staple food: there are various types of it, of which the best is *girical*[1] which is a white rice...though the lower classes eat a darker-coloured rice. . . . There is also another type of oily rice called *puloth* [*pulut*] which is white, black or red. . . . Rice is grown in wet marshy places of the lowlands. All other types of grain are grown on the upland. . . . Although the land produces rice and grains, many of the natives buy from Javanese merchants all the grain and all the rice they can procure, to sell it again in periods when there is an increase in the cost of provisions and periods when the land is unproductive. These calamitous epochs occur quite frequently because of the troubles and wars which lay waste Malacca. . . .

Janssen, 1882, 8, 16, 17.

Clearly this was no rice monoculture. The role of grains other than rice, presumably millets of some description, of tubers, of livestock both large and small, and of beans and green leafy vegetables point to an alimentation

[1]*Girical* is obviously a Portuguese transliteration of a Malay word, but which? One possibility is *jereket*, 'sticky'.

somewhat more varied than that of the present. A similar view, some thirty years later, is that of Schouten whose description additionally points towards the existence of a form of plantation management employing slave labour within a system of mixed agriculture.

Beyond the suburbs and a few miles up the river *Panagy* [=Penaga] and all the land between the two rivers were mostly covered with big fruit orchards, beautiful meadows, or pasture grounds for cattle and extensive rice fields under cultivation. The black Christians (mostly slaves of the citizens) lived here. To the north and south, the seashore, about three miles from the city up to the rivers *Panagy* and *Kassang* [=Kesang] was similarly inhabited while both banks of the *Malacca* river up to the church of *Nossa Signora de Guadaloupe* (about 4 miles from the city) were also covered with very beautiful orchards, meadows, and rice fields, and were inhabited....

The village of *Naning* and *Ringy* or *Rangy* [=Renggek]...the former is inhabited by Monicabers [Minangkabau] and the latter by Malays. They planted rice, cultivated Siri [*sireh*] fruits and bred cattle and sold them in the Malacca market....*Ringy* is situated at the mouth of the River Kassong [Kesang]... having a population of 400....

Naning lies inland at about 8 miles from Malacca with 100 inhabitants....

Leupe, 1936, 88.

In the immediate vicinity of the port itself, the lower lands between tree-lined sand ridges paralleling the coast were cleared and almost certainly under rice (Boxer, 1964, pl. opp. 110).

When the Minangkabau were not skirmishing with Malacca, the intruders sold food to the town. But despite the Portuguese complaints that dependence upon imported food was unnecessary since the country nearby was perfectly capable of supporting the wants of the town, Malay land-holders were seemingly reluctant to enter into commercial production to any significant degree (Maxwell, 1911, 4). In any case the trade of Malacca was almost extinct by the time the Dutch began their blockade (Harrison, 1954, 107) though twenty years earlier Javanese rice junks had flocked to the port and earlier still the noble Lancaster had made play with Portuguese vessels bringing rice from Bengal (Purchas, 1625, 424; van Leur 1955, 128).

Like the Portuguese, the Dutch complained that the Malays would grow little more rice than sufficed for their own needs although at Naning, pepper and a small surplus of rice were available (*Dagh-Register 1641-2,* 158, 178). In 1668 the Malacca rice fields produced 76 loads of 3,000 pounds each as against an estimated requirement of 200 loads yearly (Harrison, 1954, 115–16). Production had earlier been reduced by war both in Malacca and the Minangkabau states of Naning and Rembau. The rice lands along the Malacca river were resettled by Catholic refugees following the siege but were again abandoned in 1664 for fear of the Minangkabau. To the north of the town the lands at Batang Tiga were also abandoned and were still derelict at the time of Governor Bort's report in 1678 (Bremner, 1926, 51). The threatening Minangkabau themselves suffered the destruction of Melekek village together with its orchards and

rice fields in the punitive expedition which followed and suffered again
a year later when Naning was reduced to ashes and its fields laid waste
(Chardon, 1940, 124).

In Malacca territory, in the lower valleys, Bort reported that

The lands called Marlimoèn [=Merlimau], Ringy [=Renggek] and Cassan
[=Kesang] on the south side have each a small stream running out into the sea
and level fields [i.e. *sawah*]. Black Christians of the Roman Catholic faith live
there but mostly Malays and Bugis earning a livelihood in the main from rice
plantations.

Bremner, 1926, 51.

These 'Black Christians', partly the offspring of Portuguese and Mantra
aborigines, being Catholic, were persecuted by the Dutch and had therefore moved to the rural areas not only in the south but also again up the
Malacca river to the vicinity of the church of Nossa Senhora da Guadaloupe where they occupied garden and rice lands at To' Alang, Machap,
Belimbing, Panchor and Tanah Merah. The Dutch East India Company
or wealthy burghers now owned large tracts and as Bort condescendingly
notes, some were let at 50 per cent of the produce 'to the poor inhabitants'
(Chardon, 1940, 133).

Not all lands were let out at such high rates but in the period of Dutch
occupation, rights to collect a tithe of the produce were given out to a
small group of proprietors.

The object of the Dutch government in assigning to persons designated as
proprietors, the right of levying one tenth, probably was to make it the interest
of certain individuals to introduce, encourage and extend the cultivation of the
land, but it appears that so far from taking any pains for that purpose, they never
even visited their estates, that they did not themselves collect the tenth, but rented
it in the mass once a year to a Chinese contractor... and it appears that an excess
is sometimes levied, beyond the tenth, moreover that services are retained and
labor [*sic*] exacted from the tenants, in short they are kept in a state of vassalage
and servitude quite inconsistent with the encouragement of cultivation.

Blundell, 1848, 740.

Bort's policy had been to encourage local production of rice by repos-
sessing unsown lands and giving them out to others by lending money
against future deliveries of rice (Bremner, 1926, 51). But production was
very small. The *Register* of 1668 gives a total rice production of 38,000
gantangs,[1] a tiny amount, which, allowing the very moderate yield of 100
gantangs per acre, would mean an area of only 380 acres in cultivation,
or, allowing 400 gantangs per family per year, sufficient to support 80
families. Production must have been more than double this since rice
farmers, excluding the 'Black Christians', were drawn from the Malay and
Bugis population which totalled 768 and 125 respectively (Bremner, 1926,
40–1, 51).

[1] However, it is hard to believe that this figure included all rice retained for home use.

Attemp s to promote self-sufficiency in Malacca having failed, it became policy to prohibit entirely the cultivation of rice,[1] though it may be questioned just how far this prohibition was enforceable (Blundell, 1848, 739). Yet enforced it seems to have been, at least in the immediate vicinity of the town, since Koenig's 1779 report somewhat ingenuously stated that, 'The Governor von Schillingen. . . assured me that only utter need forced the poor living there to eat sago. Whoever was rich enough to buy rice, which must be imported as it does not grow there, would never be induced to eat sago. . . .' (Koenig, 1894, xxvi, 190). Malacca was thus dependent upon rice imports from Java, the preferred source, Arakan and Bengal, exporting commodities such as wax, *dammar*, *kajangs*, preserved fish and *pinang* nuts, from which the local populace derived cash income (*Dagh-Register*, various dates).

Throughout and beyond the period of Dutch control, rice cultivation in Malacca was a matter of little consequence. Inland, beyond the enlarged Malacca and beyond the eyes of Dutch observers, the Minangkabau peoples had doubtless established their sophisticated form of agriculture, but of this nothing substantial was known before the nineteenth century. Discussion of this is thus postponed to Chapter 7.

JOHORE

Johore was founded *c*.1530 but at no time was it a significant area of rice production even though it was a major political and economic power. An appendix to the *Malay Annals* refers to an order from the founder, Ala'u'd-din, for aborigines to fell scrub for his settlement (Winstedt, 1932, 13). This, and the fact that in the reign of Muzaffar Shah, both sides of the Seluyut river were settled up to Padang Riang-Riang (Winstedt, 1932, 22), suggests cultivation, but of what?

Tung Hsi Yang K'au (1616) reported that, 'Johore does not produce any rice, and the inhabitants are accustomed to go in small ships to other countries, exchanging the products of their own for rice' (Groeneveldt, 1887, 255). From Muar small vessels were reported as blockade-running rice to the Portuguese besieged in Malacca (Leupe, 1936, 31). This rice could have come from the coastal tracts but more likely from Ulu Muar where Minangkabau peoples were settled on the Segamat river (*Dagh-Register 1641–2*, 73). But the Rio Formoso (Batu Pahat) and Muar were more noted for pepper than rice whilst, 'The fields of Johore. . . because of the war, were mostly not sown, except that some fields were already prepared for the sowing of rice and pepper' (*Dagh-Register 1640–1*, 226).

Nevertheless Johore was a rice-deficit area as numerous *Dagh-Register* entries testify and whilst rice very occasionally appears in the manifests of vessels from Johore such exciting goods as salted fish-skins, sago,

---

[1] It has not been possible to establish when this became policy. Abdullah (Hill, 1955, 212) speaking of Malacca *c*. 1823 noted that, 'In the time of the Dutch nobody had been directed to plant rice for ages past'. Blundell (1848) failed to give a date.

pinang, and *kajang* comprised the bulk of the cargoes. This deficiency in rice has never been made good, even down to the present.

PAHANG

Pahang is an enigma. Those with intimate knowledge of the state frequently hear of a wonderful 'lost civilization' usually denoted Thai but sometimes Khmer, centred around lakes Bera and Chini and based upon elaborate irrigation of rice. Apart from a few undated, unexcavated heaps of brickwork and occasional pottery of Chinese and Sawankalok provenance, together with some place-names, there is nothing to justify these speculations (Sircom, 1920; Linehan, 1928; 1936; 1947; Wavell, 1958; Southwood, 1960).

The earliest reliable report, in the *Hsing-ch'a Sheng-lan c.*1436 noted that, 'The ground is fertile and they have abundance of rice' (Linehan, 1936, 7). Around the end of the following century Sultan Abdul Ghafar had compiled a legal digest which indicated irrigation and specified that lands might be let only for a fixed rent, but because the text contains undated additions, these matters cannot be definitely ascribed to this time (Kempe and Winstedt, 1948). Certainly at some time prior to 1612 the rice supply situation had drastically changed, possibly, as Southwood (1960, 28) suggests, as a result of disastrous floods.

By 1612 Pahang was clearly a rice-deficit area as is witnessed by Peter Floris's account of its blockade by the Queen of Patani (Purchas, 1625, 329). The state then imported rice from Siam and Cambodia. From 1623, the region of the Pahang river, depopulated by raids and transportations, had become the haunt of pirates (Linehan, 1936, 39). Some economic recovery was indicated by the *Dagh-Register* but cargoes arriving at Batavia from Pahang were few, comprising items similar to those of Johore. Rice was presumably grown in small quantity but even Hamilton makes no mention of it although he lists pepper (Foster, 1930, 2, 81). On the whole, as Linehan notes (1936, 52), we know little about Pahang in the eighteenth century.

TYPOLOGY, TECHNIQUES AND THE SOCIAL SETTING

In the fifty years comprising the last quarter of the eighteenth and the first quarter of the nineteenth centuries, there was a great burgeoning of works in English relating to the Malay world. These writings serve to establish clearly the salient characteristics of rice cultivation, first in Sumatra, then in Java and the islands to the eastwards then, partly by implication, in the Peninsula (Marsden, 1811; Raffles, 1817; Crawfurd, 1820). To these must be added the rather earlier *Herbarium* of Rumpf (1741–50) and a brief outline by Stavorinus (1798, 1, 230–1). No general account of agriculture, specifically in the Peninsula, at this time exists but the detailed evidence to be discussed subsequently confirms and elaborates Crawfurd's general model which exhibits the major characteristics of rice cultivation.

TYPOLOGY

An early typology of rice cultivation was that of Poivre who was in South-East Asia in the period 1745–7 (Mallaret, 1968, 5–7). Poivre drew the fundamental distinction between cultivation on high, dry ground, and cultivation in marshes, the Sumatran and general Malay distinction between *padi ladang* and *padi sawah*, and the modern dry rice and wet rice.

These distinctions were refined by Crawfurd (1820, 1, 360–3) whose observations led him to a quadripartite typology superior to the earlier dual typology which, however, remains entrenched in the literature.[1] In the Archipelago, Crawfurd noted,

The *rudest*, and probably the earliest practised mode of cultivating rice consists in taking from the forest lands a fugitive crop, after burning the trees, grass and underwood. The ground is turned up with the mattock and the seed planted by dibbling between the stumps of the trees....

The *second* description of rice tillage consists also in growing mountain or dry land rice. This...tillage differs from the last chiefly by the situations in which it is practised. These situations are the common upland arable lands, lands, in short, which, from their locality, cannot be subjected to the process of flooding. The grain in this mode of culture is sown in the middle of the dry season, by dibbling or by broadcast, and reaped in seven or five months....In this mode of culture no lands are of sufficient fertility to yield two crops within the year, and in poor lands it often happens that a fallow of one, two, or even three years, is necessary to renovate the soil. An European soon learns to distinguish this mode of culture, by the absence of the chequered appearance produced in the marsh rice lands by the dikes of irrigation,—by the superior extent of the fields,—by their being frequently surrounded with an imperfect hedge....

The culture of rice by [the] aid of the periodical rains is the *third* mode of tillage. Of course, the grain is of that kind which requires submersion....With the first fall of the rains, the lands are ploughed and harrowed....The seed is sown in beds usually by strewing very thickly the corn [=grain] in the ear. From these beds the plants...are removed into the fields and thinly set with the hand. This practice of transplanting is universal. The plants are constantly immersed in water until within a fortnight of the harvest, when it is drawn off to facilitate the ripening of the grain....

The *fourth*...mode of cultivating rice is the most refined of all....It consists in forcing rice by artificial irrigation, and is found only to prevail in the most improved parts of the Archipelago....This mode does not depend upon the seasons, and hence we see in the finest parts of Java, where it chiefly obtains, at any given season, and in the same district; within, indeed, the compass of a few acres, rice in every state of progress....Lands which can be inundated at pleasure almost always yield a white [i.e. a cereal] and a green [i.e. a pulse] crop within the year, and to take two white crops from them...is very common...when this practice is pursued, it is always the five months grain which is grown. The rapid growth of this variety has, indeed, enabled the Javanese husbandman, in a few happy situations, to urge the culture to the amount of six crops in two years and a half....

Crawfurd's four main types require but little expansion to encompass

[1] For modern typologies see Hill, 1966a, 1970; Hill and Ühlig, 1970.

the various other classes of cultivation which must have existed at that time. Shifting cultivation was practised not only on hill lands but also to some extent in swamps and on other flat land, as in Pahang or in the eastern islands of the Archipelago (Rumpf, 1741–50, Bk. 8, Sec. 30). In Crawfurd's third type, which may be denoted 'rain rice', bunded fields were sometimes absent, again as in Pahang where permanent cultivation took place in the *payas*. Irrigated cultivation was rare in the Peninsula, being largely confined to areas settled by Minangkabau peoples. Unlike Java, double-cropping and continuous cropping[1] were unknown in the Peninsula except in the far north amongst the Siamese of Mergui (Malleret, 1968, 76).

THE ROUND OF WORK: SHIFTING CULTIVATION

The first step in the cultivation of rice under shifting cultivation, whether in the swamps or on the hill slopes, was the selection of the tract to be cleared. This was done at the approach of the dry, south-west monsoon in April or May. According to Marsden (1811, 67–8),

...the site of woods is universally preferred, and the more ancient the woods the better, on account of the superior richness of the soil....[But] if old woods are not at hand, ground covered with that of younger growth, termed *balukar*, is resorted to; but not, if possible, under the age of four or five years.

Following selection, the chosen plot, probably an acre or two in extent, was marked out by the husbandman. Upon him thus devolved rights to the use of the land so long as he should cause it to be occupied by crops or later, by fruit trees (Marsden, 1811, 68). Next the ground was cleared.

The work divides itself into two parts. The first (called *tebbas, menebbas*) consists in cutting down the brushwood, and rank vegetables [*sic*], which are suffered to dry during an interval of a fortnight, or more or less...before they proceed to the second operation (called *tebbang, menebbang*) of felling the large trees. Their tools, [are] the *prang* [=*parang*] and *billiong* [=*beliong*]...they do not fell the tree near the ground...but erect a stage, and begin to hew...where the dimensions are smaller...it is not an uncommon practice to cut a number of trees half-through ...and then fix upon one of great bulk, at the extremity of the space marked out... [and] determine its fall in such a direction as to produce the effect of its bearing down by its prodigious weight all those trees which had previously been weakened....
Some of the branches are lopped off, and when these, together with the underwood, have become sufficiently arid, they are set fire to, and the country, for the space of a month or two, is in a general blaze and smoke, until the whole is consumed, and the ground effectually cleared. The expiring wood, beneficent to its ungrateful destroyer, fertilizes for his use, by its ashes and their salts, the earth which it so long adorned....
Unseasonable weather at this period...produces much inconvenience by the delay of burning, till the vegetation has had time to renew itself; in which case the spot is commonly abandoned....

Marsden, 1811, 68–71.

[1]The term 'double-cropping' is equivocal and at present is still commonly used in both the senses of Crawfurd to refer to a 'rice—rice' succession and to a 'rice—other crop' succession. 'Continuous cropping' is equally equivocal. Some advance is made in Hill and Ühlig, 1970.

In this case, tubers such as species of *Colocasia* and *Dioscorea*, whether wild or cultivated, would have to suffice as famine food (Rumpf, 1741–50, Bk. 9, Sec. 9). More likely the husbandman whose misfortune it was to have failed to burn his clearing adequately would now seek swamp land in which to make a sawah. This was definitely regarded as second-best since any connoisseur of rice, then as now, would hold that the *ladang* rice is better-smelling, better-tasting and better-keeping than the 'watery' rice of wet fields (Marsden, 1811, 66; Raffles, 1817, 1, 118). Moreover a hill ladang, unlike a sawah, would provide a variety of vegetables, including bananas, maize, pumpkins and gourds, sugarcane and chillies (Maxwell, 1884, 81).

The next stage of cultivation was sowing; the soil normally does not require tilling, though Crawfurd (1820, 1, 360) claimed that the ground was turned up with a mattock.

Prior to the advent of Islam, sowing took place at the time of the rising of the constellation Pleiades which rises in October and sets in late March. In some districts in Malaya and in Sumatra, following the introduction of Islam, the people began the custom of planting after the end of the fasting month. This practice soon led to the agricultural year being out of phase with the seasons since the Muslim lunar year is shorter than the solar year by 11 days and the calendar thus passes through all the seasons in $32\frac{1}{2}$ years (Marsden, 1811, 71; Freeman-Grenville, 1963, 2).

When the periodical rains begin to fall, which takes place gradually about October, the planter assembles his neighbours (whom he assists in turn), and with the aid of his whole family proceeds to sow his ground.... The manner of sowing (*tugal–menugal*) is this. Two or three men enter the plantation... holding in each hand sticks about five feet long and two inches diameter, bluntly pointed, with which... they make small, shallow holes, at a distance of about five inches from each other. These [men] are followed by women and elder children with small baskets containing the seed grain...of which they drop four or five grains into every hole, and passing on, are followed by the younger children, who with their feet cover them lightly from the adjacent earth, that the seed may not be too much exposed to the birds....

Marsden, 1811, 71.

At the same time maize[1] and the seeds of a gourd, a common one being the local *Momordica charentia*, would be sown in the same field as the rice (Marsden, 1811, 72; Burkill, 1935, 2, 1485). It is also likely that the sweet *sali* millet (*Coix lachryma-jobi*) was planted around the margins of the rice fields. This practice certainly existed in the Eastern Archipelago and the crop is still known in the western parts (Rumpf, 1741–50, Bk. 8, Sec. 28). A main and a ratoon crop of sali were commonly taken.

The rice crop would have been above the ground within four or five days provided there was adequate rain, failing which sowing was repeated. At the end of a month a weeding was necessary and another a month or so later. Towards harvest time, as the crop came into bearing, a small hut

---

[1]Maize reached the Archipelago in Spanish times. See Burkill, 1935, 2, 2288–90.

was erected into which ran a series of rattans linking the post with such various bird-scaring devices as rattles, clappers and scarecrows. Around the margins of the fields, clacking 'windmills' were erected.[1]

Harvesting of the gourds began after two months, with the maize harvest following a month later. Reaping of the rice crop took place during the sixth month and again neighbours were summoned to the work. Since uneven ripening was the rule, the harvest could extend over a considerable period. Each head was cut individually by the harvester using a characteristic and probably very old type of knife, widely known as *tuai*, the Javanese *ani-ani* (see Colani, 1940). Only in Minangkabau areas was the sickle used (Marsden, 1811, 73n). The heads were then conveyed to the farmer's home where, following drying, they would be tied up into miniature sheaves and then stored, sometimes in the house itself, sometimes in special structures lined with bark. A normal yield was around eightyfold, giving between 400 and 800 gallons of unhusked rice per family, depending upon the area sown and the sowing rate.

Threshing, according to Crawfurd (1820, 1, 364), was sometimes done at once, the grain being stored unhusked. Alternatively threshing could take place as the rice was required for cooking. Crawfurd (1820, 1, 364) is emphatic that threshing by animals was never practised in the Archipelago, but Baker's account of its existence, though dying, in twentieth-century Kedah throws some doubt upon this (Baker, 1940, 43–4). Treading under the feet of women was usual, though sometimes threshing was combined with husking. Husking was also done by the women using large wooden mortars, with pestles of the same material (Rumpf, 1741–50, Bk. 8, Sec. 30; Crawfurd, 1820, 1, 365).

THE ROUND OF WORK: SEMI-PERMANENT CULTIVATION

Dry land plough cultivation is as much a form of short-cycle shifting cultivation as, a permanent form of cultivation with grass and scrub fallow. The annual cycle of work began with slashing of the scrub, where present, followed by burning it in heaps. Where the plough was to be employed, roots would be removed, but where the preceding fallow had been under grass grazed by livestock, this step was unnecessary. In Java, and probably elsewhere, a simple plough, lacking a mouldboard, was employed. Following ploughing the seed would be sown either broadcast or by dibbling, the latter being more conservative of seed. Crawfurd (1820, 1, 361) is surely in error in suggesting that sowing took place in the middle of the dry season. Not only would most soils be too hard to work at that season, but satisfactory germination would be almost impossible. Intercropping with maize and gourds was probably not practised. For the remainder of the cycle of production, weeding, harvesting, and threshing were similar to the processes already described, with the minor exception that both seven-month and five-month rices were grown under this upland

[1]This practice seems to have died out in Malaya, though other devices are common enough. Windmills are common in rice fields in Sabah.

arable system. An average yield was about a hundredfold, or between 500 and 1,000 gallons of unhusked rice per family (Marsden, 1811, 77).

The number of years during which a crop was taken was highly variable but in no case could more than one crop a year be taken. Crawfurd (1820, 1, 361) fails to make clear the number of successive years in which a crop was taken, but the range was probably from one to six years under crop, each cropping period being followed by a one- to three-year fallow under grass, usually given over to grazing.[1]

THE ROUND OF WORK: PERMANENT CULTIVATION

As Raffles (1817, 1, 115) correctly noted,

It is on the *sawahs* that the great rice cultivation is carried on; and these admit of a subdivision, according to the manner in which the land is irrigated. Those which can be irrigated at pleasure from adjacent springs or rivers, are considered as the proper *sawah*; those which depend upon the periodical rains for the whole or principal part of the water by which they are fertilized, are termed *sawah tadahan*....

The round of work on each of these types was very similar, varying only to the extent that the former type required maintenance of the means of irrigation. However, where cropping was continuous, as in parts of Java, the whole round of work would necessarily have been speeded up.

In the Peninsula, the Minangkabau certainly, some Kelantanese and a few Chinese farmers practised irrigation prior to the 1880s. For the irrigators the first stage in the agricultural year was the repair of water-wheels, clearing of ditches and the construction of temporary brushwood dams in the streams. For the others the first step was the clearing away of reeds and long grass which had grown up during the dry season. Where possible these were burnt, otherwise they were piled on the embankments (*batas*) between the fields. Alternatively the rubbish was merely slashed and left to rot in the rising water. The soil was then worked by one of several methods:

In some places a number of buffaloes...are turned in, and these by their motions contribute to give it a more uniform consistence, as well as enrich[ing] it by their dung. In other parts, less permanently moist, the soil is turned up either with a wooden [-handled] instrument between a hoe and a pick-axe, or with the plough, of which they use two kinds; their own, drawn by one buffalo, extremely simple, and the wooden share of it doing little more than scratch the ground to the depth of six inches; and the one they borrowed from the Chinese, drawn either with one or two buffaloes, very light...turning the soil over as it passes, and making a narrow furrow. In *sawahs*, however, the surface has in general so little consistence, that no furrow is perceptible, and the plough does little more than loosen the stiff mud to some depth, and cut the roots of the grass and weeds, from which it is afterwards cleared by means of a kind of harrow or rake.... This they contrive to drag along the surface, for the purpose, at the same time, of depressing the

[1]These paragraphs are largely based upon extrapolation from modern practices and upon Crawfurd (1820, 1, 361). See also Hill, 1966b.

rising spots and filling up the hollow ones, the whole being brought as nearly as possible to a level, that the water may lie equally upon it....

Marsden, 1811, 74–5.

Where the fields had been used as grazing for livestock, the initial step of slashing weeds was unnecessary where ploughing followed.

While the sawahs were being tilled a small nursery plot nearby was worked, presumably with the hoe, though the sources are silent on the point, following which the seed *padi* was thickly sown, according to Crawfurd (1820, 1, 362), usually in the ear. Two types of nursery, one wet and the other dry, were probably employed in various parts. A further type, the floating nursery, may also have been used but again the sources are silent. At the end of some forty days, the bulk of the seedlings, now five to eight inches high, were planted out into the prepared sawahs, a moiety being reserved in the nursery to replace such seedlings as might fail to survive transplantation. Transplanting seems generally to have been regarded as 'women's work' in contrast to the working of the soil which was invariably a male task. Simultaneity of planting was highly desirable to avoid the severe losses to rats and birds which would otherwise ensue at maturity. The synchronization of planting was not imposed by formal authority. In the words of Marsden (1811, 76), '...the inhabitants of a district sow by agreement pretty nearly at the same time....' Transplanting seems to have been the general rule, but in the Peninsula at least, direct sowing into sawah land was practised (*GGPWISM* 17.1.1829).

The remaining tasks, weeding, crop protection and harvesting, were identical to those of shifting cultivation, with the exception that water trapped in the fields was allowed to drain away a month or so before harvest so that a satisfactory ripening of the crop could be obtained. The harvest took place either four months or six months after transplanting though some heavy-yielding varieties took eight months to mature. The harvested yield was about 120-fold, an amount varying between 600 and 1,200 gallons per family, according to the area and the sowing rate (Marsden, 1811, 77). Subsequent treatment of the crop was identical to that grown under a system of shifting cultivation. One characteristic of shifting cultivation, inter-cropping, was lacking under semi-permanent and permanent systems. But there is some evidence to suggest that the millet, *Coix lachryma-jobi* may have been grown as a crop around the margins of wet fields. Marsden (1811, 76) noted it in Sumatra. Rumpf (1741–50, Bk. 7, Sec. 28) reported that in Java and the eastern islands of the Archipelago it was sown on the margins of the rice fields, but there is no report of this practice in the Peninsula.

RELIGIOUS SANCTIONS

The fundamental drive influencing rice growers was of course hunger and the desire of the cultivator was to fill his own belly and those of his family. If there were a market in rice, no reports of it remain, except in Kedah. But other motives existed. With the process of growing rice was associated a series of ritual acts cementing the bond between man and the world beyond the world. However un-Islamic it might have been, the cultivator observed various ceremonies at crucial points in the cycle of cultivation. The *ladang*-maker, for whom a good burn was crucial, had his set of incantations to the fire that it might clear and cleanse the soil, consuming all. The *sawah*-cultivator had his observances whilst sowing his nursery. Both believed in the *semangat padi*, the soul of the rice, and that it might not be disturbed by the sight of the reaping blade, the tuai was employed. That it might not flee and the crop be accursed, various 'harvest home' ceremonies were observed. In most places these observances were merely customary, but in Perak, as the requirement that 'Once in three months the wizard [*pawang*] will vivify the padi...' shows, they had the force of law (Rigby, 1908, 30).

The various ceremonies have been summarized by Muhammed Ja'afar (1897, 297–8),

First the elders had to hold a consultation with the pawang; then the date was fixed; then *Maulud* prayers were read over the 'mother seed' and benzoin, supplied by the pawang, was burned.... When the *Maulud* prayers are over, every man goes down to the rice-field, if possible on the same day or the next one, in order to begin ploughing the nursery plot....

When the nursery was sown with the previously sprouted seed, benzoin incense was again burnt and the plot sprinkled with rice flour, following which the 'mother seed' was planted in one corner followed by the remainder of the seed-rice.

At harvest further observances were made:

When one wishes to begin reaping the grain one must first have the *pawang's* permission and burn benzoin supplied by him in the field.... When the rice [field] is ripe all over, one must first take the *semangat* (soul) out of all the plots of one's field. You choose the spot where the rice is best.... You begin with a bunch of this kind and clip seven stems to be the *semangat padi*, soul of the rice, and then you clip yet another handful to be the 'mother seed' for the following year. The *semangat* is wrapped in a white cloth tied with a cord of bark and made into the shape of a little child in swaddling clothes....

Muhammed, 1897, 301–2.

THE SOCIAL POLITY

But the affirmation of links with an unseen world were only matters of crisis points in the agricultural year. Of greater significance than supernatural sanctions were those sanctions which regulated inter-personal relationships, both with equals and superiors, in so far as these were related to rice agriculture. The structure of society in western Malaya during the nineteenth century has been admirably described by Gullick (1958) and no more than a brief account need therefore be given here. Early in the nineteenth century the Malay population was rather mixed and it became more so as immigration continued. Some, the Minangkabau and the Javanese, were by tradition rice cultivators. Others, the Bugis in particular, were not. But whatever their origins, the mass of the people, the *rakyat*, the freemen, formed the great bulk of the population. This group was largely village-dwelling and the village, the *kampong*, comprising anything from a half-dozen family homes up to a hundred or so, was the basic unit of settlement. In part, the villages reflected a need for physical, political and especially, psychic protection. Equally, those in which the economy was based upon rice, reflected in part the imperatives of terrain and technique. To avoid the risk of crops in isolated fields being wiped out by rats or birds, simultaneous cultivation was highly desirable and this was more readily accomplished in a village-based society. Moreover a wet rice field is a miserably damp place for a dwelling and this alone would be sufficient to deter the individual farmer from living directly on his land. Dwellings were thus customarily located on piedmont slopes or in plains tracts upon levees. Around the homes were planted tree crops, coconut and areca, durian, mangosteen or langsat, along with 'kitchen-door' crops, chilly, banana, and leafy vegetables.

Below the rakyat in status and sometimes forming part of the village community, though possibly more often to be found in larger villages and towns, were bondsmen, not slaves yet not free, since their labour was at the disposal of those to whom they were in bond. Bondsmen were of two types: those in the personal service of a *raja* or other person of power and were members of his household, and those whose primary function was field labour. Yet lower in status were slaves who, unlike the bondsmen, had no prospect of earning their freedom. Bondsmen and slaves not engaged in household duties were required to undertake field labour. They were thus a form of capital and were also a useful work-force for those amongst the aristocrats who were interested in land development.

In each large village or group of smaller villages there was usually a headman, one rarely of aristocratic birth, who held authority largely by virtue of his personal powers of leadership. This *penghulu* may or may not have been formally recognized by superior authority, but he was recognized as having care of the families in the village. In many cases under pioneering conditions, such penghulus were more or less self-appointed although deriving some power from such local authority under whom they placed themselves and by whom they were recognized.

The supreme local authority was the district chief or raja who was almost always an aristocrat and who always had a following, his *kawan*, which comprised freemen, bondsmen and slaves. Since raja status descended to all legitimate, and often to illegitimate, heirs, members of this class were by no means invariably endowed with that portion of worldly goods to which they commonly felt themselves entitled. Some means of redressing any imbalance between status and possessions were outright appropriation, intrigue, or banditry, all of which found their adepts. But trade and agricultural development were more pacific. Political power had its territorial base, or rather, it had its basis in the number of a man's followers. Throughout the nineteenth century there are numerous instances not only of local chiefs, but of others with high status, *hajis* and *shaiks*, and of low-born 'social climbers' undertaking the pioneering of agricultural settlements.

Except amongst the Minangkabau, supreme authority and rights to land normally resided in the raja or *sultan*, and effectively, in colonial times, in the hands of governors or residents. In pre-colonial times the rulers themselves were sometimes active in developing rice land and the rice trade, like other forms of trade, was a royal monopoly, although farmed out for a fixed fee. Indeed royalty, the aristocracy and the would-be aristocrats had important developmental functions until these came to be usurped by non-indigenous functionaries.

LAND TENURE[1]

It was foreign to the Malay to consider that land of itself possessed value. The question therefore of ultimate ownership did not arise. Under Minangkabau law, land abandoned had 'gone back to God' (Maxwell, 1884, 173) and He, presumably, was the ultimate owner, though another Minangkabau source (Winstedt, 1953, 8) cannily implies that the territorial chief was His agent on earth and thus a fit person to receive abandoned lands. Chiefs also received the estates of those deceased without heirs.

A fundamental distinction was drawn between 'dead land', *tanah mati*, and 'live land', *tanah hidup*. In the words of the Malacca code (Maxwell, 1884, 175),

Tanah mati is that land on which there is no sign or token that it has been appropriated by any one, or any grove of fruit-trees in respect of which a proprietor can demand a payment. Regarding such land it is certain that there can be no question. If any person proceeds to plant upland or wet *padi* on such land, no one has any right to dispute it with him for it has been abandoned voluntarily by its former owner....

Land which is known as *tanah hidup* is that which is appropriated by some one, either by living on it or by planting timber or fruit-trees or by laying out a garden or enclosure. This cannot be taken by anyone and is called *tanah hidup*. This rule applies also to persons who settle on the lands or plantations of others. As long as they live there, they must obey the orders of the owner....

There was thus a clear link between use and ownership. According to the Malacca code a necessary concomitant for the conversion of tanah mati into tanah hidup was that the clearer should be a Muslim though this rule was never rigorously applied. But on land once cleared there were certain residual rights of the owner even though he might abandon it. An early Pahang law has, 'abandoned rice-fields may be borrowed or rented and returned at the proprietor's request' (Kempe and Winstedt, 1948, 5). The same was true of lands under the Perak and Malacca codes (Maxwell, 1884, 171, 177) but under Minangkabau law the period in which any

---

[1]Laws relating to land may be found in various Malay legal digests, concerning which see Wilkinson (1908) and Hooker (1968b).

residual right could be exercised was three years from abandonment (Winstedt, 1953, 8). The strength of the cultivator's right to land is measured by the fact that the Malacca code provided that even though a cultivator might make a plantation or lay out rice fields on the land of another, without the owner's permission, the cultivator was nevertheless entitled to two-thirds of the produce (Maxwell, 1884, 175–7).

The letting of land by a proprietor to another was clearly provided for in the Malacca code (Maxwell, 1884, 175), whilst the Pahang code required fixed rental in cash or kind, rents fixed at a share of the crop being specifically prohibited (Kempe and Winstedt, 1948, 13). In view of the modern prevalence of this practice, it is an interesting prohibition, though there is little evidence of tenancy during the century.

Formal written titles were issued only in Kedah and Kelantan. In Kedah, according to Maxwell (Kedah AR 1909, 14) the earliest form of deed was in the form of a written decision made by the presiding judge in cases of dispute. Such a letter, *surat putus*, when confirmed by the Sultan, gave absolute title. The same authority suggests that the next step in the evolution of titles was for owners to obtain a surat putus as a protective measure to forestall disputes. Curiously, the earliest surviving laws of Kedah, those of Dato Sri Paduka Tuan, 1667, make no reference to land beyond requiring rice fields to be fenced and buffaloes to be sent off to common grazing once the rice was planted (Winstedt, 1928, 8).

For those remaining Peninsular states under indigenous government, there is no evidence of a similar formalization of rights to land. Kedah and Kelantan were thus exceptional in this respect, possibly because rice land had become an asset worth safeguarding. In Malacca, titles for large blocks of land were held by largely absentee landlords, whilst in Penang first, then in Province Wellesley, the British-administered system of land administration began early in the nineteenth century.

This was to lead to the introduction of a concept of land as real property, hitherto absent. In turn the right of government to tax land was to be established, a right which was quite incomprehensible to the Malay (Kedah AR 1909, 15). This new tax was to replace the tax on all cultivators, known in Kedah and Perak as *rapai*, an impost which c.1820 amounted to about 100 pounds of rice per holding, an exaction which found its way into the hands of the aristocracy, not into those of the sovereign (Crawfurd, 1820, 3, 48). Nowhere in the Peninsula, except in Malacca, is there report of the levy of the tithe or higher portion of the crop, though in eastern Java up to half was exacted, amongst the Sundas a tithe or rarely a fifth, and in the Celebes a tithe, was surrendered up to the supreme authority (Crawfurd, 1820, 3, 48–51). According to Swettenham, the customary exaction of the tithe in Malacca was of Dutch introduction and he strongly attacked Maxwell's and Dickson's suggestion that the tithe was an 'immemorial custom' amongst Malays (Swettenham, 1893, 685; 1894, 5; Maxwell, 1894, ix–xi, xv–xviii).

4

The Nineteenth and Early Twentieth Centuries: The Northern Malay States

IN this and the two succeeding chapters the northern centres of rice-growing are discussed. These include Kedah and Perlis on the west coast of the Peninsula and Kelantan and Trengganu on the east. Penang and Province Wellesley were out-growths of the Kedah region and are treated in Chapter 5, while Perak, in part a minor traditional centre and in part a major area of pioneering, is considered in Chapter 6. The following chapters are concerned with the southern centre of cultivation in Malacca and Negri Sembilan and finally the remaining portion of the Peninsula in which rice-growing was not the sole or major economic activity. These accounts are inevitably unbalanced with respect to time. As the British gained control over each state, there was a rush of publications informing a presumably gratified public of imperium's latest acquisition. Later materials, where these have survived, were almost exclusively documents concerned with routine administration. Thus we know more of the geography of Penang and Province Wellesley in the 1820s than in the 1870s but little of Kedah, with Perlis, Kelantan and Trengganu, until the first decade of the twentieth century. The initial colonization of Penang and the Province by rice farmers derived from Kedah, but Kedah was not to be adequately described until nearly a century later.

During the period four major regions emerged. The first was the northern region centred upon Kedah but including the colonized lands of Penang and Province Wellesley. To the east, Kelantan, by the turn of the century prosperous and advanced in administration, contrasted markedly with the social, political and economic turmoil of Trengganu which was rather more urban and industrial craft in character. Perak, excepting the southern tin-mining areas, was much less important agriculturally than Kedah but offers a fine example of development under British rule. The second and southern region included the plains of Malacca, largely non-Minangkabau in technique, tradition and law, contrasting with the Minangkabau lands of the Negri Sembilan. The third region comprised the 'marches', areas in which rice-growing was of little importance or which were being colonized during the century. This included southern Perak, the whole of Selangor and Pahang, together with minor outliers in Johore and Singapore. The fourth region was that of the hill peoples. This region was known only in part during the nineteenth century and the

TABLE 1
MALAY PENINSULA: POPULATION ESTIMATES, 1834[1]

State	Population	Per cent
Kedah (incl. Perlis)	50,000	11
Penang	40,322	8
Province Wellesley	49,553	10
Perak	35,000	7
Selangor	12,000	3
Malacca (incl. Naning)	34,333	7
'Negri Sembilan'	27,080	6
Johore	25,000	6
Patani	54,000	11
Kelantan	50,000	11
Trengganu	30,000	6
Kemaman	1,000	
Pahang	40,000	8
Singapore	26,329	6
Total	474,617	100

Sources: SFP 26.1.1837; Newbold, 1839.

reconstruction of their agricultural economy partly rests upon a backwards projection of more modern source materials.

In any one of the states comprising these regions, the area occupied can have been rather limited since according to Newbold (*SFP* 26.1.1837) the total population of the Peninsular states, including Patani, was only about 475,000.

Generally, four zones of settlement lay between the sea and the mountains. Along the coast and up the estuaries, scattered in and amongst the mangrove, were settlements of aborigines, the 'strandloopers', together with the *bagans*, villages of Malay commercial fishermen, the settlements of pirates and of mangrove-cutters. Inland, upstream of the point at which the river-water was reasonably fresh, was the zone of agriculture, often with a screen of tree crops and in the north, bamboos along the river-banks, beyond which were the wet rice fields, usually in contiguous blocks. Inland again and upslope were the hamlets of Malay shifting cultivators separated from each other by tracts of forest from which timber and jungle products were extracted. Beyond these yet again, beyond *tanah Melayu*, the land of the Malays, were the *orang bukit*, the aboriginal hill peoples, living a largely self-contained and self-sufficient life.

The northern region was bifurcate in form, extending from the Perak valley in the south-west, through the recently-colonized lands of Krian, Province Wellesley and off-shore Penang to a major long-established centre on the Kedah-Perlis plain. In the more accessible portions of this region, rice production was specialized and commercially-oriented.

[1]For comments on the reliability of these estimates see Hill, 1973, 146n.

The eastern wing comprised a concatenation of tiny Siamese states, successors to Patani, which included Chana, Tani, Raman, Jaring and Sai, together with Kelantan and Trengganu. In these states, agriculture was rather less specialized and commercialized, though there was some export of livestock to Penang and to Singapore. Concerning the peasants of Patani, for instance, the *Jawi Peranakan* (31.1.1887) noted that,

Their livelihood is gained by planting rice and by planting things such as beans, vegetables, Malay kitchen spices and cultivating in swampy places yams and *karam*[1] which are very cheap. Of livestock they have chickens, ducks, goats, buffaloes, a few cattle and elephants whose function is like boats on land....

Between the two wings, in the north, were hills, in the higher parts of which lived aboriginal shifting-cultivators, with Malays and a scattering of Siamese, also shifting-cultivators, in the lower parts. In the centre and south was a tangle of forested mountains.

Upon this pattern came to be superimposed another. Penang and the Province were polyglot, heterogeneous, British in administration, Malay only because the great majority of the cultivators of the soil happened to be Malays, mostly of Kedah origin. Perak, too, was similar, excepting only that a core of rice areas already existed in the middle reaches of the Perak river. The coastal tract in the Krian district was the locus of a major agricultural colony overseen by British officers. The rest was purely Malay, alternately stable, wealthy, with an administrative superstructure quite sufficient for the needs of a peasant society, and fallen into a condition of near anarchy in which the preservation of the family demanded at best a tightening of the *sarong* or at worst, the employment of the ultimate sanction against oppression or natural disaster—flight.

THE NORTH-WEST: KEDAH AND PERLIS

Quedah...is entirely worthless from the financial point of view....

S.G. Bonham, 1838[2]

The cultivation of rice is enormous...Quedah is just beginning to prosper, and this owing to the ability of their noble Chief and his three brothers....

van de Ville, 1866, *SFPW* 4.10.1866.

Kedah illustrates the manner in which economic well-being, based largely upon rice with an assist earlier from pepper, fluctuated in step with changing political fortunes. The state had been desolated by Acheh in the seventeenth century (Harris, 1764, 748) and Alor Star laid waste in 1770 (Topping, 1850, 43). In the 1820s and 1830s Kedah was invaded by the Rajah of Ligor at the request of his Siamese overlord with the result that

---

[1] *Karam* = tuber? This word is not listed in any dictionary available to me.
[2] Gov. PWI to Fort William, 30.7.1838, EIC Board's Coll.

tens of thousands fled to Company territory.[1] Risings against the Siamese in 1831 and 1838–9 resulted in further depopulation, but by the 1860s the country was well on the way to recovery and in the 1880s was in flourishing condition with the colonization of new land for rice proceeding apace, having received a major stimulus not only from wise entrepreneurs amongst the aristocracy, but also an influx of refugees from Kelantan.

As has been shown earlier, Kedah was and still is an important exporter of rice. In the sixteenth, seventeenth and eighteenth centuries, pepper rather than rice provided the major portion of the economic surplus, but by the mid-nineteenth century, pepper was no longer to be found at Langkawi, its major centre of production (*SDT* 10.5.1867) and rice, exported largely to Penang, was a major source of state revenue (Sharom, 1969, 31–2).

c.1780 TO c.1880

By the late eighteenth century the centre of rice cultivation was near Alor Star. It cannot be agreed with Sharom (1969, 34) that the centre was in the coastal tract near Kuala Kedah, because Osborn (1865, 35–6) who was a member of the British East India Company's blockading force in 1838 specifically stated that, 'A dense and waving jungle of trees skirted round the town and fort of [Kuala] Quedah, and spread away on either hand....'[2]

According to Topping (1850, 43), whose information came largely from Francis Light, in the immediate vicinity of Alor Star fruit and vegetables were cultivated and beyond, some four miles away, '...a very little above Limbun [=Limbong][3] the prospect opens out into an extensive plain, on which are many miles of Paddy grounds.... During the rainy season this plain is overflowed, which greatly enriches it.' South-east of Alor Star, at Apabukit (not located)[4] was a further centre of cultivation, especially notable because the majority of the cultivators were Indians, whom Topping calls Chulias (Topping, 1850, 43). On the eastern boundary of the Kedah plain the country was forest intersected by some small villages surrounded by their cultivated lands. South of Kedah Peak was the newly enlarged centre of settlement and rice cultivation around Kuala Muda now known as Sungai Patani to which perhaps 15,000 Patani people had recently migrated. For the rest there are no data beyond the fact that the southernmost portion which became Province Wellesley in 1800 had no agriculture worthy of note. The Prai basin produced tin and was very sparsely occupied, whilst Krian produced only rattans (Topping, 1850, 44).

There can be little doubt that the establishment of Penang came to have major effects upon the agricultural economy of Kedah. In the first place Kedah was in a state of some turmoil, a fact cleverly used by the British

[1]Low estimated that 70,000 left Kedah for the Province (see C. Skinner, 1964, 160).

[2]See also Milburn, 1813, 296.

[3]There are two existing villages of this name, no great distance apart, Kg. Limbong and Kg. Kota Limbong.

[4]'Apabukit', i.e. 'apa bukit?', 'what hill?'

to gain possession first of the island and then of the Province. To these territories came migrants in large numbers, many from Kedah. This migration must have led to at least some rice lands in the state being abandoned. In the second place Penang offered a major market not only for rice but also for cattle and poultry. A rice-eating population of 22,000 just across the water was by no means negligible (*PWIGG* 10.3.1810), and as a consequence Kuala Kedah was a rice-exporting port of some magnitude (*SFP* 31.3.1839).

To a considerable extent the Kedah rice trade was a child of imperial interests. According to James Low (Ag. Res. Councillor PWI to Gov., 20.3.1838, EIC Board's Coll.), the first major sale was to the Dutch government at Batam some time before the cession of Penang to the British, the ruler of Kedah clearing the tidy profit of Sp.Drs. 10,000 on 500 *coyans* of rice purchased from his rakyat at Sp.Drs. 15 per coyan. Following the cession the average export to Penang was around 1,000 coyans worth some Sp.Drs. 50,000,[1] but by 1818–19 the amount had fallen to half this, worth only Sp.Drs. 20,000. Not all of this export was consumed in Penang, a portion of both Kedah and Moulmein rice being re-exported to China and other parts.

The total export of rice was around 570 coyans in 1785. In 1821 the amount sent to Penang alone was little short of this and the island had become very much dependent upon imports (Bonney, 1967, 8). A letter to the editor of the *Prince of Wales Island Government Gazette* (31.10.1821) complained of the 'impolicy' of Penang 'being so entirely dependent upon Quedah and Acheen for our supplies of rice. . . .' Certainly Kedah rice compared favourably in quality with that of Bengal since prices in the George Town market were much on a par (*PWIGG* 6.6.1807, 2.4.1808). There is no knowing if the rice trade was in the hands of the *raja*, or his nominees, at this time as it certainly was later, but it would seem unlikely that authority did not abrogate to itself this lucrative trade. Nevertheless continuity of supply and stable prices could not be maintained. In 1807 the average price of fine Kedah rice was six to seven *gantangs* for a dollar; coarse kinds eight to twelve gantangs for a dollar. A year later rice of all kinds was six gantangs per dollar.

The symbiotic trade relationship of Kedah with Penang was sundered by the invasion of 1821, upon reports of which the rice price promptly doubled (*PWIGG* 21.11.1821). The towns and villages of the State were put to the torch and thus began a major exodus of rice growers and others into Company territory, especially into the Province which had been but little developed since its acquisition (*PWIGG* 31.10.1821; Anderson, 1824, 7). Despite the onslaught something survived though Anderson (1824, 14) remarked that the supplies coming from Kedah were very scanty. In 1838, for instance, the unidentified Kampong Tamelan, possibly in Perlis,

. . .consisted of about a hundred neatly-built mat houses scattered through a grove of cocoa-nut trees. . .either end of the cocoa-nut grove rested on a dense

[1]Newbold (1839, 2, 3) stated that the average annual export was 2,500 coyans.

jungle which swept with a large semi-circular curve behind the village, leaving ample clearance for the ricefields and wells of the inhabitants....

Osborn, 1865, 106.

Kangar, now the capital of Perlis, was much the same and had

... only just enough clear ground around it to afford room for the growth of such rice, fruit, and vegetables as were required for the consumption of the inhabitants —the unreclaimed jungle sweeping round the cultivated land and orchards in a great curve, whose radius might possibly be a mile and a half....

Osborn, 1865, 214.

To Governor Bonham however, Kedah was 'entirely worthless from the financial point of view'. Its 20,000 inhabitants, which included only 500 Siamese, had become almost completely dependent upon their immediate environs for subsistence.[1] The suppression of the rice and poultry trade in 1838 must have been especially hard upon Kuala Kedah as may be judged from a bitterly-complaining letter from Rajahs Abdullah and Mohamed Asa-ad to the *Free Press* (*SFP* 31.1.1839). Inland, Alor Star had disappeared and possibly its nearby rice fields were, like the town, overgrown with forest when, in 1843, Kedah was finally restored to a ruler who had spent the interim living off the country (Gov. to Fort William 30.7.1837, EIC Board's Coll.; Winstedt, 1920, 35). The Kuala Muda settlement mentioned by Topping (1850, 44) had been much reduced by the end of 1821, only some rice fields remaining (Finlayson, 1826, 30).

Yet some revival of production had taken place, even some export, otherwise export duties of $15 per coyan of rice and $5 per coyan of padi would not have been imposed though this violated the Anglo-Siamese Treaty of 1826 (*SFP* 24.12.1846). In 1836–7 Kedah exported some 757 coyans of rice and padi to Penang (Ag. Res. Councillor to Gov., 20.3.1838, EIC Board's Coll.). The fact that, in the words of a correspondent of the *Pinang Gazette*, '...little more [rice] is cultivated than the quantity required for local consumption; and large tracts of beautiful land capable of being brought under tillage at a very trifling expense remain waste and neglected' (*SFP* 24.12.1846), pointed up not the alleged iniquities of an export duty but a lack of hands to put to the plough.

By mid-century the population had risen to around sixty or seventy thousand and the country could not have been 'covered with vast forests' as claimed by Pallegoix (1854, 25–6) and Bowring (1857, 2, 49). Logan's account (1851, 53–9) of the Kedah river in 1850 indicates that except for a few small hamlets amongst the mangrove, rice lands extended from the Mergong river across the northern part of the plain and well into the small tributary valleys of the eastern hills as far as 'S. Sauwi'. Along the banks of the Kedah lay a series of villages placed a mile or so apart like beads on a string (see Figure 4). In the plains tract, the actual river bank, for a depth

---

[1]For a discussion of the population of the state throughout the period, see Zaharah, 1968.

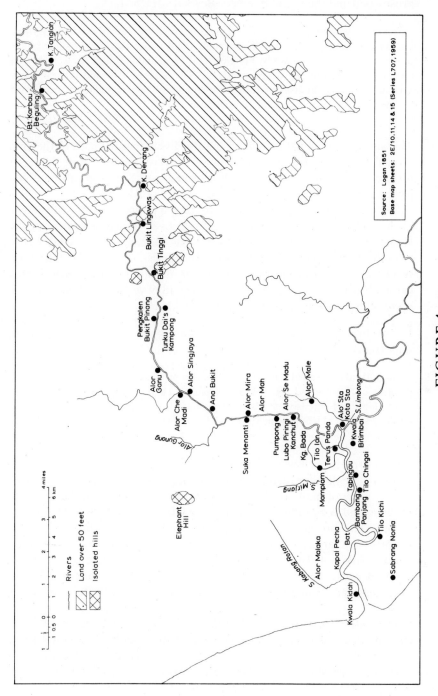

FIGURE 4

SETTLEMENT ON THE KEDAH RIVER IN 1850

of twenty or thirty yards, was uncultivated and covered with grass, brushwood and the useful bamboo. Beyond stretched,

...an immense paddy field broken at great intervals by clumps and belts of trees; but only a small part is now [September, 1850] under culture. In some places ploughs were at work drawn by buffaloes and oxen, and in others the women were already planting out the young paddy....The Malays here said that the plain was inferior in fertility to Province Wellesley, which they thought was accounted for by the latter being new land and the former old....

Logan, 1851, 55.

This supposition could be correct but it is likely that the soils of the area around Pengkalan Bt. Pinang, being well towards the hills, were lighter in texture, more leached and hence less productive. The yield of about 160 gantangs per acre was half that of the vicinity of Alor Star.

But much land was still abandoned and the population was only a half of the 100,000 or so of pre-invasion times. Even though a number of the former inhabitants had followed their chiefs back, many stayed elsewhere after the invasion (Logan, 1851, 58). Nevertheless, in places, land development was being vigorously pushed ahead despite setbacks such as that caused by the disastrous floods in October 1859 which set off yet another wave of emigration (*SFP* 17.11.1859; 29.3.1860).

In the breaking-in of new land, corvée labour, *krah*, was of crucial importance.[1]

T[unku] Ibrahim availed himself largely of this privileges [*sic*], in clearing ground, planting cocoanuts and taking crops of paddy. He has now about 400 *orlong* of paddy land and extensive tracts of cocoanuts stretching from the muda [*sic*] to the Marbau [=Merbok] which must yield him annually $5,000 at the least....

SFP 16.6.1859.

But krah, useful as it was, was not popular and its imposition to build part of a trans-Peninsular road in 1864 once more resulted in the flight back to the Province of many of those who were formerly living in the Province but who had been induced to return to Kedah (*SFP* 7.1.1864; 18.2.1864).

Yet export production had increased. The 1864 state revenues from rice exports were farmed out for $10,000 (*SFP* 30.6.1864) and two years later, van de Ville noted the burgeoning prosperity of the state (*SFPW* 4.10. 1866). Because of transport difficulties, rice exports were not concentrated at a single port but rather the crop was moved directly to small ports along the coasts and estuaries of both Kedah and Perlis. Ports included the mouths of the Perlis, Kedah, Sala and Muda rivers, Sanglang, Jerlone [Jerlun], Bagan Samak,[2] Sala and the Langkawi Islands (Penang AR 1873, 139–40). No assessment of which were the largest is possible although once the Alor Star–Kedah Peak canal was opened, either Alor Star or

[1]Sharom (1969, 67–100) has a most useful and full discussion of krah.
[2]This place has not been located but may have been on the Merbok or Muda river.

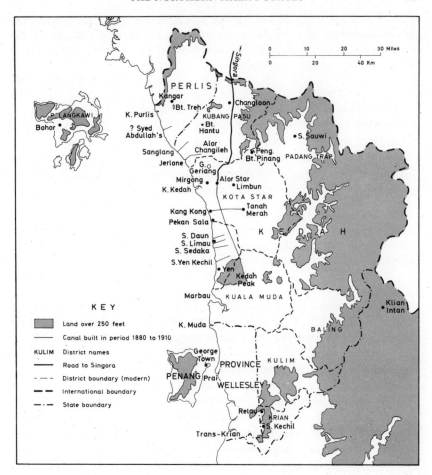

FIGURE 5

KEDAH, DISTRICTS, CANALS AND PLACES MENTIONED IN THE TEXT

more likely Kuala Muda,[3] handled the export of the newly-opened south-ern plains.

Swettenham has left an interesting description of the central and southern plains area as it was at the end of 1889. The population of the state had risen from roughly 50,000 in 1850 to around 70,000 Malays plus a 'few thousand' Chinese. It is noteworthy that the rice-growing peasantry was already at this early date a relatively depressed class.

[3]It is not clear from the sources at which point rice cargoes were assembled, if indeed they were.

price of padi had been very low but was now better and with a rice mill recently erected the people are doing better, but even now rice growing will only pay the small owners who cultivate their own fields with their own labour and that of their families: it will not pay to hire labour.

                                        Gov. SS to CO, 23.11.1889, CO 273/162.

At this time the southern plains were just beginning to be developed for cultivation and in this, a steady influx of Kelantanese refugees fleeing first from a hurricane, then from famine and pestilence, must have played a part. According to a subsequent report (*JP* 26.9.1887), about 2,000 refugee families entered the state and these were supported at government expense until, within two years, productive *bendangs* could be made.

On being examined again concerning what work they could take up, they were found to be servants (*hamba*) and peasants (*rakyat*) already accustomed to the cultivation of wet rice, that being the life of humble folk. The government was pleased because [now] all the padi sawahs in the state of Kedah were fully used....

                                        JP 26.9.1887.

Thus, finally the state was restored to something like its condition prior to the invasion of 1821 and was now on the threshold of a large agricultural expansion which involved the construction of extensive drainage works.

DRAINAGE AND LAND DEVELOPMENT

Several modern writers (Bonney, 1967, 8; Sharom, 1969, 3) have referred to the economic importance of Kedah rivers as a communications network and for irrigation. The latter claim is erroneous since irrigation connotes the control of water in the amount and timing of its application. Control of the water was impossible because gates and other works were lacking. Moreover, water levels were usually slightly below field levels and water-raising devices were absent. As noted by Topping (1850, 43), the plains were inundated annually by rain-water and by the overflowing of the rivers. This supplied the water for planting which seems usually to have begun in April or May at the onset of the south-west monsoon. As the rains tapered off in December and January, water levels fell and the rivers now acted as drains. Nevertheless the cutting of canals was of major significance in several ways. One important function was to carry off surplus water and to maintain a gentle flow through the fields thus preventing stagnation with its deleterious effects upon plant growth. Another function was to provide drinking water (Gov. SS to CO 23.11. 1889, CO 273/162). Yet another was their role as routeways and this must be regarded as their primary function. In this, the carriage of cargoes of rice and padi was but part of a larger transportation function. Wan Mat's famous Kedah Peak to Alor Star canal, for instance, not only carried padi but also a large traffic in timber (Kedah AR 1906–8, 38).

The early 'artificial rivers', *sungai korok*, are described by Sharom (1969, 33–6) and the cutting of these, like the later ones, was presumably accompanied by a linear spread of settlement, just as happens with road-building today. Some artificial rivers were genuine canals, but many, especially those normal to the coast, were merely natural water-courses straightened and deepened. The most famous canal-builder was a state minister, Wan Muhammed Saman, whose Alor Star–Kedah Peak canal[1] laid the foundations for the development of an estimated 100 square miles of swampy jungle lying south of the Kedah river (HC, FMS to CO 12.1. 1910, CO 273/360). Wan Mat obtained royal permission to undertake the work which began in 1885. He was to make the canal at his own expense, receiving the concession of,

Twenty *relongs* of land on either side of the canal when excavated,[2] with the provision that he was to sell this land to intending settlers at a uniform rate of $3 per square *relong*.[3] He was allowed to charge an annual rent of fifty cents per [square?] *relong*, and it was expressly provided that *raiats* might take up his land, and pay him rent and thereby become exempt from liability to forced labour....Settlers poured in, and were given strips of land on either side of the canal, with a *relong's* frontage on the canal and the full twenty *relongs'* depth. Each *relong's* frontage thus represented a lump sum payment of $120, and an annual rental of $20, whereas the cost of making a *relong's* length of the canal had been between $50 and $55. (The land for which these settlers paid $3 a *relong* now changes hands at $60 a *relong*)....

Kedah AR 1909, 24.

The success of this scheme encouraged the builder to undertake the first irrigation scheme reported in the state, a canal $6\frac{1}{2}$ miles long from Tanah Merah to the S. Kangkong, but as an irrigation work it was a failure because the levels were faulty.

Other people of high birth obtained concessions to forward canal-building and colonization elsewhere: Wan Yunus on the Daun, Limau and Sedaka rivers; Syed Osman at S. Yen Kechil; the Sultan himself at Alor Changilih, north of the Kedah river; Syed Abdullah, the State Treasurer, north of that; Wan Yahia at Sanglang. But the gravest defect of these canals as a means of intercourse was that they did not connect with one another (Kedah AR 1909). Moreover they cannot have been particularly efficient as drains, there being no record of side drains being cut, and they were useless for irrigation as well. Yet they were the marvel of their day.

A number of conclusions emerge from this account of the southern plains region. Of greatest importance is the role of Wan Mat as an agricultural pioneer. Doubtless he had everything to gain personally, power, prestige, money, but apparently without attracting royal jealousy. Following him were others, well-connected with the royal house, by virtue

---

[1]Maxwell (Kedah AR 1909, 23) refers to this canal as being generally known as 'Sungei Korok Wan Mat'. Modern maps refer to it as 'Sungei Wan Mat Saman'.

[2]There is a conflict of authorities as to the type of labour used in the work. Maxwell (Kedah AR 1909, 24) stated that Wan Mat used Chinese coolies but Swettenham claimed that forced labour was used (HC, FMS to CO, 12.1.1910, CO 273/360).

[3]Possibly Penang relongs, see Hill, 1973, 162n.

of position or personal wealth being able to mobilize capital or labour or both. The role of agricultural pioneer was one played by others of position elsewhere but never on quite the same scale and under the British, the aristocracy quickly lost its taste for this form of investment together with the concern for the common man which accompanied it. A further conclusion is that by the 1880s land had come to be regarded as real property and had acquired a monetary value. Although the sources do not specifically state this, it is likely that the lands given out to the settlers were not cleared of their wild vegetation. Thus even undeveloped land had acquired intrinsic value and became the object of investment by capitalists, since who else, by 1909, could afford to buy land at $60 per relong?

If this interpretation is correct, then a new class of landowners had come into existence. Previously the ruler had given grants of land to whomsoever he desired, usually to aristocrats. These then controlled the revenues of their domains, revenues which were often judiciously increased by the development of unused land by the application of forced labour and capital. There is not the slightest evidence that in so doing a 'capital gain' or an increase in the value of the 'estate' was envisaged. Land had no value other than the revenue derivable from it. But by the end of the century this was changed and land had become of inherent value. Thus the emergence of a non-aristocratic, capitalist, 'commercial' land-owning group is indicated. Trade was largely in their hands (Kedah AR 1906–8, 3) as were the revenue 'farms' especially the right of collecting the export duty on rice and padi. As Sharom (1969, 30) justly observes,

Having agreed to a fixed annual rent on the [revenue] farm, the more rice that was produced, the greater their profits would be. One way in which the Chinese revenue farmers ensured a large and regular supply of padi was available for the export market was to get the Malay peasants into debt....What normally happened of course was that the raayat [sic] was unable to honour the loan on time, and this meant that he had either to hand over a more than proportionate share of the harvest or lose the land.

Foreclosure on mortgages, however, can have been only one way in which capitalists gained land, and outright purchase was probably of more importance.

Another group of 'capitalists' was clearly the first settlers. Twenty Kedah relongs is equivalent to about fourteen acres, an area considerably in excess of the acre or two required for the support of a single nuclear family and more than such a family could work.[1] The fact that lands were sold off in blocks of this size must have led to the emergence of a 'wealthy peasant' class of which the members, whilst themselves cultivators, rented out land on a share-crop basis. An alternative interpretation is that extended family working was the rule. Wage labour seems not to have been employed since it was uneconomic to do so (Gov. SS to CO 23.11. 1889, CO 273/162).

---

[1]Marshall (1954, 57) has estimated that a family of two adults and five children would require one acre yielding 400 gantangs/acre to feed itself for a year.

The process of land development also led to strikingly new forms of settlement pattern and possibly to new field patterns. Whereas in the north, the rice villages had a 'beads on a string' pattern along the rivers, in the south, homesteads formed a continuous line along the canals. Inland from the homesteads, around which were clustered fruit trees and 'kitchen garden' crops, extended the rice fields. Where levels permitted, the holding may have been cultivated as a single field, in which case the farm would have been markedly strip-like in form. In any case the elongate shape of holdings contrasted markedly with the irregular and rather square shapes of holdings in Kelantan.

KEDAH AND PERLIS *c*.1910

The only comprehensive contemporary accounts of Kedah during the period were those of Maxwell and Frost (Kedah AR 1909, 22–7; Perlis AR 1910), although the report on the census of 1911 provides valuable supplementary data which permit the construction of a statistical profile of the two states. The major focus of settlement was a broad belt of wet rice land extending from the Perlis hills in the north to the foot of Kedah Peak in the south. On the west the rice land boundary lay probably at about two to four miles from the coast, the intervening area still being largely in mangrove. To the east, hills and plain interdigitated, with both wet rice and shifting cultivation in the valleys and shifting cultivation only on the hills. The second focus was around Kuala Muda which was a port for both commerce and fishing as well as being a centre for the exploitation of the mangrove and *nipah* swamps along the coast (Cavendish, 1911, 62–93). Rice was grown in the vicinity. The third focus lay to the south of Kedah Peak, in the tin-mines and estates of Kuala Muda, Kulim and Krian. In this region the proportion of Malays and related groups was less than in the north and rice-growing was less important.

Amongst the areas, the northern districts were predominantly agricultural, which throughout the state, on an occupational basis, meant rice-growing to the virtual exclusion of anything else. Only in the Kuala Muda, Kulim and Krian districts was the proportion of rice growers to total economically active persons below 80 per cent (see Table 2).

Amongst the communities, few differences can be discerned except for the Chinese. The Malays, the immigrant Samsams (Siamese-speaking Malays) and the Siamese were all largely rice growers though the proportion varied from district to district in step with the proportion of people in these communities resident there. In other words, the fewer Malays, Samsams and Siamese in a district, the lower was the proportion of the people in groups which were engaged in growing rice. The Chinese were by no means unimportant as agriculturalists since two-fifths were so engaged, ranging from 22 per cent in the Pulau Langkawi district to just over half in the Kuala Muda district, mainly however, as estate coolies. Their contribution to the rice-growing work-force was negligible. The great majority of the Chinese rice growers were in the Kota Star district

TABLE 2

KEDAH AND PERLIS: PERSONS ECONOMICALLY ACTIVE AND IN RICE CULTIVATION BY COMMUNITY AND DISTRICT, 1911[1]

District	Malays, Samsams, Siamese			Chinese			Total			
	Economically Active	Rice growers	Rice growers as % Econ. Active	Economically Active	Rice growers	Rice growers as % Econ. Active	Economically Active	Rice growers	Rice growers as % Econ. Active	Malays, Samsams, Siamese as % Total Pop. Econ. Active
Kota Star	52,760	46,078	87	6,797	1,291	19	59,557	47,369	80	89
Padang Trap	5,245	4,965	95	64	20	n.a.	5,309	4,985	94	99
Kubang Pasu	15,496	14,015	90	715	3	1	16,211	14,018	86	96
P. Langkawi	4,167	3,419	82	730	9	1	4,897	3,428	70	85
Yen	7,508	6,706	89	621	78	13	8,129	6,784	83	92
Kuala Muda	11,014	8,211	75	8,237	60	1	19,251	8,271	43	57
Baling	15,121	13,255	88	1,152	41	4	16,273	13,296	82	93
Kulim	4,289	2,540	59	7,297	3	1	11,586	2,543	22	37
Krian	2,675	1,837	69	2,935	18	1	5,610	1,855	33	48
Kedah total	118,275	101,026	86	28,548	1,523	5	146,823	102,549	70	80
Perlis	19,947	17,560	89	1,240	98	8	21,187	17,658	83	94
Total	138,222	118,586	86	29,788	1,621	5	168,010	120,207	72	82

Source: Cavendish, 1911.

[1] Persons listed in the 'Indian' and 'Other Races' categories have been omitted from this analysis because their number was insignificant.

where they comprised a fifth of the economically active Chinese of that district.

The production of the single annual crop was commercialized to a considerable degree and trade was almost exclusively in the hands of the Chinese. In the Kota Star district, for instance, there were 102 Chinese rice dealers, compared with only seven Malays (Cavendish, 1911, 64, 80). The petty dealers would buy up the rice during the planting season, by so doing obtaining prices well below those prevailing during the harvest. The crop would then be sold to larger merchants in Alor Star, Sungei Sala (Pekan Sala) and Sungei Limau, who in turn milled it at the only steam mill in the region or exported it to Penang in the husk.

The total production is not known, but based upon an average annual rice consumption of 100 gantangs per adult and a dependency ratio of 40 dependents per 100 workers, the total annual production would have been of the order of 28 million gantangs. The total export from Kedah to Penang in 1909 was 3,278,000 gantangs of rice and 7,950,000 gantangs of unhusked rice (padi) (Kedah AR 1909, 25). This volume, reckoning a recovery rate for padi of roughly half, would give an average annual surplus per person engaged in rice cultivation of just over 70 gantangs of rice, worth perhaps ten dollars.[1] While this is no great sum, due allowance must be made for comparatively low prices of desired commodities.

More importantly, there was a very much lower dependency ratio at that time than at present. This ratio may be expressed as the ratio of economically unproductive to economically productive persons. Analysis of the 1911 Census data shows that the ratio varied from 31 per cent in Padang Trap district to 44 per cent in the Langkawi district, with the ratio for Kota Star being the same as the state average of 40 per cent. This may be compared with a modern (1957) dependency ratio for Malays of all classes of 64 per cent.

There was some variation of rice-farming systems, organization and settlement from district to district. The Perlis plain, Kota Star and part of the Yen district formed a single unit within which older riverside settlements contrasted with those of the mostly newly-developed lands along the canals, the most extensive of which were south of the Kedah river. This region, unlike the others, was one of a virtual rice monoculture except in Perlis where stock-rearing was of some significance (Ridley, 1911, 38). The largely humanized landscape of the vicinity of Gunong Geriang has been described by Ridley, a botanist (1911, 30): 'On both sides of the [Kedah] river, and in fact over the whole district the land is or has been cultivated, and is covered with ricefields or villages, so that whatever the indigenous flora was, it is almost all gone now.' Across to the east, the wet rice fields of the Kedah basin terminated at the appropriately named Kepala Batas, 'head of the rice-field embankments' (Ridley, 1911, 33). In the north, the rice fields did not cover the whole plain and Ridley's mention of 'rice-field and pasture' (1911, 38) suggests the existence of a

[1]For details of this computation see Hill, 1973, 171.

grass fallow or short-cycle shifting cultivation system. Bounding the region in the south was Kedah Peak, in the foothills of which were the fine fruit plantations of Yen, which district also included the rice lands of the Sala, Limau and Yen river-basins.

To the north-east of the rice plain lay two sparsely inhabited districts, Kubang Pasu and Padang Trap, forming an arc from the inland edge of the coastal rice fields on the west, with part of Perlis and Singgora on the north and east. These districts were beyond the rice plain, beyond Kepala Batas, and although there were some bendangs, most of the cultivation was in the hill clearings of *huma* cultivation, in which rice, maize, manioc, yams and plantains were grown, largely by Malays, Samsams and Siamese (Kedah AR 1909, 22–3). These crops probably made no significant contribution to the export economy or even to a local market economy. Rather, cash income was derived from the herding of cattle and buffaloes, of which there was a large number (Kedah AR 1906–8, 4). Off the northern part of the west coast lay the Langkawi islands. By 1910 the famous pepper fields had largely disappeared. The largest island produced 'enough rice and cocoanuts to supply the needs of the people who are mostly fishermen or boat-builders on a small scale' (Kedah AR 1906–8, 7).[1]

The districts to the south of Kedah Peak contained some stretches of rice land but nothing on a scale approaching that of the Kedah plain. The coastal tract between the Merbok and the Muda was 'very fine' and in the upper reaches of the Muda, in the Baling district, a large population of Malays, mostly the descendants of immigrants from Patani, planted rice on the level plains on either side of the river. Cut off from outside markets by difficulties of transport on the Muda, rice production was likely for local consumption only, although the tin-mines of the Klian Intan area may have provided some local demand. South of the Muda river were two small districts topographically forming part of the hinterland of Province Wellesley but politically part of Kedah. Rice was grown on the banks of the Muda in the Kulim district, and at Relau and Sungei Kechil in the Krian district, of which the trans-Krian portion had been hacked off and given to Perak in 1848.

By 1910 therefore, well-marked regional contrasts had developed. The Kedah-Perlis plain was the centre of a largely commercialized, export-oriented economy of which the social and especially the entrepreneurial basis was still 'traditional' in nature. This modernized traditional economy owed its existence to a combination of factors, notable amongst which were the existence of Penang, a voracious consumer of the basic staple, and home of aggressive commercial interests which found in Kedah a field for profit despite the admitted vagaries of a state modernizing its administration at its own rather than at foreign initiative. Flanking this region was another to the north-east, east and south which was sparsely inhabited and still largely subsistence in economy though doubtless with some local market orientation. The third economic region was discontinuous and represented modern mining and rubber estate interests, the

[1]The Census of 1911 does not bear out Hart's observation.

latter clustered in blocks along the Singgora road in Kubang Pasu district and in the Kuala Muda and Kulim districts to the south.

THE NORTH-EAST: KELANTAN AND TRENGGANU

The banks of the Kelantan River are very beautiful; the admixture of coco-nuts and clumps of bamboos, with stretches of bright green paddy, with a background of dark forest makes a pretty picture.

W. Davison, 1890, 89.

These two states stood somewhat apart from the others, being separated from the Kedah centre of cultivation by mountains on their western boundaries, boundaries in the nineteenth century as yet undefined. To the south of Trengganu lay more mountains and hills, with possibly a sprinkling of fisher-folk along the coast. Only the north was open to the free movement of peoples, and like Kedah, Kelantan was in receipt of ethnic Thais whose slow southward drift continued into the present century. In Kelantan, the basin of the river from which the state takes its name formed a single settled unit, though doubtless not all the lowland was occupied. To the south, the Trengganu basin formed the major settled area but with minor settlements in the Besut basin in the north, and the valleys of the Marang, Dungun, Paka and Kemaman rivers to the south of the state capital at Kuala Trengganu.[1]

Neither of the two states was notable as a rice-production centre, but both are interesting in that they are excellent examples of thoroughly Malay states both politically and economically, owing but little to the affairs of imperium. Such scanty information as exists, mainly in newspaper and travellers' reports, would suggest that these areas had diversified peasant economies coupled with, to foreign eyes, anarchic political systems. Kelantan seems to have been at least self-sufficient in the basic staple and at times exported rice. The population totalled about 50,000 in 1834 (SFP 26.1.1837). Trengganu, in contrast, was urbanized to the extent that nearly half of a total population of thirty or forty thousand lived in the capital at Kuala Trengganu (SFP 26.1.1837; Malcom, 1839, 105–6). The state as a whole seems to have been rice-deficient from the 1860s when rice exports were forbidden (SFP 30.10.1860; Ord, 1868, 19), though in some years prior to this time there was some export. This deficit was made good by imports purchased with the proceeds from the sale of fish and other marine products, pepper, cloth and weapons which were exported, mainly to Singapore.

KELANTAN TO c.1900

No coherent account of agriculture in the state can be given until late

---

[1]Newbold (1839, 2, 62) stated that the population of Kuala Trengganu was 15–20,000. Marang, Dungun and Paka contained 400, 1,000 and 100 houses respectively. Newbold (SFP 26.1.1837) reported a population of 1,000 for the semi-independent Kemaman district but this was not confirmed by Abdullah in 1838 (Coope, 1949, 65).

in the period but the famous story of Abdullah bin Abdul Kadir (Coope, 1949) dating from 1838 gives tantalizing glimpses of life in the coastal tract which alone Abdullah saw. At Kampong Laut the *munshi* noted that, 'The orchards and rice-fields were very fine.... Whenever I came to an open space or a rice-field, I found it full of cattle and buffaloes and goats and sheep....' (Coope, 1949, 43–4). The importance of livestock would suggest the existence of extensive areas of grazing which would be required to support the stock during the rice-planting season, though Abdullah visiting the area at the end of March saw them grazing stubble. The existence of grazing would in turn imply either that there was permanent grazing land here or that significant areas of rice land were cultivated only at intervals, between which they lay fallow under grass and were used for pastoral purposes. Either or both are likely in this 'sand-ridge and swale' terrain. Abdullah further reported a small export of rice and also an early example of the modern Kelantan custom of planting maize during the dry season (Coope, 1949, 39).

In the coastal tracts fishing was combined with rice cultivation and livestock rearing, though whether the same people were both fishermen and farmers is not clear. Concerning 'Sabak' (=Kampong Sabak) a place with a population of six or seven hundred, the munshi noted that,

The people get their living by fishing and rice planting.... We walked along the ridges between the rice-fields which spread out before us like an ocean; the fields were clean and contained no trees or stumps. We walked for about two hours, traversing many homesteads, full of coconut and betelnut trees and fruit trees. And I saw cattle and buffaloes by the hundred....

Coope, 1949, 49, 51.

In mid-century Kelantan had some export of rice (*SFP* 16.7.1852) but towards the end of the century the state suffered a series of disasters which severely affected its economic life. In 1870 a severe cattle plague, probably rinderpest, prevailed '...so that the country had been almost devastated' (*SDT* 20.7.1870). This was a serious matter, because, as following the further cattle plague of 1887, the people lost not only a source of wealth but a source of traction. As the *Jawi Peranakan* reported (22.8.1887),

Because buffaloes and other livestock were dead the cultivation of padi suddenly came to a halt. When cultivation ceased famine came to Kelantan. Whoever had buffaloes continued to plough. (These people plough up for padi growing with buffaloes only). When people who possessed buffaloes for ploughing suddenly became poor they were in effect landless and therefore took up reaping but not planting work....

The famine which ensued forced the emigration of several thousand families, most, presumably, rice growers. Some settled at Kemaman, some in Selangor, about a thousand families went to Muar (possibly Ulu Muar), and two thousand families settled in Kedah where they were promptly given food and land. Most likely all set up rice-growing colonies where they settled.

What were the full effects of the hurricane[1] followed by cholera and smallpox epidemics which the state had experienced several years earlier there is no telling, but whole villages were wiped out and whereas in 1875 there were 100,000 people living in the immediate vicinity of Kota Bharu, by 1893 there were no more than 50,000 in the whole state (*SFP* 26.7. 1893).[2] Undoubtedly considerable depopulation occurred since Norman (1895, 567) reported as commonplace, '... places where at one time there had evidently been a small and flourishing community... but now virtually deserted, the houses empty and falling to pieces, the cultivated land lapsing into jungle again. . . .' Emigration of some of the survivors occurred as a result of all these natural disasters and the upshot was a spread of skilled rice growers.

By the end of the century the state seems to have made a fair recovery from these disasters since the population rose from about 65,000 in mid-century (Pallegoix, 1854, 24; Bowring, 1857, 48) to around 300,000 in 1911 (Graham, 1911, 482). Unlike its southern neighbour, Kelantan was largely agricultural with some gold-mining carried out by Kelantan-born Chinese in the Galas district in the *Ulu*.

KELANTAN c.1910

Foreign observers seem to have regarded the state as highly prosperous, although based largely upon agriculture. Graham, for example, spoke of Kelantan as having '... one of the largest as well as richest rural communities of the whole peninsula' (Kelantan AR 1903–4, 3). Clifford (1897, 37) indicated that the state was deficient in rice. By the 1900s the production of rice was usually little in excess of local requirements, although in very good years free exportation was allowed (Kelantan AR 1904–5, 5–6). There was however a considerable internal trade in the staple, because, although many Malays and some of the Chinese in the predominantly mining districts of the interior were agriculturalists and some parts of Ulu Kelantan, for example the Lebir valley, were rice-surplus areas, the Ulu as a whole was deficient and required imports from down-river (Clifford, 1897, 33–4; Annandale, 1900, 518; Waterstradt, 1902, 9).

Four agricultural zones may be recognized. The first comprised the lower valley and the delta. Here the predominant type of rice land was *tanah chedong*, land for transplanting, upon which standing water, supplied either by irrigation or by rainfall, was maintained within low embankments during the greater part of the time the crop was in the ground. This class of land was planted annually (Graham, 1908, 71). Livestock

[1]Wyatt-Smith (1964, 202) gives the year of the hurricane as 1883 but a search of the *Straits Times* newspaper files for that year and the first three months of the following year failed to reveal any mention of a hurricane in Kelantan. Browne (1949) stated that the exact date is uncertain, whilst Clifford writing nearer the event (1897, 14) gave 1880, a date which could not be checked from newspaper sources. The standard authority, Graham (1908, 15), merely states, ...some 30 years ago' whereas a modern Malay historian, As'ad Shukri Haji Muda (1962, 122) has the date as 1880.

[2]This would seem to be a gross underestimate, however, since Graham, who had been in the service of Siam, gave a population of 300,000 in 1911. See Graham (1911, 482).

were less important than in the second zone because the land was under
crop most of the year. Moreover, village lands formed large contiguous
blocks (Coope, 1949, 49) leaving little space for grazing during the growing
seasons. These lands were in parts intersected with canals, such as those
linking Kota Bharu with Tabal and Bachok, but by 1905 these were so
silted up as to severely reduce the formerly considerable boat traffic upon
them (Kelantan AR 1904–5, 30). But as to whether these particular canals
were also used for irrigation there is no report, although the existence of
irrigation elsewhere in the state is undoubted.

The second zone lay inland and up-river from the first. Here *tanah
tugalan*, land for dibbling, was predominant. This land was put to the
plough but once in three years. The land was neither irrigated nor bunded
(Graham, 1908, 71–2).[1] On these higher grounds, large herds of cattle and
flocks of sheep and goats were depastured, and of these, when disease was
absent, several thousand head were annually exported (Kelantan AR
1903–4, 18). It may be surmised that the grass fallows of this zone provided
grazing for the traction animals of the first zone during the rice-growing
season. In other words a sort of 'horizontal transhumance' was practised
between the two zones.

The third zone comprised the more remote valley lands in which shifting
cultivation was practised by Malays. Graham (1908) does not suggest that
the making of *ladangs* was confined only to the aboriginal tribes of the
interior or to hill lands. This zone also included gold-mining. In the fourth
zone aboriginal peoples combined shifting cultivation with, to a limited
degree, the collection of jungle products, but on the whole their economy
was self-contained and their relations with Malays were hostile (Clifford,
1897, 33).

In the zones of permanent agriculture, rice was by no means the only
product of importance. Coconuts were extensively grown in well-kept
plantations, fortunately free of the rhinoceros beetle. Indeed, the high
price of copra and oil in the mid-1900s resulted in considerable areas of
rice land, especially in the northern districts, being converted into coconut
plantations which, though they might be slightly less lucrative than padi,
required considerably less toil (Kelantan AR 1903–4, 26). This process,
however, did not lead to a significant overall reduction in the area of land
under rice because rice land, fallow since the disasters of the 1880s, was
once more being brought under cultivation (Kelantan AR 1904–5, 14).
In addition to rice, maize, tobacco, tapioca, sugarcane, croton and castor-
oil seeds and still a little pepper were grown, though the production of
pepper was doubtless much less than a century earlier when Raffles quoted
a combined Kelantan and Trengganu production of 2,000 tons annually
(Raffles, 1817, 215n). In 1905 rubber planting had just begun (Wright and
Reid, 1912, 171).

Like Kedah, Kelantan had a system of land registration, inaugurated
in 1882, by which a title deed or grant was issued, initially only to fresh

[1]As late as 1933, a quarter of the total padi land of the state was under annual cultivation
in 'dry', unirrigated, unbunded fields; see Craig, 1933, 664.

applicants but later to those who already held land (Kelantan AR 1903–4, 25). A number of the duplicates of these documents survives but most are in too poor a condition for consultation and hence could not be used for statistical analysis. One volume (Kelantan Land Office Records 1903) for the mukim of Surau Sabak, was consulted and this shows that most holdings were remarkably irregular in shape and of very small size, the latter suggesting that these were additions to existing lands, the general

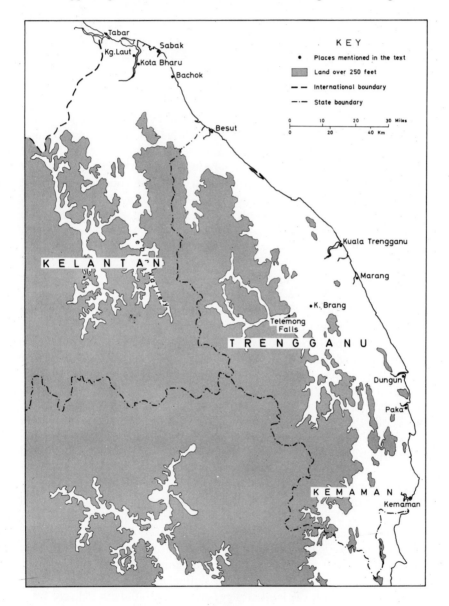

FIGURE 6
KELANTAN AND TRENGGANU: PLACES MENTIONED IN THE TEXT

area having been settled at least as early as Abdullah's visit. The predominant land uses were for *padi chedongan* (transplanted rice) and *padi
tugalan* (dibbled rice), but other uses included coconut, *nipah*, *dusun*
and fallow.

The overall picture then is by no means black, and though chieftains
doubtless arrogated to themselves much of the economic surplus (Kelantan AR 1903-4, 3), life for the peasant, if not easy, can have been by no
means unpleasant, provided that he did not fall foul of authority. The
corvée (*krah*) was enforced and although certainly, by Western standards,
misused for personal gain, it was also used for the general good, including
the repair of irrigation works (Kelantan AR 1903-4, 3, 17).

TRENGGANU *c*.1910

Relevant Malay sources are lacking and the only comprehensive account of Trengganu is a somewhat lurid one by Clifford (1897). Neale
(1852, 124) merely visited the town, while Ord (1868, 19) commented that,
'But little is known of the country'. It is clear that by the 1890s the state
was in a condition of near anarchy. The local chiefs had lost most of their
power even where such officers still existed and the country was preyed
upon by the *budak raja* (Clifford, 1897, 16-17). But the political crisis
was paralleled by and probably not unrelated to a major economic
crisis.

Trengganu had been a major producer of pepper, but this was not all.
Silk-weaving of a widely-celebrated type, the manufacture of cotton
sarongs, including weaving and dyeing, was a major industry, as was work
in brass which, because of its high quality, enjoyed a Peninsular-wide
market. In addition a wide range of weapons, *kris*, spears, swords, knives
and choppers was produced. Various articles in wood were also manu-
factured for export. Not unjustly did Clifford (1897, 27) describe the state
as 'the Birmingham of the Peninsula'. In addition to the export of pepper
and manufactures, shipbuilding flourished and not only Trengganu trade
but also that of other states was carried in Trengganu ships. Fishing,
although confined to the off-monsoon period from March to November,
was modestly lucrative, there being trade with the inland area in salt and
dried fish as well as some export (Trengganu AR 1910, 7; Graham, 1911,
483). Of agricultural products, coconuts were exported to Siam and salted
limes to other markets (Davison, 1890, 87).

The agricultural economy was based upon rice, pepper being no longer
of consequence. According to Clifford, the preponderance of plough land,
70 per cent of the total, was unusual in an independent state and this was
to be accounted for by a high population density. About a tenth of the
rice land was 'irrigated', though by this Clifford almost certainly merely
meant bunded, 60 per cent was unbunded plough land probably annually
cultivated, and the balance was under shifting cultivation. Some pressure
of population upon the land is suggested in that after the rice crop was
garnered, maize, tapioca and yams, generally regarded as poor substitutes
for rice, were planted in the dry season (Clifford, 1897, 31). In 1910, Scott

(Trengganu AR 1910, 11) reported that all the land on both banks of the Trengganu and Nerus rivers was under wet rice with dry rice on the hills. Even soils of the swales and sand ridges of the coastal tract from Kuala Trengganu to Marang were cropped, Scott (Trengganu AR 1910, 11) remarking that it was '. . . extraordinary that this sandy soil should produce good crops. . .'. Indeed it was, but its use was merely a reflection of population pressure.

Trengganu was as vulnerable to internal political strains as to forces outside it. The imposition of British control reduced the demand for Malay-style weapons, while competition with the cheap, machine-made products of Birmingham and Manchester had begun to destroy manufacturing crafts. The result was the beginning of agrarianization, a process probably substantially complete by the 1930s.

But in 1895, the country between the capital at Kuala Trengganu and the impassable Telemong falls above Kuala Brang on the Sungei Trengganu, already contained a population of about 33,000, making that area one of the most densely populated tracts in the Peninsula. Clifford (1897, 31) remarked that '. . . all the suitable [rice] planting land below the Kelemang [sic] falls is owned, and cannot. . . be taken up by anyone who has a mind to do so, as is the case in most parts of the Peninsula.' Moreover, the existing cultivators, some two-thirds of the populace, produced virtually nothing in excess of consumption at this time, although forty years earlier there were hints of a larger surplus (SFP 29.5.1856). It is also likely that a reduction of grazing land occurred as the population grew. The Straits Times newspaper (ST 11.9.1875) reported that Singapore was supplied with beef cattle from Trengganu whilst much earlier, in the 1830s and 1840s, the native craft manifests in the Singapore Free Press frequently included the item ghee[1] imported from Trengganu. Yet by 1911, this trade had disappeared (Graham, 1911, 483).

For some the answer to increasing impoverishment was emigration but this seems to have been confined largely to fishermen whose villages are still to be encountered southwards on the coasts of Pahang and Johore. For the rest the answer was a loss of traditional skills and a move to the farming of already crowded land.

---

[1]Clarified butter. The production and export of this commodity, one now rarely used in Malay cuisine, is an interesting indication of the degree of commercialization of pastoral farming in the state.

5

The Northern Centre:
Penang and Province Wellesley

The produce of the Prince of Wales's Island, is wood, cattle, hogs, poultry, canes and rice where cultivated, together with fruit and vegetables, all in the greatest abundance, and at the most reasonable prices.

Elisha Trapaud, 1788, 18.

IF the burgeoning production of rice in the Kedah-Perlis plain were the child of imperial interests, then these interests were no more than foster-parents. In contrast Penang and the Province were their natural children, both being virtual wildernesses at the beginning of British control. Superficially, rice production in the colony was much the same as in the northern Malay states, but this similarity went only as deep as the landscape. The institutional milieu was quite different.

In a sense the presence of the Malays was accidental. Before 1821 some thousands had settled in the colony but it was the rape of Kedah by Siam which triggered migration and subsequently resulted in large-scale land development especially in the Province. The role of the Malays in a non-Malay state was to be subordinate to the real business which was shop-keeping on a large scale. One part lay in land-clearing, at which the Malays were held to be particularly adept, and following their role as hewers of wood, they were to be relegated to the growing of a cheap staple, since, in the words of one Lieutenant-Governor, '... Malay Inhabitants... are incapable of any labour beyond the cultivation of Paddy' (Leith, 1804, 27). Yet their achievement was considerable. By 1910, both Island and Province were fully cultivated except for the hills whose deforested slopes were the result of a completely commercialized, sometimes highly profit-able yet unstable system of agriculture which contrasted with the partially commercialized, poorly-paying yet stable rice agriculture of the plains.

Nevertheless it would be absurd to suggest that the institutional milieu, with its alien forms of land tenure, and its individualistic and its com-munalistic social structure, with its thoroughly commercial economic structure, had effects upon the processes of land development and settle-ment, upon systems of cultivation significantly beyond those in the Malay states. Only on one score, the minor conflicts between sugar-growing and rice-growing in the Province, were differences actually reflected in the landscape. The examination of land development and of systems of cultivation is facilitated by the detailed documentation available for the settlement.

THE SPREAD OF AGRICULTURE

Whereas in Kedah, the large-scale development of the lowlands for at least partly commercial purposes preceded the development of the uplands, in Penang, though not in the Province, the pattern was reversed, and the initial clearing was for the cultivation of spices on the uplands, rice apparently not even being grown as a catch-crop (Guthrie et al., 1861, 6). At the outset both Penang and the Province were clean slates. Though in 1786 the Island was, according to Crawfurd (1828, 29) 'wholly uncultivated', and scarcely inhabited,[1] some sixty years earlier there had been a fair-sized settlement of 2,000 or so people with land in fruit trees, and from Macalister's description (1803, 23), permanent plough agriculture. The Province too, on its Cession in 1800 was likewise uncultivated (Crawfurd, 1828, 35) though not, as Crawfurd suggests, quite uninhabited (Topping, 1850).

DEVELOPMENT TECHNIQUES

Little is known of the techniques by which the immigrant rice growers developed their lands. Certainly the sources make no mention of planned and directed enterprise on the scale of Kedah in the 1880s. Rather in the settlement it must have been every man for himself, though in undertaking the clearing of the virgin forest, Macalister (1803, 24) implied that co-operative working was the rule. 'A dozen of strong Malays', he said, 'armed with cane-handled axes, will clear away a great deal of ground in a very short time.' This was done by partially cutting through the trees such that when once one was completely felled the rest were thrown down, each by the other. The next step was presumably firing of the trash following drying. This was followed by the planting of rice, coconuts, *pinang*, fruit trees, plantains and sugarcane, presumably in separate plots. After three years the stumps and trunks were sufficiently decayed to permit the use of animal traction (Tregonning, 1958, 319–20).

Little is known of the cost of clearing, Newbold's 1838 estimate of $1,000 per acre referring to land for spices (Lee, 1957, 44). In any case a rakyat was scarcely in the habit of costing his own labour. Nevertheless there was a price in human health to be paid, at least in some areas. Certain newly-cleared tracts were 'peculiarly unhealthy', and a period of two or even three years was often required for 'the amelioration of the climate'—a nineteenth-century euphemism for the stabilizing of populations of malarial mosquitoes, doubtless *Anopheles*.

PENANG ISLAND

On the island the amount of land topographically suitable for rice cultivation was rather limited, being essentially the land below the 50-foot

[1]See Hill, 1973, 189n.

contour. This totalled about 36 square miles from which the sand flats of the George Town plain and the sand ridges and coastal mangrove must be deducted.

The initial clearance for rice-planting was in the vicinity of Sungei Kluang where in 1788, Light reported that sixty families (250 persons) had cleared about 600 orlongs from which an initial yield of 2,700 pounds of rice per acre was obtained. A further strip of cleared land lay between the Kluang and the Penang rivers. Here the crops included rice, coconuts and pepper, a combination chosen to include a carbohydrate staple, a source of fats, and a cash crop which would come into production within three years (Tregonning, 1958, 319–20). At Nipah river each family was given lands with a frontage of between one and five linear orlongs, with the depth dependent upon how far each decided to cut (Tregonning, 1958, 321). In a later report, Light noted that the Malays, some of them immigrants from Borneo, Celebes, Java and Sumatra, had cleared and planted about 2,500 acres which yielded 10,000 maunds of rice, a yield which would double in the following year as much of the land was still tree-covered (Great Britain, IOL, Home Misc. 434). The same report mentioned that '. . . among the Malays are five familys [sic] of principle [sic] note whose connections are extensive and dependents numerous, the others about 600 in number a sober industrious people employed in agriculture. . . .' The former likely played an entrepreneurial role as did Light himself, on whose death were bequeathed to his widow a life interest in a hundred orlongs of rice land at Sungei Nibong together with forty buffaloes and implements. This land was probably worked by slaves and offers a rare example of a large-scale rice estate (Cullin and Zehnder, 1905 12).

The increase of developed land cannot be systematically traced but two years later the total population was said to be 20,000[1] with an estimated 7,000 orlongs '. . . principally in villages with surrounding orchards and paddy grounds' (Great Britain, IOL, Home Misc. 434). The east coast rural districts, Pulau Tikus, Jelutong, Glugor and Sungei Kluang, each had populations of between 1,400 and 2,400 by 1810 when their population totalled some 8,000, just over a third of the total for Penang as a whole (PWIGG 10.3.1810). The 'great Western Bay', Balik Pulau, was yet undeveloped, the Company taking the initiative to send a group of Malays there to clear the land and to plant rice (Leith, 1804, 12).

Yet much of the land initially cleared for rice cultivation was quickly put into other more profitable crops. As Leith (1804, 32) noted,

No considerable supply of either Paddy or Cattle, can ever be expected from our Island, as the value of land is so high, and the price of labour so great, that no man will ever appropriate any part of his land to Pasture or Paddy Fields, which can possibly be turned to any other purpose of a more profitable nature; very little Paddy is consequently cultivated, and no cattle reared on the Island. The former is merely for the use of the Slaves, who perform the labour.

[1]This must be taken with a grain of salt since Leith (1804, 29), quoting official sources, gave populations of 6,937 and 10,310 for 1797 and 1801 respectively.

The 'slaves' producing rice were across the channel in Kedah whence came grain '. . . cheaper than the price of agricultural labour in our island' (Macalister, 1803, 11).

So strong was the influence of this economic fact of life that in the 1830s, Low estimated that the total area of *sawah* did not exceed a mere 900 acres, with perhaps another 270 acres under shifting cultivation at any one time (Low, 1836, 83). Yet this seems to be something of an underestimate since an Admiralty survey of 1832 shows significant concentrations of what appears to be lowland rice cultivation in the Ayer Hitam valley, in the upper valley of the Sungai Dua, in the lands north of 'James Town' (the modern Kg. Pulau) and an extensive stretch at Bayan Lepas (Woore, 1832). In the west, the rice area was landward of Permatang Tengah in the upper valley of the 'Red River', i.e. the modern S. Kongsi, in the vicinity of the modern small town of Balik Pulau.

This general pattern was confirmed by Thomson[1] (1865a, 46) who added that the land-use pattern of the Peniagre plain, on which George Town stood, was highly varied with plantations of coconut and *pinang* alternating with rice and sugar fields with, here and there, the country houses and nutmeg gardens of the European speculators. Thomson may, however, have somewhat overstated the matter in suggesting that the Balik Pulau plain was 'pretty well cultivated': an Admiralty chart of 1832 (Woore, 1832) clearly shows that it was not.

The subsequent changes in these main rice areas are difficult to trace by reason of lack of sources. As George Town grew, the north-eastern areas presumably gave way to market-gardens and suburbia, a process already suggested by Dyce's view of quite extensive gardens on the outskirts of the town (Dyce, 1847, fol. 41 recto). The remaining areas of eastern Penang remain to the present. In 1860–1 the total area was 10,713 acres (*SSAR* 1860–1, 45). Some seaward extension was in progress in 1869 both in the south-east and the west.

The drainage of the Sungy Nibong, Ralaw [= Relau] and Bayan Lepas plains is far superior to the larger paddy tracts of the Province, and the Rice crops, where cultivated by the Chinese, are equal to the best in the Province. . . none of the fields looked better than some lately reclaimed from the mangrove swamps. . . . The Bali Pulo [= Balik Pulau] paddy fields, which were cleared a few years ago, are an illustration of what can be done with mangrove swamps with capital, energy, and skill, under liberal terms of purchase.

SDT 25.9.1869.

To the west, Küchler (1968, map 10) has shown that by 1886, lands seaward of Permatang Tengah were under rice almost to the coast. In this tract holdings were notably smaller and more elongate than in the older area east of the Permatang. At some time subsequent to 1886 the cultivation of rice in the inland tract was abandoned. Down to the end of the period there is little knowing what was happening to rice-growing on the Island, though the Straits Settlements Government felt that it was of

[1]Thomson was in Penang and the Province in the 1830s.

sufficient local importance to allocate funds for a bund at S. Acheh and sluices at Dusun Lada and Pinang Tunggal (*SS Estimates* 1893, 3275; 1897, 2224).

PROVINCE WELLESLEY

Province Wellesley was acquired by the British partly as a result of the fright Light had received in 1791 when the ruler of Kedah had cut off the supply of rice and other commodities.[1] The Island would never have provided sufficient food for its own support, partly because the area of suitable land available was too small, and partly because production of rice was unprofitable. As Leith noted (1804, 32), 'By acquiring a tract of land on the Continent, we should have the satisfaction of knowing, that in a short time we might reasonably expect to be independant [*sic*] of all countries for our supplies of Rice....' Actually the supply from Kedah was resumed, though with a major break in supply in 1808, when as a result of an epidemic of cattle disease and consequent lack of traction, there was a great scarcity of rice (Low, 1836, 155). Though some land was taken up and Leith (1804, 34) claimed that more people were 'daily resorting thither', there was no significant development. In the Province, land was in sight but out of mind before 1819, up to which time the official documents made but four mentions of the matter (Stubbs-Brown, 1963, 216). The arrival of large numbers of Kedah fugitives transformed the situation, very much to the advantage of the English land proprietors since it cleared their jungles and gave them a settled population as well as the prospect of a secure food supply within a brief space of time (*PWIGG* 31.10.1821; Low, 1829; Warren to Gov. PWI 20.3.1839, EIC Board's Coll.; Thomson, 1865a, 156).

The Government of Prince of Wales Island, ...anxious to provide for the numerous fugitives who had voluntarily placed themselves under its protection, ...considered it advisable to appoint a Resident at Province Wellesley, who had authority to portion out small tracts of land to such families as might wish to settle permanently and cultivate; to make small advances of cash repayable within a certain period, in grain, and to give every encouragement to the cultivation of paddy; and the rearing of cattle and poultry....

Anderson, 1824, 14.

Thus, whereas in Penang there had been a few individual entrepreneurs working on some scale, in the Province the disruptions of a foreign war led the Government to undertake this entrepreneurial role, just as the Kedah government was to do sixty years later. The Penang government clearly saw that not only would a prosperous peasantry in the Province solve the food supply problem but also would provide a captive market for British manufactures (Ag. Res. Councillor PWI to Gov. 20.3.1838, EIC Board's Coll.). In this developmental role the provision of roads by government was crucial. These were constructed by convict labour and

[1]For a description of Kedah-Penang trade see Light (1787). Khoo (1959) has a number of relevant statistics.

settlement by Malays growing rice swiftly followed (Low, 1836, 325). The easiest terrain in which to build roads was along the crests of the *permatangs*, narrow sand ridges which lay parallel to the coast and at varying distances from it. Between the ridges lay alluvial soils 'superior in fertility to that of lands of the same class in Pinang' (Newbold, 1839, 1, 102). Thus evolved a pattern of settlement which was linear to the roads, just as in the south Kedah plain settlement was to be linear to the canals (see Fig. 7).

The great bulk of the land initially given out was to the north of the Prai river and here Malays were a considerable majority though by no means the only group present. The total area under rice cannot be satisfactorily estimated, but Low suggested that in 1825 about 5,000 orlongs were under rice with three times that area so cultivated by 1836 (Low, 1836, 83). Many of the grants of land made in the early 1830s are still recorded in the Penang Land Office. The documents are sufficiently detailed to allow a statistical analysis and this is presented in a following section (p. 76 ff).

The impetus of land development for rice continued during the 1840s, even though with the return of peace in Kedah, some of the Malays returned, selling their lands to Chinese and Europeans for the large-scale production of sugar (Balestier, 1848, 142). Most land for sugar was opened in the southern parts, eight new estates being opened in 1845–6 alone (Logan, 1887, 20n). Nevertheless '...some planters seemed inclined to purchase paddy-lands for making sugar plantations, rather than clear waste tracts for that purpose' (Logan, 1887, 18). But on the whole the owners of rice land were preserved from the temptation to sell out to sugar interests by the smallness of their lots which ranged from fifty down to two or three orlongs (Logan, 1887, 20). This made it virtually impossible to purchase from a multitude of owners an area sufficient for a sugar estate (Jackson, 1965, 225).

But Chinese interests were by no means confined to large-scale commercial sugar plantations, although these were paramount. From an unknown date but probably after 1833 since the Land Office records do not give details, Chinese from Macau had settled at a number of points. Logan (1887, 19) who visited the area in 1845, reported that, 'At Duraka I found from forty to fifty Chinese engaged in the cultivation of paddy, about eighty at Pau, as many at Paoyu [=Puyu], twenty to thirty at S. Susat [=Sesat]....' Some twenty years later, Chinese and Malays together were opening lands along the Muda river. Chinese also owned rice mills though these were primitive to a degree. 'The Chinese seem to have taken as much to rice cultivation as the Malays. There are several large plots of paddy land owned by Chinese in Tulloh [Telok] Ayer Tawar, Penaga, Qualla Muda, Permatang Poh [Pau] and near Bukit Maratajam [Mertajam]' (*SFP* 13.10.1864).

Although in the 1840s some Malays had sold up and returned to Kedah, the flow of migration again reversed in the 1860s when Malays from Kedah, most in fact people who had once been living in the Province, returned to British territory to avoid krah. These folk had been treated like aliens in their land of origin, many being merely tenants-at-will (*SFP* 18.2.1864). They thus had double reason to return to the Province where suitable freehold land was still available, largely on the Muda river.

By 1861 the total area under rice was 41,493 acres (*SSAR* 1860–1, 45). Most of the cultivators were Malays who comprised about 83 per cent of a total population of about 64,000, ten times that of 1830 (Earl, 1861, 4).

The proportion of Malays is greater in the northern district than elsewhere, as the nature of the country is peculiarly favourable to the mode of life in which they most delight. Their dwellings are erected on the permatangs or sand-ridges, under the shade of the coconut trees with which they are thickly studded, and the bulk of the male population is employed during the intervals of planting and reaping the paddy lands in farming and tending the fishing weirs which extend far out to sea on the bank that lines the shore, and which yield an abundant harvest of excellent fish. . . . Shrimp-catching is also an important branch of industry on the sandy shore between the.Mudah and the Prye. . . .

In the districts lying between the Prye and the Junjong the bulk of the population is still Malay, but the proportion of Chinese and Klings is greater than to the north, as many of the former [i.e. the Chinese?] are employed as planters of rice, sugar cane, fruits and spices. . . .

In the district south of the Junjong, where the culture of sugar-cane is more extensive, the male population of Chinese is greater than that of the Malays. . . .

Earl, 1861, 4–5.

The subsequent change in the area under rice is impossible to document adequately, though that area south of the Krian river, termed Trans-Krian, was surely amongst the last in the Province to be agriculturally colonized. Trans-Krian was fully developed by the mid-1870s, when Weld (in Lovat, 1914, 371) suggested that almost the entire area of the Province was under cultivation. The great bulk of the rice land of the whole settlement, a total of 63,444 acres (*SSAR* 1876, 490), was in the Province which probably had around 50,000 acres of that area. The area subsequently remained stable at around that figure, reaching 63,000 acres twice in the 1870s and otherwise remaining at around the 40–50,000 acre mark (see Table 18). From 1860 until the end of the century the lowland was almost entirely taken up for cultivation (Hill, 1900, 604).

PROVINCE WELLESLEY—A STATISTICAL PROFILE, 1829–33

The survival of some twenty-two volumes[1] of duplicates of early land grants allows the gathering of a fair range of statistical data. The relevant data include the name of the grantee, the district, rent payable, the size of holding and type of land. A good number have sketch plans of the lands to which they refer and a few have endorsements concerning subdivisions subsequent to the issue of the document. The great majority refer to individual lots in the northern part of the Province, thereby encompassing the greater part of the rice land at that time. The reconstruction of farm

[1]For details concerning these volumes see Hill, 1973, 202n.

data from lot data is a matter of some difficulty and the principle adopted was admittedly hit-or-miss. If two or more grants in the same district bore the same name spelt in the same way, then it was assumed that they were the same person, otherwise each was considered a separate farm. On this basis 82 per cent of the farms turned out to be single-lot farms though the number of multiple-lot farms may still be over-estimated.

The analysis which follows is largely based upon farm rather than lot data but there are in fact no really noteworthy differences between the two. For example, the mean and median lot sizes were 3.5 and 2.6 orlongs respectively, compared with mean and median farm sizes of 3.8 and 3.0 orlongs respectively.

LAND USE BY REGIONS

The greater proportion of dry land in the centre and especially the south is illustrated in Table 3.

TABLE 3
PROVINCE WELLESLEY: LAND USE BY REGIONS (LOTS),
1829–33

Major Area	Wet Rice Land		Dry Land		Total	
	No.	Per cent	No.	Per cent	No.	Per cent
North: Northern section (S. Muda–S. Abdul)	484	94	31	6	515	100
Southern section (S. Abdul–S. Prai)	574	77	172	23	746	100
Centre (S. Prai–S. Juru)	217	68	104	32	321	100
South (S. of S. Juru)	79	13	508	87	587	100
Total	1354	62	815	38	2169	100

Source: Calculated from Penang Land Office Records 1829–33.

Although both wet rice land and dry rice land were found in the various districts in varying proportions, on individual farms, lands were usually of one type or the other (Table 4).

As would be expected in a pioneer situation in which the inheritance of or the purchase of separate plots of land were not yet operative, the degree of fragmentation, as measured by apparently the same person holding more than one lot, was rather low. Nevertheless it existed in some degree as is indicated by an average of 1.23 lots per farm. Table 4 suggests that the degree of fragmentation was a function of land use deriving from the desire of a farmer to have some dry land for his house, fruit trees and kitchen garden crops. This is not to suggest that half the farms in fact had

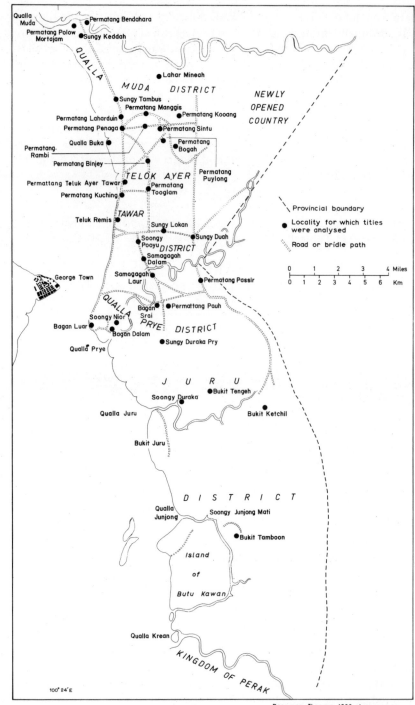

Qualla Muda
Permatang Bendahara
Permatang Polow Mortajam
Sungy Keddah
QUALLA
Lahar Mineah
MUDA DISTRICT
NEWLY OPENED COUNTRY
Sungy Tambus
Permatang Manggis
Permatang Laharduin
Permatang Kooang
Permatang Penaga
Permatang Sintu
Qualla Buka
Permatang Bogah
Permatang Rambi
Permatang Binjey
TELOK AYER
Permatang Puylong
Permattang Teluk Ayer Tawar
Permatang Tooglam
Permatang Kuching
TAWAR
Teluk Remis
Sungy Lokan
Soongy Pooyu DISTRICT
Sungy Duah
Samagagah Dalam
Samagagah Laur
Permatang Passir
George Town
QUALLA PRYE DISTRICT
Permattang Pauh
Soongy Nior
Bagan Srai
Bagan Luar
Bagan Dalam
Qualla Prye
Sungy Duraka Pry
J U R U
Soongy Duraka
Bukit Tengeh
Qualla Juru
Bukit Ketchil
Bukit Juru
D I S T R I C T
Qualla Junjong
Soongy Junjong Mati
Bukit Tamboon
Island of Butu Kawan
Qualla Krean
KINGDOM OF PERAK
100° 24' E

Provincial boundary
Locality for which titles were analysed
Road or bridle path

0   1   2   3   4 Miles
0 1 2 3 4 5 6 Km

Base map: Thomson 1839, place-names
from Penang Land Office records 1829–33

FIGURE 7
PROVINCE WELLESLEY: RICE-GROWING LOCALITIES, 1829–33

TABLE 4
PROVINCE WELLESLEY: LAND USE ON ANALYSED LOTS, 1829–33

Land-use Class	Farms		Lots	
	Number	Per cent	Number	Per cent
1 wet rice only	873	50	1133	52
2 $>\frac{3}{4}$ in wet rice	211	12	178	8
3 $>\frac{1}{2}-\frac{3}{4}$ in wet rice	27		20	
4 $>\frac{1}{4}-\frac{1}{2}$ in wet rice	20	3	20	2
5 $<\frac{1}{4}$ in wet rice	10		3	
6 no wet rice, dry crops	624*	35	815*	38
Total	1765	100	2169	100

Source: Calculated from Penang Land Office Records 1829–33.
*Calculated from a 25 per cent sample of lot data.

their house sites in wet rice land as might be suggested by Table 4 but merely that the proportion of dry land was so small that it was not indicated on the original documents. Subsequent land subdivision was such that few subdivided lots were so small as to be uneconomic in size. The second generation thus usually received an economically viable unit on inheritance.

TABLE 5
PROVINCE WELLESLEY: NUMBER AND PROPORTION OF LANDOWNERS OF EACH SOCIAL GROUP, 1829–33
(LOT DATA FOR ALL CLASSES OF LAND)

Group	Number		Per cent	
1. Malays	1524		89	
1 *Rakyat, penghulu, serang, nakhoda*		1166		68
2 *Shaik, wan, syed*		47		3
3 *Haji, imam, bilal, lebai*		180		11
4 Women		125		7
5 Royalty (*ungku, tungku, raja*)		6		
2. Non-Malays	189		11	
1 Chinese (including *babas*)		74		4
2 Thais		38		2
3 Europeans and Eurasians		15		1
4 Others		62		4
Total	1713	1713	100	100

Source: Penang Land Office Records 1829–33.

OWNERSHIP

Joint ownership of land was not a significant feature of land tenure and the Province Wellesley data show that only 2 per cent of the lots were so owned. Of greater significance are the questions concerning who owned the land, how much and where. In analysis nine different classes of landowners were recognized, the total numbers and proportions in each of which are given in Table 5. The Malays emerge as the larger group and within it the rakyat are most numerous, though the proportion of *hajis* is quite striking for this early period when the *haj* was by no means lightly undertaken. Although under Islamic law, women could inherit estates of the deceased, though not equally with their brothers, the proportion of women owning land was very small. None of the remaining classes of society call for particular comment.

More significant are the patterns of land use associated with the various classes of owners. These are shown in Table 6.

TABLE 6

PROVINCE WELLESLEY: PROPORTION OF FARMS IN VARIOUS LAND-USE CLASSES BY SOCIAL GROUP OF OWNERS, 1829–33

Landowner Group	Land-use Class (%) 1 Rice only		2 & 3 >½ in rice		6 Dry only		Total	
1. Malays	91		90		89		89	
1 *Rakyat* etc.		71		63		67		69
2 Women		7		9		7		7
3 *Shaiks* etc.		3		5		5		4
4 *Hajis* etc.		10		12		4		8
5 Royalty		–		1		1		1
2. Non-Malays	9		10		11		11	
1 Chinese		3		4		6		4
2 Thais		2		3		3		2
3 Europeans etc.		1		–		2		1
4 Others		3		3		5		4
Total	100	100	100	100	100	100	100	100

Source: Calculated from Penang Land Office Records 1829–33.

Table 6, being based upon numbers, understates the importance of minority groups because the area of land owned by them is not taken into consideration. On this basis, Table 6 shows a slight concentration of the rakyat on farms classed as exclusively rice-growing, with a slight preference by non-Malays for dry land. As far as Europeans and Eurasians were concerned, it is perhaps a little surprising to observe that they owned any rice land at all. Doubtless they possessed establishments like that of

Light on the mainland. One John Sneider, for instance, owned some 20 orlongs of rice land at Permatang Penaga. James Low, the Company apologist, held 311 orlongs of wet rice land and dry land at Bagan Bahru in the Teluk Ayer Tawar district, naturally on the easiest of terms, viz. rent-free for five years. This was not his only holding, his lands in the Province at this period totalling 630 orlongs, making Low the largest single landowner there.

FARM SIZE

Farm size is an index of major importance because it reflects the social structure, besides having its own intrinsic interest. The distribution curve of farm sizes is skewed and for this reason the median value is a better measure of central tendency than the mean. The size data, median and mean sizes of farms for various classes of owners is given in Tables 7 and 8.

Since the data have been kept in orlongs because it has been found impossible to confirm that the orlong was, at this early date, equivalent to the one-and-a-third acres it came to be later, uncertainty clouds discussion somewhat since if it were the same as the Kedah measure, 0.7 acre, the question of what was an economic holding becomes quite different. Assuming that the data refer to orlongs of one and one-third acres, some

TABLE 7

PROVINCE WELLESLEY: PROPORTION OF FARMS IN VARIOUS
SIZE CLASSES BY SOCIAL GROUP OF OWNERS, 1829–33

Size Class (orlongs)[1]	Class of Owner			
	All Malays	Rakyat, etc. Women	Shaiks, Hajis, Royalty, etc.	Non-Malays
	%	%	%	%
< 1.0	13	13	11	15
1.0– 1.9	19	20	16	19
2.0– 2.9	18	18	17	15
3.0– 3.9	14	14	15	12
4.0– 4.9	11	11	9	10
5.0– 6.9	12	11	15	10
7.0– 9.9	8	7	10	6
10.0–19.9	5	5	5	6
20.0–49.9	1	1	2	6
50.0 and over	–	–	–	6
	101	100	100	101
Farms enumerated	1244	1058	186	144

[1]An orlong probably equalled 1.33 acres.

TABLE 8
PROVINCE WELLESLEY: MEDIAN AND MEAN FARM SIZES BY
SOCIAL GROUP OF OWNERS, 1829–33

Social Group of Owner	Median (orlongs)	Mean (orlongs)
1. Malays	3.0	4.2
1 *Rakyat* etc.	3.0	4.0
2 Women	3.8	4.0
3 *Shaiks* etc.	3.5	4.2
4 *Hajis* etc.	3.4	4.7
5 Royalty	n.c.	n.c.
2. Non-Malays	3.1	6.2
1 Chinese	3.8	6.5
2 Thais	2.6	5.0
3 Europeans etc.	4.3	16.5
4 Others	2.7	3.9

Source: Calculated from Penang Land Office Records 1829–33.

salient points concerning farm size may be indicated. First is the rather even spread of sizes from under an orlong up to almost seven orlongs. This probably reflects the varying abilities of the owners to carve out holdings for themselves, in turn reflecting the family structure of the pioneers. A family with a number of able hands was obviously better placed to handle a large holding than one with husband, wife and young children. On the other hand a holding worked by young adults would more quickly reach its maximum productive capacity, soon resulting in a further search for land.

Amongst the Malays, there can be no doubt that social status and size of holding were mutually reflective, though the large median size of lands owned by women may be surprising to those who would think of women of that time as a depressed class.[1] The Malay 'middle class', the shaiks, wans and syeds, together with others whose status derived from religious matters, on the whole, owned larger farms than the rakyat, though the question as to whether they held more land because of their status or had higher status because they had more land is, perhaps, moot. Once fully developed these holdings were capable of supporting more than one family. Whether this group included landlords or not there is no knowing, but the lands could have supported both a tenant and an owner-farmer. Do we see here a Malay equivalent of the Russian *kulak* class? The conclusion is tempting.

So far as the non-Malay groups were concerned, there was a greater spread of farm sizes. Some, the Thais and certain of the Chinese, had very small holdings, many less than an orlong in size. Other Chinese had

[1]They never were in Minangkabau states and these data suggest that some were not outside it, however relatively disadvantaged they might be in matters of inheritance under Islamic law.

moderately large holdings as did some but not all of the Europeans and Eurasians.

Mixed wet rice and dry land farms, with median and mean sizes of 5.1 and 7.2 orlongs respectively, were almost twice as large as farms growing only wet rice (2.8 and 3.8 orlongs) and a little over six times as large as dry land farms. The small average size of the dry land farms is a surprise since in modern times, peasant dry land farms are on the whole larger than wet rice farms by a factor of at least two and more usually three. The reason is not hard to find. In the 1830s the only successful dry land crops

TABLE 9
PROVINCE WELLESLEY: MEDIAN SIZE OF 'RICE ONLY' FARMS
BY MAJOR AREAS AND DISTRICT, 1829–33

Area	No. of Farms	Median Size (orl.)
1. *North: northern section*		
1.1 On S. Muda: S. Kedah, Permatang P. Mertajam, Permatang Bendahara, Lahar Mineah	70	1.73
1.2 Coastal: Permatang Penaga, Permatang Lahardiun, S. Tambus	64	2.90
1.3 Part coastal, part inland: Permatang Sintu, Qualla Buka	49	3.58
1.4 1 mile inland: Permatang Puylong, Permatang Rambi	67	2.56
1.5 3 miles inland: Permatang Bougah, Permatang Manggis, Permatang Kosong	61	1.88
2. *North: southern section*		
2.1 Mainly coastal: S. Pooyu, Teluk Remis, Permatang Kuching, Permatang Teluk Ayer Tawar	76	2.71
2.2 2 miles inland: Permatang Binjey, Permatang Tooglam	98	3.22
2.3 3–4 miles inland: S. Lokan, S. Duah	79	2.84
3. *Centre*		
3.1 3 miles inland (with 9 farms nr. Prai): Bagan Dalam, S. Niar, Bagan Luar, Permatang Pauh, Bagan Srai, Samagagah Luar, S. Duraka Pry	76	2.61
3.2 5 miles inland: Permatang Passir	54	2.37
3.3 2 miles inland near S. Prai: Samagagah Dalam	132	4.07
4. *South*		
4.1 Juru	47	2.53

Source: Calculated from Penang Land Office Records 1829–33.

were coconuts and areca (pinang), in Province Wellesley usually grown on the permatangs, and pepper, nutmegs and cloves, usually grown on the clay soils of the hill slopes. Except for a few largish holdings, the uplands were settled by small-holders who seemed to have managed to make a living on their small plots. Some of these were owned by Chinese market-gardeners as at Aur Gading (Earl, 1861, 11).

A further use to which farm size data can be put is to plot their areal pattern (Table 9). A number of factors would seem to account for areal variation in the size of peasant farms. One, of course, is type of land use; another is the amount of land required to support a family under given soil, drainage and locational conditions, including possibilities of part-time, off-farm employment. Yet another factor is the period during which land has been occupied. Since most farms would, in fact or in effect, be cut into at least two parts every generation, areas in which the farms were small might be expected to be those which had been longest occupied.

Some explanation is clearly called for since the median sizes in certain of the northern districts are less than half those of the centre. Moreover there is some tendency for the farms in the inland districts to be larger than those along the coast. In the northern section, a string of villages on the south bank of the Muda river lay along a line beginning some two miles upstream of the river-mouth and within half a mile of the bank (group 1.1 in Table 9). In this area, settled by Patani people in the eighteenth century (Topping, 1850, 44) rice farms were comparatively small. Along the coast, farms were larger even though it might have been expected that farms in the coastal zone would be smaller than inland because fishing was available as a supplementary source of income. This seems not to have been the case and the size of farms could reflect specialization of activities into farming on one hand and fishing on the other. Inland, the farms were smaller and this indicates a coastwards drift of settlement resulting from later colonization. In the southern section, farms were a good deal larger than elsewhere, but a similar pattern of smaller farms inland and larger farms nearer the coast again prevailed, presumably for the same reasons. In the central region, between the Prai and the Juru rivers, farm size was remarkably uniform but again there is the suggestion that farms nearer the coast were larger and hence likely more recent than those inland. The Samagagah Dalam area[1] was almost certainly of recent settlement having been colonized from swamp land along the Prai river. In the south, rice-growing was of no great importance and the farms were almost the same size as in the centre.

CULTIVATION TECHNIQUES AND NATURAL HAZARDS, THE ROUND OF WORK, YIELDS

The technical aspects of rice cultivation have already been discussed in Chapter 3, in which a typology was presented along with a broad sketch

[1] The village formerly lay on the banks of the Prai river just north of Bagan Serai.

of the agricultural year. All that is necessary here is to indicate briefly the main differences and similarities between the general model and the reality of the Province.

TYPOLOGY

Of the four main types of cultivation outlined by Crawfurd (1820, 1, 360–3), only two were present in significant degree, shifting cultivation (huma) and 'rain-rice' cultivation in wet fields. To these may be added an ephemeral type appropriate to pioneering. Shifting cultivation scarcely existed. Low (1836, 92, 94) mentioned varieties of upland rice (padi huma) and refers to 'irregular and fugitive cultivation' which contributed some 4 per cent of the total production of rice in the Province.[1] By the 1850s there 'was no regular cultivation of it though a few patches are to be found ...planted by Chinese' (Vaughan, 1857, 131).

Because it took some years to satisfactorily clear and level a bendang to the point at which a plough could be used, Low (1836, 111) noted that 'no uniform system' had yet been adopted. But even on lands sufficiently cleared for the use of the plough, it was nevertheless not employed, possibly because the rakyat were as yet too poor to purchase the necessary implements and tractive animals (Vaughan, 1857, 128). For some, the hiring of a herd of buffaloes to mire the land prior to planting was not only cheaper than ploughing but also gave higher yields (Low, 1836, 115) and was easier where tree roots had not yet rotted.

The provision of water on the fields was largely dependent upon the weather, but the topography aided matters since the small streams mostly ran parallel to the north-south trending permatangs and, being thus impeded, inundated the swales between them. In some places a form of irrigation was practised by which ditches were cut through the permatangs to convey water onto the fields (Vaughan, 1857, 127). True irrigation, in which control of the amount and timing of water application is possible, was lacking amongst the Malays. As Low (1836, 95) noted,

The Malays here have not attempted double-cropping[2] as on the continent of India. There are no tanks and it is only at a very few spots that they could be made. Most Malayan wet land rice requires so long a period to reach maturity, that there would be a deficiency of water for a second crop...the Malays are obstinate in asserting that, were water abundant still the rice sown here will not fructify[3] after the rainy season has passed.

The Chinese rice growers, however, though few in number, rendered themselves nearly independent of the weather by conveying water to their land from neighbouring streams by means of ditches, and where necessary, by nibong palms split lengthways to make small, open pipes (Vaughan, 1857, 130).

[1]Low's estimate.

[2]The Chinese, certainly, and possibly also the Kedah Malays, had short-term varieties but this did not lead to double-cropping (Low, 1836, 94–5).

[3]This is by no means as unsoundly based as may at first appear, since many rices are markedly photo-sensitive.

If irrigation was largely lacking, so seemingly was drainage, at least in the rice areas, until comparatively late. Not a source mentions drainage prior to 1862–3 when some preliminary works in the northern district were completed (*SSAR* 1862–3, 20).

Another technique that was certainly lacking was manuring. The Province lacked the limestone caves which provided the bat guano used by the Kedah farmers, and no attempt was made to substitute for it with the undoubted result that yields fell after the initial boost in soil nutrient status given by the burning of the forest. 'I was informed by several Malays at different places', noted Logan (1887, 18), 'that the crops of paddy had been inferior for some years past'.

THE ROUND OF WORK

The round of work was in no wise dissimilar to that described earlier (p. 41), but Vaughan's account (1857, 127–9) adds so much detail concerning the life of the rice farmer that it is worth quoting just a few of his sentences.

After the first fall of rain which indicates the approach of the wet season, his first care is to clear the fields of grass and weeds; this is done with an instrument called *tajah* [= *tajak*]; it resembles a scythe, the blade is short, heavy, and wedge-shaped and the handle is short and fixed at right angles to the blade. It is used with both hands, is raised above the head and brought down with a swing to the ground; its weight and sharpness renders it a very effective instrument, it cuts down everything as it falls and sinks several inches into the ground, uprootings [sic] the weeds. The latter are then drawn to the sides of the fields...and the ground is ploughed with a very primitive instrument called a *tangala* [= *tenggala*], it is nothing but a crooked timber with a short and a long log, the former is pointed and shod with iron, the latter has a bar of wood fastened across the end to which men or buffaloes are yoked....The ground is then cleared of any weeds that may be left with a rake or *pangara*; finally a curious roller, with six or seven sharp edges, resembling the cogs of a wheel, is drawn over the fields to crush the lumps of earth.

The work of the males now ceases; the women sow the grain in a nursery and when the plants are about a foot high, they are transplanted and put into the ground, about two feet apart, in bunches of three or four plants, and in regular rows about two or three feet apart....

The planter experiences much trouble as the paddy begins to ripen, and incessant watching is required to prevent birds picking the grains out of the ears by day, and pigs uprooting the plants by night....Small watch-houses are erected on the outskirts of a field...[and] from watch-house to watch-house lines are led, to which branches of trees, leaves, rags etc. are attached and the watchers incessantly move these lines to frighten the birds away....

If the fields happen to be near the jungle, horns are blown at intervals during the night to frighten the wild hogs off. Rats also do much harm....

The paddy is usually stored in the ear and when rice is required for consumption a sufficient quantity is taken out of the store-house and beaten on the ground till the grains are cleared from the stalks. They are then husked in a rice pounder or *alu* (literally a pestle)....A simple method of separating good from indifferent paddy is the following. A platform or stage is erected, about eight or ten feet above the ground, and when a moderate breeze is blowing the paddy is poured from the top of the stage, the wind carries away all the light useless grain and the good paddy falls on mats which are spread below to receive it. . . .[1]

A similar but earlier description by Low (1836, 96–102) adds a little. He noted that a planting fork or dibble was used to push the seedlings into the mud, at distances usually six to eighteen inches apart. At harvest the sickle was used to cut the grain when it had been laid down by its own weight or by the wind. Otherwise the Malay harvesting knife was used, partly because the grain was often not ripe all at once, and partly 'because the ryots do not readily walk out of the path which their forefathers followed' (Low, 1836, 102), but then Low obviously knew nothing of the semangat padi, the soul of the rice.

CROP YIELDS AND NATURAL HAZARDS

It has often been maintained that under the wet system of rice-growing, yields do not substantially diminish even after extended periods of cultivation. The matter has not been put to the test in a rigorously scientific manner but historical materials can nevertheless throw some light on the question. Where, as in many parts of the Province (Vaughan, 1857, 127), the soil received an annual, natural 'top-dressing' with alluvium, yields remained high. But inevitably there comes a time when such natural inundations become increasingly rare and increased leaching of soil nutrients, only partially obviated by surface flooding, and a continuous export of nutrients in the form of the crop would, in the absence of manuring, lead to a fall in soil nutrient status and hence average yield. The Province was 'new land' and in Malay opinion its yields were higher than the 'old land' of the Kedah plain and piedmont tract (Logan, 1851, 55). Even in the Province itself Logan (1887, 18) reported a diminution of yield of a number of years' standing. Certainly a district-by-district yield report for 1884 showed substantially lower yields or wider ranges of yields in the older established areas such as Permatang Bendahara, Penaga and Ara Rendang districts as compared with newer lands at Nibong Tebal and Trans-Krian (Skinner, 1884).

However, yields were highly variable from place to place and from time to time. The range from area to area was given by Logan (1887, 19) as from 180 to 600 gantangs per acre, though this estimate seems a little on the high side having regard to modern yields and to Skinner's report of 1884 (Skinner, 1884). The latter gave ranges of 60–180 gantangs per acre in the Simpang Ampat district, the lowest, up to ranges of 120–450 gantangs per acre in the Nibong Tebal and Trans-Krian districts, the highest.

The pattern of variation from place to place is considerable enough but the pattern of variation from year to year is virtually impossible to document. What for one was an 'abundant crop' might be for another

---

[1]The writer has never seen such a structure, which would seem unnecessarily elaborate for the requirements of a normal household. A common modern method of winnowing is to suspend a basket from a tripod and to pour·out the grain on a windy day. Many housewives eschew even a tripod for support.

merely 'quite good', and these are the terms in which harvest reports were couched. Nevertheless some sort of rough analysis can be made from the nineteen harvest reports available for the years 1846–97.[1] Not unexpectedly the good years balance the bad, giving lie to Low's claim of a bad year once in twelve, but this hides both the severity of bad years and the reasons for them. In 1855, for example, cholera was so prevalent that much difficulty was experienced in getting in the crop (*SFP* 8.3.1855). Disease, this time amongst buffaloes, made severe havoc from 1871 until 1873, resulting in substantial areas of land not being planted for lack of animals to plough it up (*SDT* 6.12.1871; 24.11.1873). The same thing happened in 1882, though in that year the crop itself was 'exceptionally good' (*SDT* 15.12.1882).

Other natural hazards included drought, that occurring at the end of 1891 being exceptionally severe, and flood. The area adjacent to the Muda river seems to have been rather vulnerable, as in 1859 when the whole area from that river to Penaga was severely flooded shortly after the seedlings had been planted out. But the severest natural disasters occurred in 1897 when actual famine resulted during which the people had to fall back on roots and jungle fruits for sustenance (Penang AR 1897, 274).

TENURE AND LANDLORDISM

But regardless of the vagaries of weather or the onslaught of epidemic disease, for some a major consideration was the source of the annual rent and for all was the question of adequate income from their farms.

The tenure system of the Province can best be described as 'two-tiered'. All holders of land, whether outright owners by virtue of holding grants, or tenants by virtue of holding long-term leases, were required to pay an annual rent to the controlling authority, initially the East India Company and from 1858, the British Crown. The sums exacted as 'quit rent' were never large, although the terms, at least initially, favoured the large capitalist, though this was merely a reflection of the nature of the crops usually grown by them, namely, spices. The rice-growing peasant had, in 1829, merely to pay a quit-rent of 60 pice per orlong, from 1839 reduced to two *copangs* (Penang Land Office Records 1829–33). In many cases, even this low rent was unpaid and in the event of land being resumed by government for non-payment and subsequently auctioned off, the sole bidder was often its occupier who bid less than his arrears of rent (*SSAR* 1855–6, 9). In many cases, rents were worth less than the expense of their collection. This was not the case throughout the whole of the century, of course. In 1887 it was reported that the rate on land was to be 5 per cent of the annual value (Penang AR 1887, 1266) but even this was hardly excessive. Any notion, therefore, that the peasantry was being ground down by the exactions of government would thus be false.

Equally false would be a picture of a sturdily independent peasantry,

---

[1]Full details are given in Hill, 1973, 222.

each family on its lands producing enough for subsistence with some surplus for sale. Right from the very beginning of British interest in the Province there were those who saw the possibility of carving out for themselves a domain upon which slaves and near-slaves would work in plantation fashion. Light did this in Penang, Low did it in the Province. But much earlier various people had been somewhat informally granted permission to clear lands which, from the size of the plots concerned, must have been worked either by tenants or by wage-labour. One 'Soongh Gluam' had 16 orlongs of rice land at Sungei Dua, the Panglima Muda had 154 orlongs at the same place, 'Aullong' had 64 orlongs, whilst yet others had smaller plots (Stubbs-Brown, 1963, App. VE). As the names indicate, many of these large owners were Malays, or at least Muslims. Of one such, Kader Mustan of Ulu Jeru, Thomson (1865b, 84) has a thumb-nail sketch.

He was a jawee Pekan (an Arab Kling) who had settled for many years amongst the Malays for the purpose of paddy-planting, trading and making his fortune. By his intelligence and industry, he had amassed some wealth, which was principally invested in rice-fields, coconut-groves, opium, cloth, nails, and tobacco, houses, slaves, and concubines.

The manner of working such large tracts, whether by tenants or by wage-labour, is difficult to establish. Low's own 'budget' outlined in his book (1836, 111–15) is based upon the use of wage-labour. Other large owners may also have worked in the same manner but of this there is no record and it seems likely that most were merely landlords. The terms and conditions upon which tenants occupied lands varied from time to time and from place to place. In one instance, that of a large village on the S. Susat, the rent payable was half the produce (Thomson, 1865a, 133). Low's data permit the conclusion that money-rents were at about half the rate of rents-in-kind which ranged from one-third to two-thirds of the produce (Low, 1836, 113, 116). Low suggested that a net annual return of 16 Spanish dollars per orlong could be obtained from rents in kind. Now this was equivalent to 370 gantangs of padi on Low's own quoted price. But the very highest rate of production was 600 gantangs an orlong, at which rate simple arithmetic will show that a tenant was paying at least 60 per cent of his crop as rent in kind. This is on a par with the very highest levels existing at present (Hill and Arope, 1969, 63). This would mean that a peasant with two orlongs of the best rice land would have just sufficient rice to feed his own family after having surrendered the rest to his landlord. Those occupying land of poorer quality therefore must necessarily have had larger farms, or paid rent at a lower rate or starved.

The other story told by Low is rather different. According to him (Low, 1836, 116), the highest money-rent was 4 Spanish dollars an orlong, with rent in kind double that, i.e. money-rent was equivalent to 1/6 of the produce and rent-in-kind 1/3, rates which cannot be considered excessive. Yet Low's own statement that '...16 dollars an orlong...will nearly correspond with the rent in *kind* received from the best land' (Low, 1836,

113), clearly shows that rack-renting had at least begun at this early date. Certainly, as in Kedah, many peasants '...although nominally the usufructaries of the land, in reality they [were] merely the dependants of agents residing in town, by whom they are supplied with food, and who, in return, receive the whole of the produce, with consequent profits....' (*SSAR* 1859–60, 18).

If some received less than their just recompense from middlemen, others suffered directly at the hands of corrupt Company officials, amongst whom, on suspicion only, must be ranged James Low. In referring to the 'nonia of the East India Company's chief official' and her relatives, Thomson (1865a, 103–4) was biting, if not libellous, in his indignation: 'The paddy (rice) field of the ryot is seized for back rents and sold for bagatelles to those sycophants...'. This was not an isolated case, and Thomson, for all his vehemence, cannot be altogether wrong in alleging malicious expropriations and outright swindles at Bukit Pelandok, Permatang Pau and elsewhere (Thomson, 1865a, 110–9; 1865b, 13, 84).

Another minor point of conflict between the peasant rice growers and commercial interests arose over the question of sugar-growing. This industry began largely in the southern parts of the Province in the 1840s. On the whole, however, whilst some planters bought up rice lands for sugar-planting, conflict of interests were not significant in the Province because most sugar plantations were developed from waste land. This was by no means the case in Krian to the south where such conflicts were of some importance. Moreover, in the Province, large-scale irrigation was not developed. Furthermore, at least *c.*1880, there is the suggestion that growing rice was more profitable than growing sugar. Were this not so, why was developed rice land rented for sums from 6 to 12 dollars an orlong whilst sugar land was let at prices only up to 6 dollars? (Penney, 1881, 614).

PRODUCTION AND PRICES

The only description of the economics of producing rice is that of Low (1836, 111–14) whose manner of working his own land would seem to have been on plantation lines, although he also gave estimates of income and expenditure for tenants and small proprietors. On a farm with a cultivable area of 20 orlongs, it was estimated that a capital investment of about 510 Spanish dollars was required, of which 400 Spanish dollars was for clearing the land of forest. Running expenses would have totalled 76 Spanish dollars per year, excluding depreciation, which Low failed to allow for, or about 145 Spanish dollars, allowing 20 per cent depreciation a year on movable assets such as buffaloes, implements of cultivation, and carts. The return Low gave as 480 gantangs of padi per orlong fetching a total of 420 Spanish dollars at 35 Spanish dollars a coyan. Assuming that no loan interest was payable, this would have given a net profit of 275 Spanish dollars a year, or allowing interest on capital at 10 per cent, a profit of about 230 Spanish dollars. Clearly at this rate, the investment

would have more than returned the whole capital in less than two years.[1]
Low's estimate was higher, being a total annual profit of 16 Spanish
dollars an orlong for the third and subsequent years.

Growing rice, therefore, was by no means an unprofitable undertaking
for those who owned their own land or who had sufficient resources to
pay money-rent in advance. The level of profitability would be even greater
for those who could obtain off-farm employment. In the pioneering phase,
such employment could not have been difficult to obtain. Government was
pressing ahead with road-building, though convicts were regularly in this
employment. More important, there was a steady capital inflow from the
1830s, which increased markedly from 1845, as sugar lands were cleared
in the Batu Kawan and Juru districts and brought into production, and
wage-labour was employed for this task (*GGPWISM* 5.12.1829; *SFP*
15.1.1846).

But with a steady diminution of the uncleared lands and a growth of
the agricultural population, the prospects of seasonal off-farm work must
have declined and competition for rice land increased. Indeed Low (1836,
118), saw that this would be the case within 'a very few years'. Certainly
by 1881 rice land seems to have been in strong demand, fetching from $50
to $250 per orlong although little of it changed hands (Penney, 1881, 614).
At the same time costs of production were higher in the Province than in
the newly-opened lands of Krian to the immediate south. One reason for
this was certainly that rents were now, in 1884, assessed at 1/10 of the
annual value and leases, for 999 years, were sold by auction, though the
assessment was reduced to 1/20 in 1887 (Penang AR 1884, 725; 1887,
1266).

TABLE 10
PENANG: PADI PRICES, 1807–61

Year	Price (Sp. $/coyan)[2]	Source of data
1807	33–35	*PWIGG* 6.6.1807
1808	47–53	*PWIGG* 2.4.1808
1819	20–21	*PWIGG* 24.4.1819
1821 (Kedah invaded)	130	*PWIGG* 21.11.1828
1825 (April)	40–45	*PWIGG* 20.4.1825
1825 (September)	25–27	*PWIGG* 17.9.1825
1826	30–37	*PWIGG* 29.4.1826
1829	25–27	*GGPWISM* 19.11.1829
1836	35	Low (1836, 113)
1860–1	40	*SSAR* (1860–1, 45)

[1]Low's book-keeping was nothing if not erratic. The cost of clearing, a capital out-going, he
charged to 'working expenses'. His own estimate was that at the end of the second year a
clear profit of 70 Sp. dollars would have been made after the capital had been returned.

[2]All prices have been converted to Sp. dollars per coyan of 800 gantangs, allowing one
gantang of rice as equal to two gantangs of padi where necessary.

Incomes, of course, were very much dependent upon price levels on the Penang market. Of these it is not possible to give a coherent account because from 1829 they were no longer published for that market. Although James Low (1836, 113) suggested that prices had been stable 'for many years back', the fragmentary evidence quoted in Table 10 indicates that prices in fact varied considerably from year to year and even within years. It might be suspected that fluctuations resulted as much from manipulations of the market by merchants as purely from supply and demand. In 1819, for instance, private merchants imported 16,491 bags of rice from Bengal, a year of notably low prices (Phipps, 1823, 245). One undoubted result of such fluctuations was, for the producer, the ease with which he could overcommit himself financially and end up in the hands of the middlemen.

CONCLUSION

The whole *raison d'être* of rice-growing in Province Wellesley was the need to safeguard a supply of the staple, both for the support of the Penang population and for trade. This supply could never have been secured from the Island itself, partly because production was cheaper in the Province, but more importantly, because the area of suitable land was extremely limited. The 10,700 acres under rice in 1860–1 (*SSAR* 1860–1, 45) almost certainly represented a maximum possible under the prevailing market conditions. Yet even with supplies from the Province, the settlement as a whole was not self-sufficient, the deficit being made up from Bengal and Kedah (Phipps, 1823, 209, 245; Low, 1836, 92). Nevertheless the British aim of a secure food-supply was achieved, although more by good luck, in the form of an influx of Kedah refugees, than by good management.

In a sense Province Wellesley was an extension of the commercialized peasant production of the Kedah-Perlis plain. In detail there were certainly differences. The rice area reached its maximum extent in the Province long before the south Kedah region came to be developed: extensive drainage works were lacking, plantation-style operations existed in the settlement but not in Kedah, and the incidence and oppressiveness of landlordism, though probably not of middleman dependence, were probably greater than in Kedah. Yet by the end of the period both Kedah and the settlement were part of a single economic unit focused on Penang.

6

The Northern Centre: Perak

The principal products of the state are tin, rice and ratans.

T.J. Newbold, 1839, 2, 23.

The country is remarkably populous, and abounds in Campongs of fruit and other trees. Paddy is grown in sufficient quantities to meet the requirements of the population....

J.W.W. Birch, 1874, *SDT* 14.5.1874.

ALTHOUGH the name 'Perak' means silver, it was not silver but tin which was the major product (Wray, 1886). In this respect Perak was unlike its northern neighbours. Some degree of regional self-sufficiency in rice probably existed, though this is a question upon which it is difficult to reach a firm conclusion because information is scanty. Nevertheless a few major facts can be ascertained, partly on the basis of Anderson's report (Anderson, 1824, 169–90). Along the mangrove-bound coast, settlements existed only on *terra firma* at the heads of some of the major creeks. Rice may have been grown by shifting cultivation on the very limited areas of sand ridges in the vicinity of these settlements, as Sinclair was to report in 1877 (*ST* 25.8.1877), but the main rice areas were some distance away.

The deltaic tracts, some four or five feet above high tide mark, were virtually uninhabited. The large tract between the Sepitang and the Krian rivers was uninhabited except for a line of villages on or near the Krian river.[1] Equally empty was the area between the Perak and Bernam rivers, except for a scattering of villages along the lower reaches of the Perak. In a similar state was a vast area of fresh-water swamp south of Bruas and west of the Perak river, a region even today largely unoccupied.

Along the main valley of the Perak and its tributaries, closely hemmed in by the surrounding hills, lay the main settled area, a straggle of villages on the river terraces and in the upper delta, on the levees. Two concentrations of settlement existed, one in the vicinity of Bandar and Rantau Panjang in the lower Perak valley, and a smaller one near Kuala Kangsar.

[1]At this time the southern boundary of Province Wellesley lay along the Krian river, on the Perak side of which lay several villages, containing Kedah refugees and their families, some 2,000 persons in all, growing rice. The largest village was at Bagan Tiang (see Asst. Res. Councillor to Res. Councillor, Penang, 7.2.1848; Gov. to Fort William, 12.2.1848, EIC Board's Coll.). Butterworth, however, gave a population of only 300 in 1847 (Gov. to Fort William, 23.6.1847, EIC Board's Coll.). The Province boundary was shifted to its present location under the terms of the Treaty of Pangkor, 1874 (see Sadka, 1968, 1n).

Of these centres, the latter, in the delta, was probably not of much agricultural significance, if the modern lack of rice-growing in this vicinity is any criterion. The smaller centre was an area of permanent rice cultivation.

Away from the main valley were two minor centres of wet rice cultivation, one in the north around Selama, and the other far to the south at Slim on the Bernam. For the rest, shifting cultivation, by Malays as in Kinta, or Patani folk as in Upper Perak or by aborigines as in the eastern hills and mountains, was the ruling mode of culture. The piedmont zone, including the Kinta, Batang Padang and Tanjong Malim districts, was rich in tin and extended beyond the state boundary into Selangor to form part of a broad 'march zone' in which rice-growing was mostly of little significance. This region is discussed in Chapter 8. Most of the State would seem to have been more or less self-sufficient with probably some surplus in some years. On the other hand, Malcom claimed that little land was cultivated and that the inhabitants depended upon the sale of tin and on fishing for the purchase of rice (Malcom, 1839, 103–4; Newbold, 1839, 2, 22ff).

CHANGES PRIOR TO INTERVENTION

Apart from the devastation of civil war which most seriously affected the Larut area, this pattern of agriculture and settlement was little changed in the period down to British intervention. Immediately following the transfer of the Krian area from Kedah to Perak administration, the Kedah rice growers who had settled there during the Siamese invasion removed to Kedah leaving the area almost desolate (*SFP* 3.5.1849). To the south it was possible that the development of the Larut tin field initiated by Long Ja'afar in the 1840s resulted in some abandonment of rice lands, but this cannot be documented (Sadka, 1968, 19).

Nevertheless a form of 'transhumant' cultivation without permanent settlement, which had existed since around 1830, seems to have continued. Persons living in Penang '. . . annually cultivated lands in Krean [*sic*]. . . living part of the year in that District and resorting during the remainder to Pulo [*sic*] Penang. . .' (Gov. to Res. Councillor, Penang, 4.2.1848, EIC Board's Coll.). The practice continued at least until 1860 when it was reported that lands at Krian, Bagan Tiang and Kurau had settled populations which were swelled three or fourfold during the padi season by people from British territory. Local Perak chiefs exacted a poll tax of one dollar which entitled the planter to as much land as he could plant at a rental of $1.50 per orlong (*SFP* 26.4.1860).

The British, in adopting the 'hands-off Perak' policy crystallized in the 1826 Treaty with Siam, effectively placed the State beyond the direct influence of the Penang capitalists. Not that the capitalists did not attempt to force an entry since in Province Wellesley, by 1868, 'A few scattered patches of sterile and swampy ground are all that now remains [*sic*] to Government. . .' (Man, 1868, 2). In 1861, Sultan Ja'afar attempted to farm out the whole of the Krian district for a period of twenty years to a European capitalist, W.T. Lewis, who was to have the land rent-free for one year and $5,000 a year thereafter. Lewis actually made a start on his settlement.

> In the 20 days I remained at Krean [*sic*] 654 families none of which took less than 5 orlongs of Paddy land were Registered by me and more have been daily coming in, so that for the ensuing Paddy season of 1861/62 it may be fairly estimated that the number will exceed 1,000 families. The good effect of such a cultivation may be shewn as not only being a gain to me but greater to the cultivators.... These grounds are notorious for their fertility yielding far more than what the lands of Penang do, estimated to be at least 1,000 gantangs per orlong, to be on the safe side in such a calculation say that each family will have returns (for the 5 orlongs cultivated) of 3,600 gantangs and allowing each family to average 5 souls (parents and children) that 600 gantangs be struck off for their food it would leave 3,000 gantangs to be disposed of equal for 1,000 families to 3,000,000 gantangs of Paddy or say 75,000 Peculs of Rice which may be estimated to be worth 150,000 Dollars.
>
> Lewis, in Khoo, 1967, 161–2.

Obviously a very promising speculation for Mr. Lewis, who was also to receive a clearing rent of one dollar per family per year as well as a rice rent payable after the second year, of three dollars per *relong*, not to mention duties on timber, rattan and tin! In the event, Lewis ultimately failed to obtain his concession, though at least some of the settlers seem to have stayed put, the area being partly settled when it passed under British protection.

The Dindings area too was seen as a suitable place for Penang capital to have free play in raising rice and sugar. Colonel Man made a preliminary investigation with the objective of colonizing the area, though the British claim was based upon a very considerable stretching of the Pangkor agreement of 1826 (Stanley to Lord Granville, 26.4.1869, CO 273/35).

Thus even before British intervention in 1874, there had been some development of land for rice cultivation. Production was in good heart since Anson listed Krian, Dulang and Trong amongst the mainland ports shipping rice to Penang, though it is highly probable that the two last were no more than transhipment points for cargoes from the hinterland (Penang AR 1873, 140). That some expansion of cultivation took place rests upon the slightly shaky ground of population estimates. Newbold (1839, 2, 24) estimated that 35,000 Malays and 'a few others' dwelt in the state *c*.1837, a figure accepted by Malcom (1839, 103). The mining population, mainly in Larut, was estimated as 10,000 in 1868 (Man, 1868, 5) and '20 to 30,000' in 1874 by Swettenham (1880b, 169). Leaving aside J.W.W. Birch's estimate of a total of 200,000 in 1874 (*SDT* 14.5.1874) as wildly unrealistic, and accepting the 1879 Census figure of 57,000 (*Singapore and Straits Directory 1881*, 95), as the best estimate to that date and leaving aside say 18,000 of a total Chinese population of 20,000 as being miners, it can be suggested that the remainder, largely agriculturalists and their dependants, was about 60,000 in 1879. The agricultural population had thus almost doubled in forty years. The corresponding increase in the cultivated area took place mainly adjacent to existing centres of cultivation.

PERAK IN THE MID-1870s

Though parts of the State were seriously affected by the civil war, the broad pattern of agricultural activity was quickly re-established following the traumas of conflict. Three classes of areas may be distinguished. In the first, settlement was permanent and cultivation was also largely permanent. In this category can be included the lands of the Perak valley and its northern tributaries, the narrow valleys of the Selama and far to the south, the Slim district. These may be termed core areas. The second category comprised areas newly resettled. In this class may be included the coastal lands of Krian, Kurau, Larut and Matang, lands lying immediately landward of the mangrove belt. These areas were largely abandoned during the civil war. The remaining portions of the occupied area of the state were thinly peopled by Malays or aborigines whose lands formed part of larger units which are discussed in Chapter 8. Statistical data in a form corresponding to these divisions do not exist but the Census of 1879 gives at least some indication of the relative importance of the various districts.

TABLE 11
PERAK: AREA UNDER CULTIVATION (ALL TYPES) AND MALAY POPULATION BY DISTRICT, 1879

	Area (orlongs) [1]	Malay Population	Density (Persons per orlong cultivated land)
Perak basin:			
Upper Perak	4,047	15,845	3.9
Lower Perak	9,986	19,533	1.9
Selama	730	1,918	2.6
North-west:			
Krian	4,871	3,718	0.8
Kurau	2,435	3,134	1.3
Tin areas:			
Larut	3,715	7,671	2.1
Kinta	2,126	7,863	3.7
	27,910	59,682	Mean: 2.1

Source: Singapore and Straits Directory 1881, 95.

[1] An orlong probably equalled 1.33 acres.

The data of Table 11 show how small was the cultivated area compared with that of Province Wellesley. The core area, Upper Perak and Selama stand out with above average densities, whilst in Lower Perak, Krian and Kurau, where agricultural expansion had just began, densities were much lower. The values for the tin areas of Larut and Kinta were presumably partly inflated by the presence of Malays engaged in tin-mining, but both areas contained pockets of well-established agricultural settlement.

AREAS OF ESTABLISHED SETTLEMENT AND CULTIVATION

By far the largest of these areas was that extending along the banks of the Perak river northwards from the vicinity of Pulau Tiga as far as the downstream end of the great series of rapids which prevents navigation in Upper Perak. Parts of this strip had felt the backwash of the war. But this was merely a passing phase. A special correspondent of the *Pinang Gazette* after visiting Kota Lama, near Kuala Kangsar, reported that,

Every house had bags of rice in it, and some were regular granaries. Flocks of goats and fowls were seen everywhere, and there was a considerable amount of paddy-ground...Plantain groves...there were in great abundance; and the number of boats and nets showed that fishing was not neglected.

D'Almeida, 1876, 366.

J.W.W. Birch (1875, 379), however, clearly indicated an almost closed subsistence economy in which, 'Some few cultivate sugar and Indian corn for sale', but perhaps this was merely a temporary effect of events. These reports lead to the conclusion that whilst there was a rice surplus in some places and at some times, the staple did not often feature in the external and local market economies of the Perak basin. The more common market crops were maize (Indian corn), coffee and, especially in Upper Perak, tobacco (D'Almeida, 1876, 363).

Elsewhere, agriculture was little affected by events. In the isolated Selama district agricultural development by a group of around 1,000 Rawa men was well under way by 1877. Their leader, Che Karim, financed the enterprise partly from his profits as a tin-miner of some substance, and partly by a loan from Penang chetties. His tenants had cleared 2,000 orlongs by Low's estimate, 10,000 by Che Karim's, much of which was to be irrigated. To the immediate south, Kampong Ijok, Batu Berdinding and Kota Tampan were settlements surrounded by their rice fields, but in total these amounted to very little (Low, 1877; *ST* 4.8.1877; Deane, 1880, 238).

The only other region of established rice cultivation lay far to the south in the valley of the Slim, a major tributary of the Bernam. The main river from Slim to the sea was inhabited only at two points, at its mouth and at 'Raja Itam's' rice-growing village, 25 miles upstream (*SDT* 22.9.1874; Swettenham, 1880a[1]). But at Slim were

...a number of very flourishing kampongs situated on spots of high ground surrounded by stretches of wet padi land irrigated by a number of small streams flowing from the hills to the East. The large majority of the inhabitants are foreign Malays, principally Mandelings, and their style of cultivation is certainly superior to that of the Malays in other parts of Perak, for which they reap their reward in the crops they get. The average yield is of 800 to 1,000 gantangs of padi to the orlong, this...from land cultivated year after year without manure.

Leech, 1879b, 36.

[1]Swettenham made the journey down the Slim and Bernam rivers in 1875. Surprisingly, Swettenham (1942, 45) later stated that the whole of the Bernam lacked habitation.

Since the Slim rice fields produced a surplus over local requirements, rice was supplied to the settlement located in the mangrove zone, a practice which likely occurred elsewhere.

TECHNIQUES OF CULTIVATION

Whilst documentation of the whereabouts of cultivation is relatively easy, material concerning the details of cultivation methods and round-of-work at this time is scanty and reliance must therefore be placed largely upon later sources. The existence of 'large herds of cattle' in every village along the Perak river (*SDT* 22.9.1874) would suggest that grass fallow was common as well as the use of the plough, though 'cattle' here could include buffaloes, of which the presence in some number would indicate the practice of buffalo-trampling to prepare the wet rice fields (D'Almeida, 1876, 365). Both ploughing and trampling techniques followed by harrowing and rolling were successively employed in the preparation of the fields. The raising of seedlings was fairly sophisticated with seed of three sorts, heavy-yielding but slow-growing, medium-yielding with a medium term of growth, and light-yielding but rapid-growing, being set out in three divisions of the nursery, *semai tuah, semai penegah* and *semai mudah* (Kuala Kangsar MR 4/1894, 202). This practice was not reported in other northern states. Cultivation was thus more sophisticated than in the newly-colonized lands of Krian where cattle and ploughs were unknown and the tajak was the only tool.

On the whole, however, cultivation methods conformed to those elsewhere in the north. It may be doubted, however, that irrigation was widely used, though fields were commonly bunded to trap water and these bunds were breached to allow the water to drain away as the crop ripened. Yet some knowledge of the technique must have existed amongst the people since in the 1880s and 1890s there occur numerous references to loans by government to Malay leaders for the purpose of building irrigation works. Irrigation was initially confined to the inland portions of the state where 'the people rely on running water for a portion of their supply' (Perak Land Dept. AR 1895, 239). But which people? All or just some, and if some, which? It is tempting to speculate that knowledge of irrigation was introduced by immigrants from Sumatra and elsewhere in the Peninsula but that the Perak Malay was ignorant of the technique. For this to be true it would be necessary to establish that the majority of applicants for aid to build dams and ditches were foreigners and though in many cases they were, the evidence is suggestive rather than conclusive. For example, D.H. Wise, speaking of several villages in the northern part of the Perak valley, noted that,

The difference between these kampongs which are all inhabited by Patani Malays and those of the natives of Perak is striking. The Patani men grow sufficient rice, tobacco, sireh, and other products for their own use, and rear a large number of poultry, and their kampongs and bendangs are kept in good order, the latter being well irrigated and planted every season.

Kuala Kangsar MR 6/1889, 613.

In Slim the same was true of the Mandeling settlers but in the Perak valley proper, amongst true Perak Malays, even annual cultivation was not always practised. Wray (1886, 13) noted that manure was quite unknown, though irrigation would have been at least a partial substitute, and that, '...after several years' cultivation, fields are sometimes, but not necessarily, allowed to lie fallow for several seasons before they are planted up again'. This system of fallowing was thus exactly like that described by Munshi Abdullah in Kelantan and by Hill in modern Trengganu (Coope, 1949; Hill, 1966a).

Bush-fallowing was by no means uncommon and a series of government orders in the late 1880s and early 1890s attempted to prohibit it (Kuala Kangsar AR 1888, 351; Perak Govt. Notices 1889). It is probable that at least some land was cultivated in this manner each year, with the amount rising when the *bendang* crops failed as a result of lack of rain (Kuala Kangsar MR· 7/1889, 659). In such cases the customary crop was not rice but maize and bananas (Maxwell, 1882a, 14). Such shifting cultivation thus falls into the 'supplementary' class of Watters (1960, 65).

NEWLY-SETTLED AREAS

This region comprised the tract south of the Krian river, including Kurau, the war-devastated lands of Larut and a thinly-peopled region to the south backing the Matang mangrove forests. When Noel Denison set up British administration in Krian, the Krian and Kurau tract

...was scarcely anything else than a vast jungle of growth in every stage. Paddy and other cultivation had been carried on in it to a considerable extent, but in irregular patches along the river side or adjacent to the creeks it abounds in... these disjointed attempts at cultivation were almost abandoned.

SDT 13.9.1881.

Following the early enactment of a series of laws aimed at promoting settlement, coupled with the vigorous efforts of Denison, within five years the scene was transformed into '...golden groves of waving [sugar-] cane and large tracks [sic] of paddy land' (*SDT* 13.9.1881). Just what the initial proportions of rice and sugar were is difficult to determine at this early date, though much of the land, and the roads and canals were developed by Chinese sugar growers.

But Malay entrepreneurs were equally quick on the scene with the object of obtaining grants of large blocks of land upon which they might settle their fellows as tenants. One Mahomet Sahan, for instance, asked Hugh Low for 100 orlongs or more for rice cultivation, on which 100 families from Kedah were settled at Parit Buntar (Low, 1877). Low also noted that in the Tanjong Bakau–Tanjong Piandang area 4,135 acres were under cultivation, mostly by Malays growing rice though some had given up this in favour of growing pumpkins and other vegetables for the Penang market. Here the lands were owned by small-holders, their holdings averaging $5\frac{1}{2}$ acres each. On the Kurau coast nearby, 1,000 acres were held by 165 families. Thus it was the peripheral areas with easy water transport which were first resettled.

Another centre of resettlement was that in Larut, separated from the Kurau centre by undeveloped land in the Selinsing basin. While the greater portion of Larut was devoted to tin-mining, certain sections, especially to the south and east of Taiping, were agricultural (Larut MR 3/1891, 210). Though Larut had been devastated by war, resettlement had begun by 1876, since D'Almeida (1876, 359) spoke of rice as being the only cereal cultivated, in part under irrigation (Murton, 1878, 106).

THE COAST AND THE PERAK ESTUARY

This region was very thinly peopled. On the actual coast there was but one village, Simpit, in the Dindings, and another, Bruas,[1] between the Dindings and the mouth of the Perak (*ST* 25.8.1877; Cowan, 1951, 91). From its mouth to Batak Rabit, the river-side was all covered with heavy jungle except for a few recent clearings, amongst which was one being vigorously opened by a Chinese (Knaggs, 1875, 26). This tract was covetously eyed with a view to development for rice and the Dindings for rice and sugar (Cowan, 1951, 91). Of the former area, Knaggs (1875, 26) said,

I saw enough to satisfy me that they are very valuable, and that in a few years they will probably supply both Penang, Singapore and Deli [in Sumatra] with rice. . . I do not think that anything would pay better than a very large rice growing company, preparing their land by steam, and cleaning their rice on the spot by suitable machinery; and then growing a second crop (after that of rice) either of Dhurra, Maize or Imphee.[2]

DEVELOPMENT: MOTIVES AND SCHEMES

By 1892 the regional pattern of cultivation had already substantially changed from that of the mid-1870s. Table 12 gives very rough estimates though those of potential rice land are wildly optimistic since much of the land in the Matang, Larut, Batang Padang, and Lower Perak districts was under fresh-water swamp forest and drainage and bunding on the scale of the Netherlands polders would have been required to make it usable.

The extension of rice-growing was intimately bound up with the inflow of 'foreign Malays' from without its borders, though the core of cultivation by Perak Malays was undoubtedly extended and methods of culture became more intensive and more sophisticated. A report by Swettenham noted that

The largest areas of existing rice fields in Perak are in Krian, cultivated mainly by immigrants from Kedah, and in Upper Perak, cultivated by immigrants from Patani. But in the Larut, Kuala Kangsar and Lower Perak districts there is a quantity of rice growing done by Perak Malays, well-to-do people who possess good houses and orchards, and do not by any means depend for their livelihood on the produce of their rice-fields.

BR Perak to Gov. SS 16.3.1893, CO 275/46.

[1]The 'kampong Bruas' visited by Edward Sinclair in 1877 would seem to have been on the coast, probably either at Pengkalan Bahru or Pantai Remis.

[2]According to Watson, 1868, *dhurra* is *Sorghum vulgare*. *Imphee* is not listed.

TABLE 12

PERAK: BENDANG LAND UNDER CULTIVATION AND POTENTIAL,
1892

District	Under Cultivation (acres)	Potential (acres)
Krian	40,000	60,000
Selama	1,000	not reported
Matang	10,000	100,250
Larut	9,775	73,390
Upper Perak	1,300	3–500
Kuala Kangsar	4,000	10,000
Kinta	a few hundred	10,000
Batang Padang	small extent	many thousands
Lower Perak	2–3,000	unlimited
Slim	not reported	not reported

Source: Ag. BR Perak to Col. Sec. 5.4.1892, CO 275/46.

The government initiated development schemes, as for instance the Krian irrigation scheme, provided administrative services through district officers and also supported projects of land settlement and irrigation initiated by Malay entrepreneurs. Some schemes were, to use Treacher's term, 'scientific' in conception and scale of execution but in many of the smaller projects, initiative, design, control and execution were largely, often purely, Malay, though partly financed by government.

MOTIVES FOR LAND DEVELOPMENT

Though the administrative apparatus was neither large nor overly elaborate, nevertheless a large, established, agricultural population was felt desirable to bear some of the cost of modernizing that apparatus whether the people wanted it or not.

The recommendations of the District magistrates all point to the policy for Government opening up the available, but still uncultivated, bendang land by the expenditure of public funds on bridle-tracks, roads, irrigation works, drains, water-gates, and so forth. This expenditure would prove remunerative by attracting rent-paying padi cultivators from neighbouring unprotected Native States of the Peninsula, from Sumatra and from Banjermasin (Borneo), and eventually, by keeping in the country a considerable portion of the large sums...now expended...in the purchase of foreign rice.

Ag. BR Perak to Col. Sec. 5.4.1892, CO 275/46.

In addition to being a self-supporting scheme for rural development and saving of foreign exchange, it was held that only rice cultivation would prove of permanent value to the State, since it alone would supply Perak with a settled population and a permanent revenue (Perak AR 1895, 493). Again, the replacement of the wilderness by waving fields of grain and a sturdy rakyat was an intrinsically desirable goal in Perak as in New Zealand where Governor Weld had, as a young man, done his share in a similar transformation.[1]

DEVELOPMENT SCHEMES, REALIZED AND UNREALIZED

The recruitment of the necessary hands to transform nature was a matter which considerably taxed the government. Land was available rent-free for three years together with loans to support the settlers until their lands were productive, and these were major inducements to settle, though in some cases the settlers merely opened temporary clearings and later decamped. Despite these favourable terms, and although Kedah, Patani and other 'foreign' Malay agricultural settlers entered in some numbers, some 2,600 in 1891 alone, these were considered to be insufficient (BR Perak to Col. Sec. SS 5.4.1892, CO 275/46). Government officers had at various times proposed colonization by non-Malays.

One such scheme, worth examining in some detail especially since it may be one of the earliest proposals for 'scientific colonization' in Malaya, was that of MacGregor (1886). He proposed that Indians should be settled on lands in the vicinity of Teluk Anson where land was to be cleared at government expense and each settler provided with materials for a house, a set of tools and seed for the first year. Each family was to receive three acres, to be fully cultivated at the end of three years, with provision for common grazing lands. Where necessary, employment on government works was to be provided to give a cash income. Major works, embankments, and an irrigation system were to be the responsibility of government which would recover the costs from revenues generated by the settlement. This plan was criticized at several points by Belfield, then acting Commissioner of Lands, notably on the notion that government should clear all the land and on the point that it should provide off-farm work. Nevertheless, there seems little reason to believe that, given suitable migrants, the scheme would not have worked, but for one fatal flaw. As in similar schemes implemented in Australia and New Zealand forty years earlier, how, except at the point of a bayonet, could settlers be kept on the land if more remunerative pursuits beckoned?

Some Indians were in fact assisted to settle in the Teluk Anson area as rice farmers (Perak AR 1886, 1212) but few continued in its cultivation. Rather more successful, possibly because religion gave cohesiveness to the efforts of the settlers, was the Tamil Catholic settlement in Krian. By 1892, some 550 men, women and children were settled on 400 acres of land (Ag. BR Perak to Col. Sec. SS 5.4.1892, CO 275/45).

Amongst Chinese, rice-growing had little appeal though Krian could muster 200 engaged in it in a good year, whilst in Larut and Kuala Kangsar they numbered just a handful. With wage-labour offering in the Kinta tin-mines 60–80 cents per day (1892), the Bishop of Malacca was undoubtedly correct in suggesting that the 'Chinese will never take to padi

[1]See Lovat, 1914, and Hill, 1965, 32–8.

fields. Hard labour is too highly remunerated to make padi cultivation pay'[1] (quoted in Ag. BR Perak to Col. Sec. SS 5.4.1892, CO 275/45).

It was thus left to the Malays to push forward settlement, largely at their own expense and exclusively by their own labour. The upshot was that most rice farmers were Malays and this was true throughout the districts with the minor exception of Krian which contained some 500 Indians and 160 Chinese.[2]

EXPANSION OF THE ESTABLISHED CORE

In spatial terms, two main patterns of land development may be distinguished. In the first case expansion takes place along a broad front, limited only by topographical and edaphic factors and by competition from alternative land uses. Associated with this form of spread is the setting up either of temporarily-occupied buildings usually located at that distance at which it is found burdensome to return home for the night, or new, more or less permanently occupied subsidiary settlements. In the second case the home base or jumping-off point is separated from the newly colonized land by intervening space, in some cases water, in others land. Both forms of expansion can be documented for Perak. In the first case expansion was from well-established bases in the valley tract of the Perak river centred upon Kuala Kangsar, in Selama, Larut and Slim, the second largely from bases outside the State.

THE PERAK VALLEY

Topographically, this region comprises the narrow valley of the Perak itself together with a strip of levees at the debouchment. Also included are the valleys of the major tributaries such as the Kangsar. These are short and narrow. Excluded are the valleys of the Kinta, Bidor and Batang Padang, rivers which join the Perak only in the delta. The core of the region centred upon Kuala Kangsar and its nearby villages, with downstream, as far as the vicinity of Pulau Tiga,[3] a series of villages surrounded by their rice lands but separated from each other by unused lands. Upstream of Kuala Kangsar, lands along the river as far as Sorli came to be opened in the 1890s, but beyond that point there were no settlements and rice lands until the first Patani Malay village of Ngor. The region from Ngor upstream[4] may thus be distinguished from the remainder by the fact that it was largely settled, and that but recently, by Patani folk, and also because not only were the areas which were topographically suitable for wet cultivation very limited, but these were also rapidly taken up, leaving little or no suitable land unused.

[1]A colony of Chinese agriculturalists was in fact ultimately settled at Sitiawan but they did not grow rice (FMS Conference of Chiefs, 1903, 17).

[2]For details see Hill, 1973, 249.

[3]The Pulau Tiga *mukim* lay, then as now, in the Lower Perak district, but in respects other than administrative, it belongs with the riverine settlements.

[4]This sub-region almost exactly corresponds with the administrative district of Upper Perak.

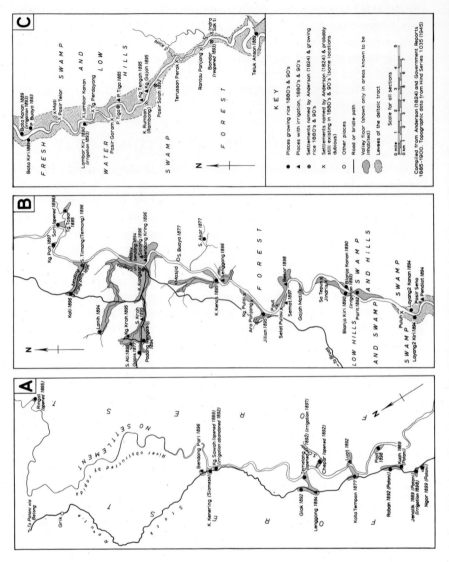

FIGURE 8

PERAK VALLEY : RICE-GROWING AND SETTLEMENT IN
THE LATE NINETEENTH CENTURY

In the Perak valley it must be presumed that the wet rice lands adjoining the villages were increased in extent though reports of specific times and places are few. This increase seems to have begun about 1888, in which year Orders-in-Council prohibiting *ladang* cultivation were issued (Kuala Kangsar AR 1888, 351). By 1890–1 it was claimed that bendang cultivation was replacing ladangs in the region (Perak Land Dept. AR 1890, 339). There were, for example, large blocks of land opened near Blanja, but the allotments were excessively small, one block of a hundred acres being given out to 100 people, a fact which would seem to indicate a considerable pressure of population upon land. This is further supported by data from monthly and annual reports of the period (see Hill, 1973, 252). But too much should not be read into these evidences since the objective of the Perak Malay was self-subsistence (Kuala Kangsar AR 1891, 809).

Irrigation, by means of small-scale works, was rapidly adopted, though with varying success. In promoting irrigation, government interest lay in the provision of finance, rarely in sufficient quantity to meet the whole cost, and in the provision of technical expertise in the taking of levels for ditches. Amongst the people, persons of position and authority, the Datoh Sri Adika Rajah, Sri Maharajah Lela and a commoner, Luakong, the Chinese *penghulu* of Blanja, were especially active (Kuala Kangsar AR 1898, 1). On the other hand certain dam-builders, one Ngah Mat Rasin and another Wan Hussein, were positive saboteurs, depriving downstream bendangs of water or in another case flooding them, by ill-considered constructions (Kuala Kangsar MR 9/1894; 10/1896, 773).

The usual technique was to tap the headwaters of small streams by means of a dam from which a ditch, *tali ayer*, led the water to the fields. The amount of storage was necessarily rather small because of the limitations of using timber and earth in the construction of the dams. Equally the streams thus held back were necessarily small. There is no evidence of damless, run-of-the river irrigation on the Igorot, Balinese or Javanese pattern though this does not mean that it did not exist. In a number of areas, the river banks were too high or the river too large for this form of irrigation but the local Malays, unlike the Minangkabau people, had no technique to meet this situation though District Officers reported attempts to install current-driven, under-shot water-wheels for raising water on the Plus river and at Kampong Gajah (Kuala Kangsar MR 5/1896, 423; Lower Perak AR 1908, 5). The peak period of activity in the construction of irrigation works was in 1894, when five small schemes were initiated, but in the other years of the decade to 1900, at least one, often two, were opened to give a total of 20 for the period. In some cases though, the lightly constructed dams were swept away by floods.

Despite the implementation of irrigation works, the position of the peasant in this district was still precarious and vulnerable to natural calamities, the effects of which were intensified by human factors. Towards the end of 1896 for example, the countryside first was ravaged by a cattle murrain, probably rinderpest, which destroyed the peasants' means of

traction, thus preventing ploughing. To this was added six months of
severe drought followed by the longest-lasting flood on record. The
peasantry had been forbidden to plant ladangs and few had reserves of
capital, having sold their rice in advance at a very low price. The result
was starvation and dependence upon government hand-outs (Kuala
Kangsar AR 1896, 138).

UPPER PERAK

In the northern sub-region, the Patani Malays would seem to have been
better placed to withstand the buffets of adverse Nature. There

> ...each 'klamin' [family] plants from two to ten acres of padi land, and thus
> produces considerably more padi than is required for its own consumption, the
> balance being sold to Perak Malays in Kuala Kangsar and down-river, where a
> klamin seldom cultivates more than one acre, though it may own two or three.
>
> Kuala Kangsar AR 1891, 809.

And not only did each family produce more rice, but also made some
attempt to diversify production by growing tobacco and sugarcane though
not in large quantity (Upper Perak AR 1889, 230).

The main problem facing the Patani people was lack of land. By 1891
it was reported that '...so much of this district is either mountainous or
else subject to sudden floods; only a small amount of land is available for
bendangs, and that is almost all occupied' (Upper Perak AR 1891, 955).
A partial answer was intensification of cultivation and where possible
this was combined with extension of the cultivated area, as for instance
at Temmelong where unoccupied land was first irrigated and then sold
off at a premium of $7.20 an acre, sufficient to cover development costs
twice over (Upper Perak MR 8–9/1897, 921)..This premium was much
higher than elsewhere in the State and reflected the strong demand for
land in the district. Elsewhere existing wet land was irrigated though 'for
divers reasons' some schemes were unsuccessful (Upper Perak AR 1891,
954). At Jenalik, intensification of cultivation extended even to the cutting
of the hillslope terraces upon which bendangs were established, this being
the only report of terracing in the whole Peninsula (Kuala Kangsar
MR 10/1893, 983).

SELAMA

Like Upper Perak, Selama was isolated from the rest of the State, only
more so. Similarly it contained Patani settlers and, following the Kelantan
cyclone, some Kelantanese, though the bulk were long-established Rawa
folk. The core of cultivation and settlement was around Selama village.
As in Upper Perak the potential areas were rather limited and only small
tracts of land were opened for bendangs, as at Sungei Sega, Padang Lal-
lang, and Pantai Besar in 1894 (Selama MR 1/1894, 83; 6/1894, 395).
Elsewhere new irrigation works led to increased production and in some
cases but for irrigation no crop would have been obtained. Increased
production was also assisted by the enforcement of regulations requiring

simultaneous planting thereby reducing the ravages of animal pests (Selama MR 3/1891, 213). Certain of the newly-opened lands were abandoned, as for example at Blah and Tebing Tinggi, but elsewhere the picture was of quiet prosperity, there being sufficient locally-produced rice for all, with some surplus and some further cash income from the production of tobacco and areca-nut (Selama MR 4/1889, 428; 2/1890, 167; AR 1898, 2; 1900, 2).

SOUTHERN MATANG AND LARUT

The Matang administrative district can be divided into two sections, a northern section centred on Selinsing, and a southern section along the coast. The northern section was merely a southern extension of the Krian area and thus may be conveniently discussed under that head. For the rest, two rice-growing regions may be distinguished, each separated from the other by an extensive tract of forest and swamp. To the north was Ulu Kurau, a region largely of recent development in which the rice area was small and occurred in discontinuous patches. These were opened from about 1891 onwards, largely by migrants from Patani and Perlis (Larut MR 5/1891, 368).

In the northern region, cultivation amounted to very little, 50 acres here and 100 acres there, as at Relau and Changkat Prah, in the head-waters of the Sungei Ara or along the river and at Ijok. In some parts of the region settlements were reported abandoned in 1888, probably by the same Patani settlers who later settled in the southern region around Bukit Gantong (Lefroy, 1888, 143–8; Larut MR 5/1891, 368).

The south was more important. Not only were the *lalang* wastes marking formerly occupied lands rehabilitated and improved, but some extension into forested terrain was made. The most important improvements were the Ayer Kuning irrigation scheme and the reopening of the Tunku Mantri canal which provided water for the three or four thousand acres. In the former, yields were especially high, averaging from 500 to 800 gantangs per orlong (Larut AR 1890, 338; MR 3/1891, 210; Matang MR 5/1894, 441). To the Ayer Kuning area came not only Malays but also 33 families of Chinese who combined rice-growing with the culture of pepper and silk (Larut MR 6/1891, 583). To the vicinity of the Tunku Mantri canal, to Jibong, S. Lang and S. Sendak came settlers from Deli, Banjermasin and from Kedah, each group headed by its leaders (Matang MR 10/1894, 10). These people not only rehabilitated abandoned bendang land but extended their activities into virgin land (Matang MR 12/1895, 41).

One impetus to these developments was given by an economic depression in the tobacco industry of Deli, north Sumatra, with the resultant collapse of the *atap*-making industry along the Perak coast (Perak AR 1891, 417). Consequently the people turned to growing rice for subsistence, and considerable increases of the rice acreage were reported for the string of villages from Trong southward, though it is certain that most of the soils used were peaty, ill-drained and hence of low productivity (Matang

MR 12/1892, 94). By 1896 the whole of the lands bordering the road from Trong to Bruas and beyond to Dendang was under rice (Birch, 1896, 779–84).

But developments in haste led to repentance at leisure. By 1897 the lands at Padang Besar, irrigated at Government expense, were virtually unoccupied. At Jibong and S. Lang the crop was an utter failure, having been spoiled by a combination of too much rain and too much irrigation-water, no provision having been made for turning the water off (Matang MR 12/1897, 28; AR 1897, 158). From this time on nothing more is heard and seemingly the cultivated area contracted to the area to the south of Bukit Gantong which did not suffer from the drainage problems of the coastal tracts.

SLIM

Following Swettenham's visit to Slim in 1880, and a subsequent one in 1885 during which he reported the existence of a four-mile-long stretch of villages and rice fields along the river (Swettenham, 1885, 3), the area sank into obscurity. The cultivated area was extended in 1889 and by 1896 the stretch from Slim to Kuala Geliting was under padi or short grass, presumably used for cattle. Ploughs, however, were unknown (Tanjong Malim MR 9/1897, 924). Throughout the period Slim seems to have remained the only significant area of bendang in this southern corner of the state (BPDO R/89; 302/92).

THE COLONIZED LANDS

Although 'foreign Malays' played some part in the expansion of the established core, this role was rather minor. To the colonized lands, settlers came mainly from places outside Perak. In the north-west, Krian was solidly taken up for either rice or sugar by the end of the century, each crop occupying large discrete tracts of land, rice mainly in the north and sugar predominantly in the south (see Fig. 9). Elsewhere, colonies of rice growers occupied much smaller areas usually separated from each other by forest or other non-agricultural land uses. In Lower Perak, there developed a strip-like pattern of settlement along tracks, roads, rivers and the Jenderata canal, but here rice-growing was largely ephemeral.

KRIAN AND NORTHERN MATANG

The story of this region, the largest single rice-growing area in the Federated Malay States, is one of fluctuating fortunes and conflicts of interest. The area was developed on its margins by transhumant farmers in the 1860s, largely abandoned, rapidly recolonized following British control, then again partly abandoned, this time because of lack of the means to offset the effects of adverse environmental conditions, and ultimately almost fully occupied by the time the Irrigation Scheme was

FIGURE 9

LAND USE AND SETTLEMENT IN NORTH-WEST PERAK *c*. 1901

opened in 1906. These fluctuations are well illustrated by the rice trade
figures in Table 13.[1]

The reasons for these fluctuations and for other difficulties were many—
difficult terrain, bad seasons, perhaps the characteristics of the settlers
themselves, government policy—all played a part in accounting for
depressing reports of abandoned farm lands. Much of the land, 60 per
cent, was deemed second class, with widely variable yields unreliably
quoted as ranging from 350 to 750 gantangs/acre at the lower limit of

[1]Exports were largely of unhusked rice and imports largely of husked rice. Virtually all
Krian-produced rice, except that used by farmers themselves, was milled in Penang.

TABLE 13
PERAK: KRIAN, VALUE OF RICE AND PADI TRADE, 1885–1907

Year	Exports ($)	Imports ($)	Excess of Exports over Imports ($)
1885	200,405	74,563	125,842
1886	166,306	n.a.	–
1887	165,002	n.a.	–
1888	131,415	98,839	32,576
1889	86,608	107,828	–21,220
1890	24,033	112,431	–88,397
1891	191,089	81,703	109,386
1892	298,462	91,795	206,667
1893	278,702	114,038	164,664
1894	371,687	131,378	240,309
1895	32,586	192,401	–159,815
1896	313,459	140,331	173,128
1897	50,441	197,220	–146,779
1898	289,709	92,983	196,826
1899	479,182	132,415	346,767
1900	538,404	139,168	399,236
1901	175,623	274,269	–98,646
1902	265,982	274,052	–8,070
1903	35,904	n.a.	–
1904	326,335	n.a.	–
1905	633,882	n.a.	–
1906	262,637	n.a.	–
1907	628,069	n.a.	–

Source: Lim, 1968, 87, and Perak AR 1899, 1900, 1901, 1902, 1905, 1907[2]

which the owners could only just make their crop pay. Another 15 per cent was third class land yielding around 350 gantangs/acre and the rest first class land yielding from 750 to 1,000 gantangs/acre[1] (encl. HC, FMS to CO 14.12.1897, CO 273/230).

One major problem was that the land itself was little above sea-level, and exceptionally wet. Whereas in Province Wellesley topographical spot heights of seven or eight feet lie four miles inland at the most, in Krian they may be as far as 13 miles inland. Moreover along the coast the levels tend to be higher by three or four feet than those inland, creating in periods of heavy rain a vast inland lake with comparatively few outlets.

[1]These yields seem abnormally, indeed unbelievably, high. In modern Malaya, anything over 500 gantangs/acre is exceptional. The figures were possibly for orlongs, not acres, which would reduce the values by one-quarter.

[2]For comments on the reliability of these sources see Hill, 1973, 261.

Some of the soils undoubtedly contained a high proportion of organic material, the partial oxidation of which seems to have led to a lowering of the ground surface (Krian AR 1894, 406). Drainage was thus essential but at the outset resources were simply not available for the detailed levelling and comprehensive drainage scheme essential to satisfactory water control. The result was a piecemeal development of drainage that could not be dignified with the term system (Krian AR 1888, 75). Equally essential were water-gates. Along the coast they were required to prevent salt water flowing up the drainage canals at high tide (Krian MR 5/1889, 573). Inland, water-gates were required to keep the water on the land since where the government had made roads by throwing up material from ditches, drainage was too free (Krian MR 1/1891, 99). Such water-gates as were provided were in some cases inadequate to discharge heavy falls, resulting in the crop being drowned (Krian MR 10/1893, 946). There was no lack of skill in land reclamation however. The first major coastal bund in the district was built from Sungei Bharu to the Kurau river by Haji Abdulrahman, the headman of the Banjarese (Krian MR 6/1894, 394).

Climate was another factor blamed for wide fluctuations in production and planted area, though a certain inability to adjust the season of planting to the climatic regime was at least as much to blame. But why? There is no evidence that the people had managed to get their agricultural cycle out-of-phase with the seasons because they rigidly followed the Muslim calendar. For the Rawas and Mandelings from Sumatra, the wet season began at about the same time as in their homelands, that is, in September to November (Boerema, 1931, 1). For the Kedah migrants, the main rains were a good deal later in Krian than in Kedah, were less intense and slightly more variable while for the Banjermasin folk the seasons were also different since in that region the maximum rainfall was in December-January whereas in Krian, early-planted rice was by this time already being harvested (Dale, 1959, 29–32; 1960, 15–18).

Official notices in the *Perak Government Gazette* reveal the problems. Early in the 1890s, planting of the nurseries was to begin in mid-July for the long-term 'heavy' varieties and mid-August for the short-term 'light' varieties. By the early 1900s the pattern had changed in a further attempt to match the crop cycle with the climate. The early-planted, long-term, heavy-yielding crop, *padi berat*, was sown in the nurseries in April-June, towards the end of the secondary maximum. It then had to be kept alive through the July-August dry period in the hope that the main rains would be early enough. If they were not, then all was lost because late sowing would either result in the crop being drowned or it coming to maturity in March at the onset of the secondary maximum. The short-term, light crop, *padi ringan*, often scarcely repaid the trouble of cultivation, so poor was its yield. Where planted, its sowing began by law in July, one of the driest months. In Kedah, the period June to August was wetter than in Krian whilst December to February was drier, allowing satisfactory ripening and harvest. In other words, in Krian, the climatic 'slots' into which the major operations had to fit were narrower, less reliable in their occurrence and less suitable to the crop. The chances of there being too much water or too little were thus greater in Krian than in Kedah or the Province.

Technically, cultivation was at a low level. Ploughs were unknown, the tajak alone being used to slash down vegetation prior to planting, though some soils may have been too soft and too rich in organic matter for successful ploughing (Vincent, 1894, 13). Lack of proper clearing of weeds and lack of buffaloes which would keep them in control in the off-season must also have lowered yields relative to those obtained further north (Perak AR 1904, 31). Moreover the effects of water shortage must have been greatly exaggerated by lack of small bunds (*batas*) to keep water on the fields.

Lack of simultaneous planting was another hindrance to production. Whilst there was no doubt the risk that authority could be wrong in choosing planting times, there were greater risks attendant upon piecemeal planting which permitted rats and birds to move from field to field over an extended period. Perhaps, too, the ravages of the padi stem borer would have been less had the land been better drained, since only low-lying land was seriously affected (Krian AR 1889, 223). The havoc caused by this pest should not be underestimated, it being sufficient to retard development 'to a most alarming extent' in the period 1886–8, for example (Krian AR 1888, 86). In part, rat damage was inevitable in a pioneer situation in which stumps and logs still lay in the fields and shelter-ed the pests, but equally no attempt seems to have been made to keep weedy growth at bay during the off-season (encl. HC, FMS to CO 14.12.1897, CO 273/230).

To all these factors may be added two related factors, disease and lack of clean drinking water. In a low-lying terrain without proper wells or latrines, cholera recurred regularly simultaneous with drought periods and the combination of the two precipitated more than one exodus. At the nadir of affairs in 1889, only 7,500 acres out of some 36,500 acres alienated were actually planted (Krian AR 1889, 223).

To those problems were added several social ones. It is clear that the capitalists who had been originally responsible for settling tenants on their lands, either could not or would not aid them. There seems to have been a fair incidence of landlordism in the district (Larut & Krian AR 1909, 3,5). But it cannot be concluded that landlordism led to lower production. Indeed, as in modern times, the contrary was probably true (Hill, 1967, 107–8). Nevertheless many planters had become indebted to shopkeepers and others for advances of rice, as usual repayable after harvest. But there were occasions when there was no harvest and the debtors, lacking the much-needed services of an agricultural bank, not unnaturally went elsewhere to avoid their creditors (Krian MR 9/1890, 616).

Parenthetically, it may be noted that there is not the slightest evidence of rack-renting, insecurity of tenure or of a 'landless peasantry' as claimed by Lim (1968, 107). There was plenty of empty land and having moved once, settlers were ready to move again if need be. Indeed, there may be some justice in the suggestion that many of the settlers were not really settlers in the true sense of the term (Perak AR 1895, 492). Some seem to have been farmers in Krian only part of the time as in pre-protectorate days (Krian AR 1894, 405).

A partial answer to the problems of Krian was drainage, irrigation and a proper water supply but government attention and finance were attracted elsewhere, notably to railway construction. A proposed irrigation-cum-drainage scheme had first to be paid for out of state accumulated revenue and subsequently by the cultivators themselves. The farmers, generally, received the notion with favour, provided that taxation was related to the productive capacity of the land (Krian AR 1894, 405). By this time settlers had come flocking back, to the extent that land was still available only in the Bagan Serai area, where 15,500 acres were already occupied, and in the Kuala Kurau mukims (Perak Land Dept. AR 1895, 239).

Extension of the cultivated area was continued to the north-east, in places on a considerable scale. W.H. Tate attempted to set up large-scale commercial production on a block of 1,300 acres and to set up padi mills throughout the district (Perak Land Dept. AR 1895, 239) though the fate of this enterprise is not known. The Sultan of Perak himself held a 'good deal' of rice land and one Kwa Chu Seng planted 700 acres in a single block (Larut & Krian AR 1909, 3, 5). To the south-east, extension of the rice area had begun around Selinsing and Kampong Dew by 1893 and significant areas must have been under cultivation by 1898 when European and Chinese sugar interests were reported to be buying up padi land. The rice trade had received a major fillip, first by a rise in price and second, by the prospect of a regular supply of water from the Irrigation Scheme, finally put under way in 1898 (Perak AR 1898, 5, 6).

But despite a boom in the last years of the century, conflict of interest between peasant rice growers and commercial sugar growers continued. From the 1870s both forms of cultivation seem to have existed alongside each other despite the differing requirements of the crops, sugar requiring more drainage than rice as well as canals for the cheap carriage of cane to the mills. More important was the fact that large-scale production was efficient and since this required large contiguous blocks, commercial interests steadily displaced rice growers, especially in years of poor rice harvests.

Though sugar was the more profitable crop, government intervened lest the hard facts of the market-place prevail and result in the failure of the policy of reducing dependence upon imported rice or lest government be placed in the curious position of having provided an expensive scheme of irrigation for rice when its culture was decreasing. What seems to have happened is that the Malay small-holder cleared the land, grew a few crops of rice on it and then sold out. Although it was official policy to protect the interests of Malay rice growers (Perak AR 1899, 17) and although newly-alienated lands within the designated Irrigation Areas were required to be planted with rice, this provision did not apply to previously alienated land. Thus the rice area extended at the periphery of settlement, only to be mopped up at the core by sugar interests.

It would be tedious to recount the story of the Krian Irrigation Scheme,[1] the only major scheme to be constructed in British-administered Malaya during the period. A few pertinent questions may be considered, however. Was the Scheme necessary? What were some of the problems involved and what degree of success was achieved? Accepting the need to reduce the dependence of the Federated Malay States upon imported rice as axiomatic, irrigation was essential for two related reasons. One was to increase and to stabilize production by adjusting water-supply to the water-requirements of the crop by supplying water in dry spells during the main growing period from September to November, and draining it off in wet spells, the latter possibly of even greater importance than the former (encl. Gov. SS to CO 14.12.1897, CO 273/230). The second need was to reduce the incidence of disease by providing potable water thus leading to greater stability of residence, improved health and efficiency in work (Vincent, 1894).

Even before the Scheme was implemented, major problems were foreseen, notably that the terrain was so flat that it was a matter of great difficulty to secure a grade, sufficient to avoid silting, for the canals (*SFP* 18.9.1894). Actual construction was delayed by personal disputes between the Irrigation Engineer and the State Engineer, and by wide variations of estimates of cost and of areas to be irrigated. The earliest estimates were a cost of $300,000 and an area of 52,000 acres. The ultimate cost was $1,600,000 whilst the estimate of area was too low by about one-third. It is uncertain what proportion of it ever grew rice though it was boasted that 70,000 acres was irrigated. In 1897, for instance, 40 per cent of the proposed Irrigation Area was uncultivated (HC, FMS to CO 14.12.97, CO 273/230).

The success of the Scheme is rather hard to estimate for lack of statistical data. Certainly the hope that assured crops would place the rakyat beyond the reach of the middleman remained very much only a hope. Although $10,000 was loaned to new settlers at Gunong Semanggol, Selinsing and Briah in 1909, with the objective of preventing people from falling into debt, it is clear that many were already heavily indebted. An agricultural bank was proposed by men on the spot in Krian but its advent was to be a mere half a century in the future (Larut & Krian AR 1909, 4).

Equally chimerical was engineer O'Shaughnessy's vision of two crops a year, one of a long-term, heavy variety and the other of a short-term, light variety (encl. HC, FMS to CO 14.12.1897, CO 273/230). Three years after the Scheme was opened it was stated that a few more years' work was required to 'make padi cultivation less dependent upon rain'. The Dato' Panglima Besar was pessimistic that there would be sufficient water for the rice growers, who in fact were still 'somewhat' dependent upon rain (Larut & Krian AR 1909, 3). His concern was not surprising since a new

[1]No single account exists. Relevant material is to be found in Vincent, 1894, in Gov. SS to CO 14.12.1897, CO 273/230, and in the various reports on the Scheme published in the *Perak Government Gazette*, e.g. *PGG* 10, 265–6, 476; 14, 5.7.1901, suppl. A further source is Anon., 1906.

canal, from near Gunong Semanggol to Gula, not provided for in the original plan, was cut exclusively to supply 20,000 acres of sugar estate land (Larut & Krian AR 1909, 5). Still, affairs were sufficiently encouraging for a modern Chinese-owned rice mill to be opened at Kuala Kurau, thus at last obviating the long haul to Penang and back. Towards the middle of the decade, the sugar industry fell on hard times and although much of the abandoned sugar land was planted with rubber, some was planted with rice (Perak AR 1905, 27; Larut & Krian AR 1909, 5).

But on balance it must be concluded that whilst irrigation did some good, it was very far from being the answer to the rakyat's prayer. Certainly, from 1906 onwards, it could be guaranteed that the district would feed itself. But allowing for about $200,000 worth of rice retained in the district to feed its own population,[1] it is clear that even prior to the introduction of irrigation, there was self-sufficiency in most years. Feeding the local populace was one matter. Feeding the whole state was another. Behind developments in Krian was always the expectation that the district would become the granary of Perak. Vain hope. In 1907 more rice was exported than ever before, $600,000 worth, but in that same year the State imported rice worth $5.7 million, of which only a small fraction was reimported Krian rice (Perak AR 1907, 2).

SOUTH-WEST PERAK

Before closing the discussion of Perak it is appropriate to refer briefly to affairs in Lower Perak and in the Dindings since in a sense this south-western region was a 'Krian-that-never-was'. The region comprised a narrow strip of terrain bounded seaward by mangrove and landward by fresh-water swamps, together with the combined deltas of the Perak and Bernam rivers forming a compact block of alluvium very similar in character to that of Krian. An inland boundary may be placed in the vicinity of Teluk Anson, between which settlement and the river-levees of the Perak lay an uninhabited tract. The whole area was extremely low-lying, so much so that the coastal areas around Rungkup, Kota Stia and Bagan Datoh were to suffer damage to the rice crop because of high tides (Lr Perak MR 12/1892, 93).

In the 1880s agriculture scarcely existed. As further north, the population was engaged almost exclusively in making atap for export to the Deli tobacco plantations (Perak AR 1886, 1212). With the collapse of Sumatran tobacco in 1891 however, and combined with an influx of settlers from Banjermasin and, to a lesser degree, from Kelantan, a series of coastal and estuarine agricultural colonies rapidly came into existence from about 1887 when it was reported that 'much additional land' had been opened for padi (Perak AR 1887, 1153; 1891, 417).

Along the coast and in the Dindings district, development was exclusively small-scale and Malay in character. Along the Perak river this was only

[1]This is estimated from data for 1905 when total production was valued at $823,882, of which $633,882 worth was exported (Larut & Krian AR 1905, 4).

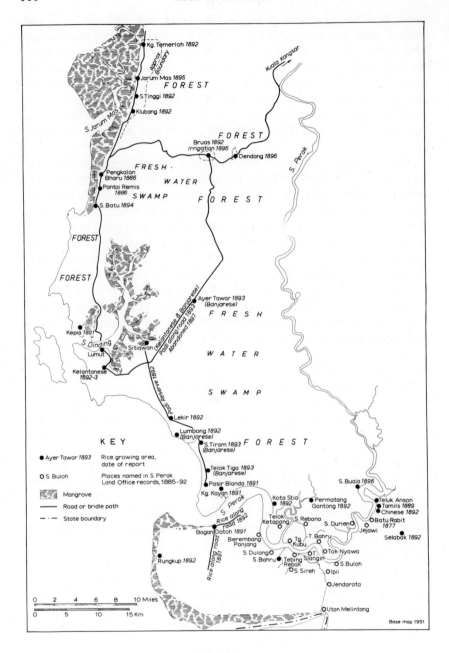

FIGURE 10
LOWER PERAK AND THE DINDINGS: RICE-GROWING AND
SETTLEMENT IN THE LATE NINETEENTH CENTURY

partly the case and large-scale developers were also active. The Datoh Panglima Kinta and the Laksamana had acquired a large tract in the vicinity of Teluk Anson (Perak AR 1896, 610). Near Lekir 1,000 acres were reserved for two Banjarese headmen. At Teluk Anson another 1,000 were granted to Fu Chu Chun with another slightly larger block at Selaba (Lr Perak MR 5/1892, 493; 11/1892, 41). At Sitiawan, the Penghulu claimed that there was rice land sufficient to support 16,000 people (Lr Perak MR 1/1893, 150). At Bagan Datoh, Javanese settlers had moved in and their rice and coconuts were said to be thriving as nowhere else in the East (Brewster, 1896, 395). In the vicinity of the Jenderata Canal[1] the land '... could be easily irrigated, and requires only population to equal the Krian district' (Lr Perak MR 3/1892, 229).

Achievement fell far short of promise. By mid-1896 the Panglima Kinta and the Laksamana had 50–70 acres cleared (Lr Perak MR 8/1896, 683). The Lekir and other Sitiawan lands were 'practically abandoned' a year later (Lr Perak MR 5/1897, 385) and of the developments by Chinese capitalists nothing more was heard. Far from becoming 'another Krian', Lower Perak and the Dindings became a major area of tree crops. Along the coast migrants from Banjermasin and Java planted coconut small-holdings, and so long as the new land was being pioneered, rice had its place as a catch-crop (Lr Perak MR 9/1898, 764). Elsewhere, after a false start with sugar-growing at the turn of the century, estate cultivation of rubber, mainly *Hevea* but with some *Ficus elastica*, occupied the scene. By 1907, 47,000 acres had been alienated for coconut. Only about 3,000 acres were under rice and virtually all of that lay in the Pulau Tiga and Kampong Gajah *mukims* lying within the Lower Perak district administratively but geographically part of the Perak river region (Lr Perak AR 1906, 3; 1907, 3).

CONCLUSION

Perak thus represents the final phase of an era in which land development and rice-growing were largely synonymous. These were associated with a southward extension of rice-growing, first in the Province, in southern Kedah following the establishment of peace, then in Krian and finally ephemerally, in the 'second Krian' of the Perak and Dindings swamps.

Throughout the whole of the nineteenth century there were only two possible major crops for the lowlands, sugar and rice. The Kedah government was much more concerned with the well-being of its own people than in large-scale foreign investment and sugar never became a significant crop there. In the Province, the Company and colonial administrations gave free rein to both capitalist and peasant interests, though the latter had already taken up much of the suitable land by the time estate sugar-grow-

---

[1]This canal was cut for communication between the Perak and the Bernam rivers and was neither designed nor used for irrigation.

ing had become profitable. Western Perak, from the Krian to the Bernam, remained. In the north, estate sugar and peasant rice interests reached a balance. In the south, estate interests prevailed not because of any political interest, but because of a combination of environmental and economic factors. There can be little doubt that even such skilled farmers as the Kelantanese settled in the south around Lumut found conditions difficult, though initially they obtained high yields from the newly-cleared land. Soils were rather peaty and subject to saline infiltration, and the settlers lacked brackish-water varieties of rice (Lr Perak MR 9/1891, 1004). In contrast, coconuts could withstand mildly saline conditions, at least for a time, and a good market for copra had developed.

By linking their fortunes with an overseas market and eschewing the relatively meagre returns of the production of the staple under such difficult conditions, the small-holders undoubtedly bettered themselves. Even had coconuts and later, rubber, not been alternative crops suited to the local environment, it is doubtful if the large-scale development of irrigation and drainage necessary to efficient rice-growing would have been technically feasible in most of the region. In the event, the question did not arise. The southward drift of rice-growing was effectually halted by economic as much as by environmental realities.

7

The Southern Centre:
Malacca and Negri Sembilan

Ah, Sir...I am just out of Malacca jail. I had *rumah tangah, harta banda, bindang dan kuboon* (house, valuables, rice-fields and plantations); but I mortgaged them to a chitty to pay the expenses of my son's wedding.

Penghulu of S. Baru *c.*1835[1]

If all the available padi-land were taken up and cultivated as the Chinese know how to do it, Malacca might be the granary of the Straits.

D.F.A. Hervey, 1844, Malacca AR 1884, 962.

Following the fertile valley of the Moar [*sic*] I passed through most picturesque country. Large rice-fields...studded with Malay huts and gardens, and flanked on either side by densely wooded ranges, extended for many miles....

D.D. Daly, 1875.[2]

THE southern centre of cultivation was separated from the northern centre by a large intervening tract of marchlands in which rice cultivation was of only local importance (see Chapter 8). Although the southern region comprises two political units, their boundaries do not coincide with geographical realities. Two sub-regions may be distinguished on the basis of distinctive landscapes and on occupance by contrastive social groups. The first may be denoted Malaccan and the second, Minangkabau.

The Malaccan sub-region comprised the coastal plain flanking Malacca town on the south-east and north-west. Only a portion of the coastal tract, that lying within a mile or two of the coast, was cultivated, the lands further inland being fresh-water swamp. North-west and south-east of the town, the belt of contiguous cultivation extended for five or six miles in either direction and beyond this cultivation was patchy. The area was occupied by people of diverse origins, Malays, Chinese, people of mixed race.[3]

In the Minangkabau sub-region, cultivated areas were strip-like in form down the narrow, rectilinear valleys, each of which was separated from

[1]Thomson 1865a, 319. '*Harta banda*[*r*]' is, correctly, 'town property', and '*kuboon*' [*kebun*], strictly, 'garden' not plantation.

[2]Daly, 1882, 399.

[3]A census of 1881 reported some 6,000 Malay 'padi-planters' and about 700 Chinese (*SSGG* 1881, 1367).

its neighbour by considerable tracts of steep hills which were cultivated only on their margins. This habitat was favoured by Minangkabau migrants, 'mountaineers' in their homeland. The boundary between Malaccans and Minangkabau thus lay a little to the south of the southern boundary of Naning (see Figure 11).

The drawing of comparisons between these two contrasting areas is somewhat complicated by the fact that for Malacca (the political unit) sources are richest for the period down to about 1870, whereas the Negri Sembilan[1] were little-known to outsiders until the 1880s. The two areas will therefore be discussed separately before attempting to compare them.

MALACCA (EXCLUDING NANING) TO C.1910

When the British took over the administration of Malacca from the Dutch in 1824, rice agriculture was, and had for some time been at a low ebb. Although the settlement had some export of fruits, Malacca produced sufficient rice for only six months' consumption despite a seemingly favourable environment and a strong demand in the town (*PWIGG* 1.9.1810; 24.10.1812; Wurtzburg, 1954, 70).

At Malacca, the country is for the most part low....About a mile inland it is swampy and covered with wood. The soil is a thick stiff clay, apparently very favourable for the cultivation of rice. There appears to be no want of water; yet with these advantages, the place does not raise rice for its own consumption. The Dutch...attribute this circumstance to the indolent habits of the Malayan race, who for the most part are cultivators of the soil. The cause more probably arises from the want of due encouragement to agriculture; from unfavourable terms in the tenure of land; and in part perhaps from the existence of slavery among the Dutch.

Finlayson, 1826, 39.

In these views, a native-born Malaccan, Abdullah bin Abdul Kadir[2] concurred, suggesting further that the Dutch had preferred to promote the sale of rice from Java to the detriment of Malacca (Hill, 1955, 212–13). Legislative encouragement, with the object of ensuring planting by imposing penalties for failure to plant and ensuring simultaneous planting, was soon forthcoming (RDM 1.5.1828, 30.5.1828). Government policy was that,

The improvement of their condition and the progressive amelioration of the habits of the indigenous population must at all times be considered the great end of British Administration, and whatever may be the supposed advantages resulting from the introduction of Chinese or other foreign adventurers, the Governor in Council is satisfied that they are so dearly purchased by the exclusion, depression,

[1]The political evolution of the Negri Sembilan is outlined in Sadka, 1968, 118. One of the constituent states, Sungei Ujong, which joined the confederation in 1895, lay within the 'tin zone' and is discussed in Chapter 8.

[2]This is, of course, the same Abdullah whose visit to Kelantan has already been mentioned (p. 64).

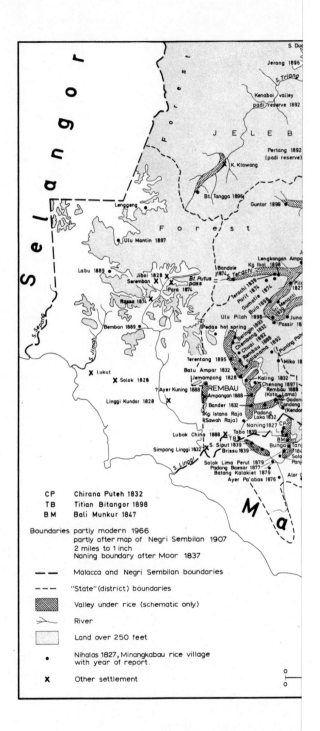

S. Dua

Jerang 1895

S. Triang

Kenaboi valley
padi reserve 1892

J E L E B

Pertang 1892
(padi reserve)

K. Klawang

Bt. Tangga 1896

Guntor 1899

Lenggeng

F o r e s t

Ulu Mantin 1897

Lengkongan Amp

Labu 1889

Bandole
1874

Kg Ibol 1898

S. Terachi

Jiboi 1828
Seremban

Bt Putus
pass

Para 1874

Terachi 1831

Pil
1827

Rassa 1874

Parit 1871

Menari

Gumatie 1871

Bula 1899

Bemban 1889

Ulu Pilah 1898

Pedas hot spring

Juno

Passir 18

Seringin 1832

Chembong 1832

Chuai 1892

Terentang 1895

Rembau 1888

Selanama 1892

Miko 18

Batu Ampar 1832

Punting Po

Lukut

Jemampong 1828

Kaling 1832

Solok 1828

REMBAU

Chenong 1897
Rembau 1888
(Kota Lama)

? Ayer Kuning 1888

Ampangan 1888

Gadon
Gondong
(Kendor

Linggi Kundor 1828

Bander 1832

Padang
Loko 1832

Kg Istana Raja
(Sawah Raja)

Naning 1827

CP

Lubok China 1888

Taba 1839

TB

BM

Simpang Linggi 1832

S. Siput 1839
Brissu 1839

Bunga Tanj

Solok Lima Perut 1879
Padang Baesar 1877
Batang Kalakiet 1879
Ayer Pa'abas 1876

S. Linggi

Solo

Panj

Alor

M

a

CP   Chirana Puteh 1832
TB   Titian Bitangor 1898
BM   Bali Munkur 1847

Boundaries partly modern 1966
partly after map of Negri Sembilan 1907
2 miles to 1 inch
Naning boundary after Moor 1837

— —   Malacca and Negri Sembilan boundaries

– – –   "State"(district) boundaries

▨   Valley under rice (schematic only)

⤳   River

▢   Land over 250 feet

•   Nihalas 1827, Minangkabau rice village
     with year of report.

✗   Other settlement

0
0

RICE VILLAGES IN TH

and degradation of the Original Malay Inhabitants of the Peninsula, who are in
the first instance entitled to our protection and encouragement.

RDM 26.8.1828.

According to Abdullah (Hill, 1955, 212–13) the effects were galvanic.

Since the English have occupied Malacca they have ordered plantations and rice-
fields to be opened up and cultivated and jungle to be cleared away so that the
people may have easy means of growing food and earning their living.

Those in the Settlement who had some capital bought rice-fields, while those
who had none of their own worked hard felling trees and cutting down bushes,
some taking up a half or a third part [i.e. share?] of a rice-field as tenants, until
the exports of rice from Malacca [to Singapore] grew to hundreds of tons a year. . . .

This boom, if in fact it existed, was short-lived since in 1828 the *Malacca
Observer* (in *PRM* 26.3.1828) noted that Malacca had merely been almost
self-sufficient and that consumption was now double the estimated
production of 700 coyans per year. Average yields at 293 gantangs/acre,
were much inferior to those of Province Wellesley where the average yield
was about 350 gantangs/acre. Moreover the yield obtained in Malacca was
achieved at the expense of a very high sowing rate, nearly 10 gantangs/acre,
compared with 3 gantangs/acre in the northern settlement (Low, 1836, 88,
219).[1] Such high sowing rates almost certainly reflect the use of poor-
quality seed, empty glumes being common (*SSAR* 1862–3, 30). As elsewhere, the yields suffered from natural calamities. Cattle disease and
consequent loss of traction was of more serious significance in Malacca
than in the Minangkabau lands where ploughs were rarely used. Floods
were no more serious than elsewhere in the Peninsula, but locust attacks
were peculiar to Malacca (*SSAR* 1861–2, 310; 1862–3, 30).

The pattern of settlement in Malacca was also unlike that in the northern
settlement and other rice-growing areas where nucleated hamlets or
villages and linear settlements were the rule. In Malacca, between the
town and Tanjong Kling, noted Logan in 1845,

The *tout ensemble* is considerably inferior to the Mooda [*sic*] and Penaga districts
of Wellesley Province. The paddy is stunted in comparison; instead of long lines
of *permatangs*, covered with trees and full of inhabitants, there are only here and
there a few scattered cocoa-nut trees, on the same level as the bindangs, with a
solitary hut beside them. [Near St. John's Hill] In front and to the S.W. lies a large
tract of cocoa-nut trees. . . . Behind [i.e. landward] the cocoa-nuts lie extensive
paddy-fields. Huts are scattered over them, but they are without any trees or other
vegetation than the paddy itself.

Logan, 1887, 4, 8.

These quotations also indicate active land development close to the town,
since by 1876, the formerly bare rice plain was dotted with clumps of
coconut and other palms, each containing a dwelling (*SSAR* 1855–6, 23;
Lovat, 1914, 278).

Although sources do not fully permit the location of newly-developed
lands, it is clear (if *Blue Book* statistics for the late 1870s onwards be

[1]Baumgarten (1849, 715) gives rather higher figures; for Malacca 360 gantangs/acre and for
Province Wellesley 480 gantangs/acre.

accepted) that a slow but steady expansion of the rice area occurred, following wild fluctuations in the mid-1880s (see Fig. 12). In part, expansion was made possible by the initiation of minor drainage works, especially along the coast, and, in the interior, irrigation works. In 1863–4, for instance, $1\frac{1}{2}$ miles of cut was made through the higher ground along the coast at Pulau Gadong (*SSAR* 1863–4, 30). Spasmodic attempts were made to clear existing drains and rivers but with the exception of small dams at Melaka Pindah, Krubong, Lendu and Melekek, all of which were in interior valleys, these works of improvement were of but little effect. Large-scale drainage and irrigation of the plains tract at no stage were more than suggested (*SFPW* 28.4.1895; 17.9.1895). Governor Clarke's policy statement of 1874 that any work should '...be of such a reproductive character as to preclude any permanent charge on the General Revenue' (*SSGG* 21.3.1874) was something of a cooler and the *Straits Times*'s (26.5.1886) suggestion that not just self-sufficiency but the supply of the whole Colony was a desirable end, was never taken up.

RICE PRODUCTION AND LAND TENURE

Interest in tenure lies not so much in its details[1] but in the question as to what extent was Malacca's comparatively poor showing in the matter of extending rice cultivation a problem of tenure difficulties as claimed by Finlayson (1826) and others (see Guthrie, 1861, 6). About the year 1817 'almost all' rice for local consumption was locally produced, but by 1828 only half was (*PRM* 26.3.1828). This situation continued through 1848 when the equivalent of seven months' consumption was of local provenance (*SFPW* 6.1.1848). Yet despite reports that the cultivated area was being extended and drainage works were being undertaken to offset the effects

Source : Straits Settlements BLUE BOOKS 1870 -1910

FIGURE 12
MALACCA: RICE ACREAGES, 1870–1920[2]

[1]These are fully discussed in Mills, 1966, Chapter 6.

[2]The *Blue Book* data for 1870–7 are suspect.

of flooding, by 1887 only three months' supply was locally grown (*SFP* 30.8.1887; 18.1.1849; 21.8.1856).

Relatively low yields have already been noted (p. 121). There is no evidence that these were the result of inferior tillage, buffalo ploughs being widely used, to the extent that considerable economic distress resulted from widespread losses of buffaloes from rinderpest and foot-and-mouth disease (*SFP* 30.8.1887; 8.2.1890; 24.7.1894). There is no evidence that at the material time the cycle of cultivation was out of phase with the seasons, though earlier, the Muslim calendar seems to have been strictly followed (Muhammed, 1897, 297). Moreover though the soil was seemingly less intrinsically fertile than in the Province or in Krian, its yields were by no means bad and these were kept up to a fair level by the use of manure (*SFP* 30.8.1887).

It must therefore be concluded that the reasons for low production lay not so much in the environmental and technical fields as with the social and legal matters. In 1827, it was reported that, as in Dutch times, '...the whole territory of Malacca, with an exception scarcely worthy of mention, is parcelled out among landed Proprietors who are as unfruitful to the Revenue as they are useless towards the advancement of local Prosperity' (RDM 11.2.1827). Although a good number of the proprietors were of Dutch origin, some were Chinese, others Malays, amongst whom Wan Chilek (Syed Mahomet bin Syed Hussein Alhabshi) was the most notable (RDM 12.3.1828; *SFP* 28.8.1887; *SSGG* 1891, 1694).

The government recognized only the right to levy a tithe on the annual produce of the lands, and once the claims of the proprietors were relinquished to the Company in consideration of an annual subvention, government took steps to collect the tithe for itself, though invariably collections fell far below the sums required to pay the former tithe-impropriators their pensions (Blundell, 1848, 738–43). The rakyat, who considered that they already held the land by ancient, unwritten right, thus became in Company eyes, tenants whose annual liability was to pay one-tenth of their crops and later, its equivalent in money to the Company and subsequently to its successor, the British Crown. In many cases the rakyat refused to pay. In Malacca, fishermen rioted and in Naning, an attempt to enforce the collection of the tithe was a cause of warfare which resulted in widespread abandonment of lands in that state (*GGPWISM* 5.9.1829; *SCCR* 11.11.1831). Yet even after the war the land tax was lauded as being only one-tenth '...instead of one-third of the produce as in other parts of India' (*GGPWISM* 10.4.1830).

By impropriating the tithe and paying off the 'proprietors' it was hoped that, 'This will set them [the 'proprietors'] at ease, and enable them at leisure to form plans of the amelioration of the agricultural interests of Malacca' (*SCCR* 10.4.1828). The hope was never realized. The 'proprietors' could hardly be expected to do anything on lands in which their interests had been bought out. The rakyat had good grounds for complaint.

The manner in which the tythe [*sic*] on paddy is collected [by Company-agents] is peculiarly oppressive, and has been the cause of most serious complaint amongst the cultivators; it is thus. When the grain is ripening, agents are sent to ascertain the quantity of paddy the harvest is likely to produce....The ryut [*sic*] is then told that he will be required to send in one-tenth of the amount thus calculated or guessed at, and it is vain to remonstrate and say that he must reserve some of the grain...for seed, some for the use of his family, or that ere it is ripe and fit to cut, a storm or a herd of buffaloes or wild hogs destroy his little plantations....

                                                                    SCCR 16.2.1832.

Government oppression continued unchecked for a long period and not only took the form described but also, by the Malacca Lands Act of 1839, included the requirement that a written title be taken out. This many Malays refused to do on the grounds that if they had no papers they would have nothing to mortgage (Malacca AR 1881, 724). Malay interests, however, were forwarded by the judgement of Mr. Justice Maxwell who found for the plaintiff in a case in which a Malay sought redress for his eviction from his house and lands by Government for non-payment of assessment, even though he continued to pay tenths. The Chief Justice remarked that,

It is well known that by old Malay law or custom of Malacca, while the sovereign was the owner of the soil, every man nevertheless had the right to clear and occupy all forest and waste lands, subject to the payment, to the Sovereign, of one tenth of the produce of the land so taken....If he abandoned the paddy land or fruit trees for three years...his rights ceased....I...hold that the custom was not only reasonable, but very well suited to any country like this, where the population is thin and the uncleared land superabundant and of no value. It must be for the advantage of the State to attract settlers to lands which are worthless as forest and swamp, and thus to increase at once the population and the wealth of the country.

                                                                    SDT 22.3.1870.

But the hoped-for influx of settlers and extension of cultivation failed to take place. Indeed the reverse happened. The area under rice fell from a rather suspect estimated figure of 52,000 acres in 1870 to 18,745 acres in 1883. Land taxes and regulations were still considered to be oppressive. For example, 'The Malays at Tanjong Kling still declare they are unable to pay rents of $1.50 per acre for padi-land, and that there is nothing to look forward to, but the seizure of their property by Government' (*SFP* 22.12. 1887). Numbers of farmers, but not their families, from Merlimau and other districts, emigrated to the adjoining state of Muar where lands were available rent-free for three years. Their Malacca lands were resumed by Government and on their return, numbers of the rakyat were convicted for trespass on Crown Lands, i.e. their own! (*ST* 26.5.1885; *SFP* 31.1.1888).

The Malacca Lands Ordinance of 1886 was vigorously opposed by Unofficial Members of the Straits Settlements Legislative Council, Shelford, for instance, stating, '...I will be no party towards assisting the Government in getting their pound of flesh from the people indigenous to the soil regardless of their customs and whether they were subjected or not to bad seasons and depressions....' (*ST* 2.7.1886). Shelford was not heeded. Further legislation in 1892 required a money payment of a sum equal to one-tenth of what the Collector of Land Revenue thought the land was capable of producing (*SFP* 20.9.1892). The enshrinement in the Malacca Lands Ordinance of 1886 of the government right to the tithe and subsequent legislation not only continued to dissuade potential immigrants from settling, especially since they could obtain land on easy terms in the Federated Malay States and in Johore (Muar), but also continued to be considered as oppressive by Malaccans.

Finlayson's view, therefore, that the relative backwardness of agriculture in Malacca should be attributed to tenure difficulties arising from the Dutch administration, cannot be sustained. As Cameron (1865, 381) noted, '. . . the unsatisfactory nature of the land grants . . . was long thought to be the chief cause of the inactivity that prevailed. But now that the soil is ready to be ·granted away in fee-simple . . . very little improvement is perceptible'.

The rakyat was still worse off under a colonial administration than his counterpart in a native state who held land rent-free for the first three years following clearance, followed by a mere 40¢ or so per acre per year as quit-rent. Nevertheless, the colonial government had a point. Since private individuals let out lands at $2 to $10 per acre, or for one-third or even half of the crop, it is not surprising that government attempted to arrogate to itself enhanced rents (Malacca AR 1887, 1286). But what government did not disclose was just how much land bore such values and could bear such heavy government revenue charges.

THE MINANGKABAU LANDS (INCLUDING NANING) TO *C*.1910

The Minangkabau lands, namely Naning and the Negri Sembilan, were only marginally known to outsiders until the earlier part of the nineteenth century though colonization from Sumatra had continued since the sixteenth century and possibly since as early as the end of the fourteenth century (Shamsul, 1964, 13–14). Gullick (1951, 39), without providing documentation, has suggested that as late as the seventeenth century little padi was grown. By the end of the nineteenth century its cultivation was hallowed by tradition to the extent that it was considered shameful not to cultivate the ancestral lands.

Newbold (1837a, b, c) considered there to be four Minangkabau states: Sungei Ujong, which was to become largely a tin-mining state (see p. 150); Rembau; Johol with its more or less independent 'dependencies,' Sri Menanti, Jempol, and Gemencheh; and Naning, the last under the Company (formerly Dutch) administration at Malacca. Newbold, however, has little information beyond noting extensive cultivation of rice in the valleys and lists of villages. The population of the various states was very small (see Table 14) but in some states sufficient rice was produced for there to be an export to Malacca.

Johol, especially, was in a state of 'high cultivation' and its rice yields

TABLE 14
POPULATION ESTIMATES OF MINANGKABAU STATES, 1828–38

	According to newspapers	According to Newbold		
Sungei Ujong	1,400	Malays 3,200	Chinese 400
Rembau	9,000	9,000	
Johol (and Gemencheh)	1,600	2,080	
Sri Menanti (incl. Jempol)	9,000	8,000	
Jelebu	2,900	3,750	
Naning	4,587	3,458	
Total	28,487	29,488	400

Sources: Newbold, 1837c, 1839; *GGPWISM* 8.11.1828; *SFP* 8.2.1838.

were superior to those of Malacca, 'one gantang of seed never producing less than a hundred-fold', which, at the usual sowing rate of four gantangs to the acre, would have yielded 400 gantangs per acre (Newbold, 1839, 2, 136). Part of the crop was exported from Johol to Malacca, as also was part of the Sri Menanti crop (Newbold, 1837b, 69).

Elsewhere production was purely for local consumption. 'The Malays of Naning [for example] do not cultivate more rice than is absolutely necessary for their private wants, and the proportion annually given up to the Panghulu [*sic*]. . . .' (Newbold, 1837c, 249). The total production in 1831 was only 16,000 gantangs of padi, of which the Penghulu's revenue was said to be 9,000 gantangs, most of which presumably found its way to the Malacca market (*SCCR* 11.8.1831). At seventyfold, yields were lower than in Johol (Newbold, 1837c, 248). But Naning was just recovering from a war[1] and in the Jasin and Rim districts to the east, hardly 100 people out of a former population of 3,000 were left, the rest having fled their lands as a result of a dispute between the Company and Rajah Borema of Muar (*GGPWISM* 5.9.1829). Naning was thus atypical of the Minangkabau lands in that it was subject to a colonial government and subjected to the trauma of political strife which, however, was later to be the lot of other areas.

It is likely that such strife led to an increase in the proportion of shifting cultivation which could be practised in the relative security of deep forest, but in ordinary circumstances the Minangkabau still commonly cultivated ladangs in tracts of secondary forest upslope from the orchards and hamlets located on the piedmont. Ladangs were cultivated not only as an insurance against failure of the sawah crop because of lack of rain, but

[1]Curiously, a measure of rice, 400 gantangs, was at issue in the Naning War. From 1776 the Dutch had levied this amount as tribute in lieu of a tithe. The Dutch governor attempted to restore the full tithe in 1822 but the Penghulu of Naning objected. The matter remained in abeyance after the change in administration until 1828 when Fullerton issued regulations that the tithe be collected again. The Penghulu considered that his rights were thereby infringed and war broke out. See *SCCR* 17.10.1835, 24.10.1835; *SDT* 23.9.1874.

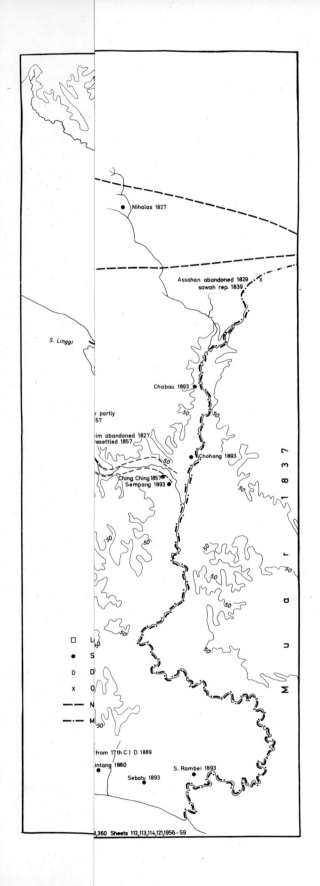

Nihalas 1827

Assahan abandoned 1829
sawah rep. 1839 · ͯ

S. Linggi

Chabau 1893

·80

·50

y partly
57

im abandoned 1827
resettled 1857

·50

Chohong 1893

·50

Ching Ching 1857
Sempang 1893 ●

M u a r   1 8 3 7

·50   ·50

·50

·50

·50

·50

·50

□   L

●   S

D   D

x   O

— —   N

—·—   M   ·50

(from 17th C.) D 1889

intang 1880   S. Rambei 1893

Sebatu 1893

,360 Sheets 112,113,114,121,1956 – 59

also because, 'The ladang rice...is affirmed by some to be sweeter and whiter, and to keep better than the produce of the sawah' (Newbold, 1839, 1, 263). For the rest of the period, it would seem that agriculture continued much as it had previously. An increasing number of sources, mainly reports of travels,[1] permit the compilation of a map (Figure 13) to show which areas were settled and where rice was grown.

Throughout the period of British administration there was a steady increase in population, partly by natural increase and partly by immigration. By 1891 population pressure in Sri Menanti had reached the point that it was 'absolutely necessary' to open up rice lands in other districts (NSSS ?/91). Elsewhere, the main valleys were fully occupied though production could still be increased by the judicious application of more advanced techniques. There were, however, lands still unoccupied in Jelebu where lands were reserved for padi in the Kenaboi and Pertang valleys, and in Gemencheh.

In strife-affected Naning, abandoned lands were still being reoccupied in the 1850s, and in Jelebu, where half the population had emigrated in the period 1860–80, lands were being reclaimed in the 1890s (O'Brien, 1884, 342). Expansion of the cultivated area on to virgin land was rather limited. On the southern margin of the Minangkabau lands, in the Jasin district, some increase in subsistence cultivation was reported in the 1890s (Malacca AR 1892, 575). Elsewhere only very minor extensions were recorded, as for instance, in the Muar valley between Kuala Pilah and Kampong Serting or in the Nerasau valley, Rembau (NSSS 833/92). At Kuala Gemencheh, settlers from Pahang had introduced the tenggala system[2] but theirs was a temporary success, the land being later abandoned (Negri Sembilan AR 1889, 422; Tampin MR 7/1898).

Data for the total area under rice and its expansion are difficult to establish. In 1891 the total was estimated at 19,423 acres and gradually increasing (Negri Sembilan AR 1891, 506). In the first decade of the twentieth century, not a single report of expansion of the cultivated area appeared. At the same time the Malay populace which had formerly been self-sufficient in rice, with some exportable surplus, was no longer self-supporting and by 1908 only 70 per cent of the total Malay rice needs were filled locally (Negri Sembilan AR 1908, 3). This was because newcomers, 'foreign Malays', who entered the region in some numbers in the 1890s were growers of maize, bananas, tobacco and coffee rather than rice growers (Jelebu AR 1892, 526). Some rice land, mainly in Jelebu, was given over to tin-mining (Jelebu AR 1894).

The Minangkabau lands were thus unlike other rice-growing areas, except perhaps Upper Perak, in that there was little expansion of the cultivated area. Lacking extensive plains suitable for large-scale working, the Negri Sembilan were unattractive as a field for significant government investment which might have otherwise been channelled to them.

[1]See, for example, Favre, 1849b; Logan, 1849; Gray, 1852; Braddell, 1853; Macpherson, 1858; D'Almeida, 1876, 374–6; Weld, 1881; Daly, 1882; Hervey, 1884.
[2]Described fully on pp. 158, 161ff.

THE MALACCA PLAINS AND THE MINANGKABAU LANDS: A COMPARISON

A comparison of the Malacca coastal plains region and the Minang-kabau areas further inland reveals considerable contrasts in almost all aspects: the physical environment, the cultural landscapes, cultivation techniques, cycle of cultivation and matters of land tenure. Moreover the occupation of hill-and-valley terrain by Minangkabau immigrants from Sumatra is a striking illustration of the manner in which a cultural preference may result in the emergence of a distinctive culture complex. It could be argued that the by-passing of the plains by the migrants was an act of political prudence, and so it undoubtedly was, but equally it must be admitted that most plain areas in the western part of the Peninsula were ripe for colonization, yet were avoided in favour of the 'hills of home'.

CONTRASTING PHYSICAL ENVIRONMENTS

[On the Malacca plain] the country...is lower and flatter than the inland parts, where...the surface of the country is undulating, now rising into high knolls, thickly clothed with jungles, and now sinking into hollows, or rather flats, about seventy or eighty yards wide, where water lodges in the rainy season, and which either form swamps or paddy-grounds, according to the industry or otherwise of the Natives in the vicinity.

Newbold, 1839, 1, 114 191–2.

The main valleys are a good deal wider than Newbold indicated, the Tampin and upper Muar valleys, for instance, being half a mile wide. In contrast, the plains region was slightly higher in its coastal parts than inland where acidic, blackwater swamplands occurred. In the rainy season, the coastal levee, like that at Krian, acted as a great bund to transform the rice areas and inland, the swamps, into a lake from which surplus water escaped with difficulty via rivers such as the Malacca, Kesang and Baru. The result was that when heavy falls of rain occurred, water remained on the land for extended periods thus 'drowning' the crop.

Drowning of the crop can have rarely occurred in the Minangkabau lands where the gradients of the valleys were much greater and where the average intensity of rainfall was also less. At Jelebu and Kuala Pilah, the average maximum intensity of rainfall is 0.53 and 0.51 inches per rain-day, compared with 0.61 inches per rain-day at Malacca (Dale, 1960, 22). In other respects too, the rainfall regime of the coast was different from that inland. The mean annual rainfall of Malacca and the Negri Sembilan together, which ranges from 65 to 80 inches is less by at least 10 inches per year, than any other important rice-growing region. In the Malaccan region this apparent deficit was compensated for by topography and by a regime markedly different from that of any other part of the Peninsula. In this small region the tendency is for there to be one maximum of about 10 inches in October, and one minimum of about 3 inches in January and February, which are the harvest months (Dale, 1959, 36). Inland, not only was the total rainfall less than at Malacca—Jelebu for example, with a mean of 65 inches being the driest place in Malaya—but the annual distribution is remarkably even, though with slight maxima in March and April and again between October and December (Dale, 1959).

CLIMATE AND THE AGRICULTURAL CYCLE

The even spread of annual rainfall may well have been a factor contributing to the difficulties experienced in Negri Sembilan in adjusting the annual round of work to the seasons. In 1889 proclamations were issued urging the people to commence to irrigate and cultivate at the proper season but ten years later there was still some doubt amongst the people as to the correct season in which to begin the agricultural cycle (Negri Sembilan AR 1889, 1586; Sungei Ujong AR 1892, 503). In 1898 at Kuala Pilah, for instance, transplanting was required to have taken place by mid-August, usually a dry month, whilst in the previous and following years, transplanting had just begun in October (NSSS 3067/98). In 1895, however, harvest was in June, indicating December planting (Kuala Pilah MR 6/1895). In 1892 in nearby Sri Menanti, according to an official Order made by the Datoh of Johol, planting should have been completed by mid-August but in fact was five months later (NSSS 931/92). The same was true in Tampin (NSSS 554/92).

It is tempting to suggest that adherence to the old Malaccan custom of planting in the Muslim calendar months of Zu'l-kaedah and Zu'l-hijjah was responsible for the confusion but in 1892 these months fell in June and July, not January; in 1895 in May and June, not December; and in 1897 and 1898 in April and May, not in October or in August. Adherence to this custom cannot be invoked for the varying commencement dates of the agricultural year. Rather, variability of the weather was the cause, since, except where irrigation from permanent sources of water was possible, the cultivators were dependent upon sufficient rain to give an adequate flow in the small tributary streams customarily used for irrigation. There is also the possibility that official planting dates were incorrect but though government minutes almost admit this (NSSS 3067/98), modern dates for transplanting invariably fall in August or September, except in parts of Jelebu where they may be two or three months later (*Warta Kerajaan Negri Sembilan*, 1967, 57, 78–81; 1970, 173–4, 179–80).

For Malacca, official reports make no mention of the failure of the planting season to coincide with the October maximum of rainfall. The sole authority, Muhammed Ja'afar (1897, 297) is equivocal.

It is the established custom in Malacca territory to plant rice once a year and the season for doing so generally falls about the month of Zilkaidah or Zilhijah. In starting planting operations, however, the object is if possible to coincide with the season when the West wind blows, because at that time there are frequent rains and accordingly the earth of the rice-field becomes soft and easy to plough.

But, as was noted earlier (p. 39) the Muslim year falls short of the solar year by 11 days and these months could not possibly have generally fallen

at the same period of the year, unless of course some local variant of the
Muslim calendar was followed. In all likelihood, the seasons rather than
the calendar were followed, at least in more recent times.

SYSTEMS AND STANDARDS OF FARMING

In these contrasting environments, the range of ecological niches was
greater in the inland hill-and-valley terrain than in the plain. Thus, inland,
rice was but part, albeit a major part, of an elaborate system of mixed
farming whereas on the plains, rice-growing was virtually a system of
monoculture. Inland, the valley floors were devoted to wet rice cultivation,
in many instances under irrigation, and to the grazing of livestock,
including buffaloes and goats. Permanently wet tracts were commonly
planted with sago. The lower slopes of the hills were devoted to orchards,
including coconut and areca. Beyond these, the slopes were occupied by
ladangs in which a wide range of crops was cultivated; hill rice, tobacco,
sugar, coffee, pepper, 'chocolate'[1] and maize (ST 27.9.1877). Even streams
bore their share of produce, being dammed up to form fish ponds from
which periodic fish-drives brought large sums in addition to a constant
supply of food. But it was from the sale of buffaloes, goats and poultry
that most of the cash income was derived (Negri Sembilan AR 1892,
6).[2] Agriculture was supplemented by the collection of jungle produce,
including damar (a resin), gutta, gum benzoin, kayu gharu and rattan which
were exported by river to Kuala Muar and by road to Malacca and Sungei
Ujong (Negri Sembilan AR 1886). On the whole, standards of cultivation
amongst the Minangkabau were superior to those of Malacca, a fact
attested to by numerous observers, and each family had a wide range of
sources of income (e.g. Gray, 1852, 370; Macpherson, 1858, 295; Daly,
1882, 399; SFP 28.4.1890).

In Malacca a range of income sources was less common. Though farms
adjacent to the low hills of the western and central plains and also along
the Kesang road included within their boundaries both dry and wet land
(see Malacca P.W.D. Survey Dept. Field Books 1876–86), the bulk of the
farms were on the plain. Apart from the growing of coconuts and areca
around the homesteads and the cultivation of vegetables in the dry season
by Chinese rice farmers, sources of income other than rice were virtually
non-existent (Malacca AR 1884, 962; Logan, 1887, 14). Jungle products
could not readily be collected because the jungle was too far away, the
terrain did not allow the easy construction of fish-ponds and none existed,
the buffaloes and cattle were employed for draught purposes, whereas
amongst the Minangkabau they were not, and moreover cattle were
frequently decimated by disease. Both regions were equally susceptible to
disease but whereas in Malacca farmers lost their means of traction and
hence could not till their lands, in the Minangkabau region the loss was

[1]Possibly cacao, though if so, this would be the earliest report of it in the Peninsula.

[2]Following British control, much of the hill land was given over to Chinese for the cultivation
of tapioca. The growing of hill rice was also prohibited (Negri Sembilan AR 1887, 1366;
Smith, 1891).

merely of one source of cash (Malacca AR 1892, 576). To cap these disadvantages, yields per unit of area were lower in Malacca than inland though this was compensated for by larger farms (Gray, 1852, 370; Hervey, 1884, 256).

IRRIGATION

Minangkabau farmers were highly skilled irrigators. Malaccans had but little idea of how irrigation might be practised. Admittedly there was less need for it in the heavy clay soils of the plains where gradients were gentle, than on the coarser soils formed from granitic detritus lying in the more steeply graded valleys of the interior. Indeed, on the plains, yields were depressed more because of too much water rather than too little (Braddell, 1853, 73). Nevertheless water shortages did occur because when the usual six-month growing-period rice varieties were used, the dry period of January-February occurred before the crop was really fully grown and ready to ripen.

Cultivation in the Malacca plain thus fell into the rain-rice category. Nevertheless supplementary irrigation was desirable and, to this end, the government had at various times constructed permanent dams in inland valleys at Bringin, Blimbing and Krubong, while on the Malacca river the rakyat constructed temporary earth and timber dams (*SFP* 14.5.1892). But on the whole irrigation and drainage were not a success.

The records show that thousands of dollars have been spent on amateur drainage schemes, many of which have not only proved failures but made things worse. Dams have been constructed in the wrong places, or else when made have been allowed to decay; drains and canals have been cut which proved useless, while useful ones have not been kept up.

Malacca AR 1893, 7.

Matters were quite otherwise in the Minangkabau lands, where governmental assistance for irrigation was refused prior to 1900 (NSSS 804/96; 2021/97). The extent to which the lands were irrigated is difficult to establish. The statement that, 'The planters. . .are now constructing dams and water-races for the better irrigation of their fields' (Negri Sembilan AR 1907, 3), would indicate a substantial reliance on rainfall.

Three main types of irrigation system were used. The simplest was that by which a stream was tapped towards the head of a rice valley and the water was led into meandering channels running more or less parallel to the main bed. In some cases the tali ayer was led along the sides of the valleys a foot or so above the general level of the fields. Nowhere was there a regular system of distributaries. This form of run-of-the-river irrigation was confined to small streams. Not a single source mentions this type of irrigation but during field interviews elderly local informants were unanimous in asserting its age.

The second class of irrigation was like the first in respect of the form of the distributaries. In this case, however, the main stream, always a fairly small one, was dammed by means of a rough construction of stakes, brushwood and mud six feet or so in height. A limited amount of storage was thus available, but since the dam lacked a sluice, stored water could be distributed only by breaking down part of the dam wall and this was rarely done since the pond also functioned as a fish-pond and as a bathroom. Both this and the preceding system were confined to small streams, many of which dried up in the dry season and complete independence from rainfall was not obtained (Kuala Pilah MR 6/1895). Both systems would seem to have been widespread though documentary sources are fragmentary.

Much more spectacular than the two systems described thus far was kinchir ayer or water-wheel irrigation.

> The contrivance is a simple one. It consists of an undershot wheel of light bamboo, which is placed in the current of the river. On the circumference are fixed short bamboo tubes, at intervals. The angle at which these are set is such that they fill with water, which, gathered at the lowest point, as the wheel rotates, is carried to the highest, where it is discharged laterally into a wooden receiver, from whence it is conducted so as to distribute the water into the surrounding fields.
>
> Jelebu AR 1892, 525.

The conduits were made of split bamboo and the whole apparatus carried on its work unattended (Daly, 1882, 399).[1]

The use of the kinchir ayer was necessarily confined to large streams where there was sufficient current to drive it. It was used mainly in the drier, inland parts of the region. In Jelebu some 2,000 acres were irrigated thus (Jelebu AR 1892, 525). Upstream from Kuala Jempol, 'Each block of padi land [was] systematically irrigated by water mills on the river' (ST 25.9.1877). They almost certainly were in use at Lenggong and Sri Menanti where they were still to be found in the early 1950s but reports from the southern portions of the region, Rembau, Johol and Naning, are lacking.

In theory, the provision of irrigation water would lead to double-cropping of rice, but in practice it would seem that not only was there insufficient water in most areas for this to be undertaken, but also that double-cropping was never contemplated even when, as happened occasionally, the crop failed. Nevertheless, in 1899 double-cropping with planting in April and October was attempted by the Yam Tuan Besar, the result, however, not being reported (NSSS 3067/98).

TECHNIQUES OF CULTIVATION

Whether the higher yields obtained in the Minangkabau region as compared with the Malacca plain are to be explained by the superior techniques of the Minangkabau, is, perhaps, moot. Although methods in both regions conformed to those presented in the general model (Chapter 3), there were significant differences, and not only in the practice of irrigation.

---

[1]No reports exist indicating the size of the machine, but one in a photograph in Wright and Reid, 1912, 170, would seem to be eight to twelve feet in diameter.

In the Minangkabau areas, but not in Malacca, the first operation of the agricultural year was the repair of irrigation facilities. Water-mills and channels were repaired and temporary dams made from stakes, rods, stones and brushwood were repaired if still in reasonable condition or torn down and rebuilt if not, as was usually the case in alternate years (Newbold, 1839, 1, 264).

Soil preparation seems not to have commenced with the cutting down of grass and weeds, as for instance in Krian. In the Minangkabau lands, grass, which had replaced the stubble of the previous year's crop, was normally well eaten down by livestock and clearing was thus avoided (Tampin MR 10–12/1887). In Malacca, the previous season's stubble was apparently trampled under water by cattle just after the harvest (Cameron, 1865, 383). This presumably delayed the growth of grass and weeds which, unless particularly tall, were later ploughed under.

Both buffalo-ploughing and trampling by penned cattle were practised in Malacca, the former being more common (Cameron, 1865, 383; Malacca AR 1894, 2). Following ploughing, first of the prospective nursery and then of the rest of the land, an iron harrow was brought into play to break up clods. On land which had remained fallow for a long while a roller was employed to knock down tall weeds prior to ploughing. Ploughing and harrowing were subsequently repeated, this second harrowing being with a wooden implement (Muhammed, 1897, 298–300). Although buffaloes were more numerous in the Minangkabau areas, except part of the Jasin district, than in Malacca, they were used neither for ploughing nor for puddling the soil. The heavy *changkol*, hoe, wielded by women, in those parts the landowners, was used for the initial stage of soil preparation, followed by harrowing (Macpherson, 1858, 298). The possession of a buffalo and plough was a major economic advantage which in 1892 was worth $10 to $12 per season. Not only was a good deal of irksome labour avoided but roughly double the area which could otherwise be cultivated could be handled by a single family (Malacca AR 1892, 576). Thus ploughing helped to offset lower yields and resulted in the larger fields of Malacca.

The remaining methods of cultivation were similar in both regions. Wet nurseries were used. Transplanting, without the aid of a dibble, was the same. Weeding of the crop was not reported though it was probably practised in the rest of the Minangkabau lands as in Rembau where the fields were much better kept than in Malacca (Hervey, 1884, 256). As elsewhere, at harvest and following the taking of the 'rice-soul', only the culms were cut, with the common tuai. Although the tuai was universally used in the inland regions, on the plains near Malacca, sickle-harvesting, described as a 'modern method', was preferred for its speed (Muhammed, 1897, 303).

Following harvest the treatment of the crop varied. Cameron (1865, 382–3) implied that in Malacca the bundles of culms were not threshed but that the grain was stripped off as and when required for husking. Bundles, not loose grain, were offered for sale. Again in Malacca, Muhammed Ja'afar (1897, 302) noted that it was a modern practice for a box to be made for the purpose of threshing the rice, and a temporary granary built to keep it in. The former practice was not reported from the Minang-kabau region. Permanent granaries, built adjacent to the house, were reported in the predominantly Minangkabau district of Alor Gajah though not elsewhere (Logan, 1849, 26). Threshed grain or unthreshed bundles were kept in the home, the receptacle being made of bark.

YIELDS

Most descriptions of crop yields are annoyingly vague, Newbold's enthusiastic report of a return of 'more than two hundredfold', for example, giving no real information since he failed to report the sowing rate (Newbold, 1839, 1, 115). Nevertheless the popular view was that yields in the Minangkabau region were superior to those of the plain (Gray, 1852, 370) which were inferior to those in some other parts of the Peninsula (see p. 121). In Johol, for example, one gantang of seed never produced less than a hundredfold, i.e. 400 gantangs/acre at the usual sowing rate of four gantangs to the acre, compared with Malacca where the yield was seldom more than fifty to sixtyfold, i.e. 200–240 gantangs/acre (Gray, 1852, 370). In Rembau the average yield was eighty to ninetyfold, 320–360 gantangs/acre (Hervey, 1884, 256). These are yields per unit of area, however, and though direct evidence is lacking, it is likely that production per farm was greater on the plains than amongst the hills where an 'average sized holding . . . gives say 400 gantangs of padi' (Negri Sembilan AR 1892, 12). But then plains farms were larger and, compared with Minangkabau farms, produced a smaller range of commodities other than rice.

SIZE OF FARMS AND FIELD PATTERNS

Usable farm-size data are not extant. The sketch plans in the Malacca P.W.D. Survey Department field books (1876–86) are not drawn to scale and provide insufficient data for reconstruction without a great deal of labour. Nor, in most cases, do they contain land-use data.

Prior to the extinguishing of the Malacca tithe-impropriators' rights, holdings were to be measured in square miles. Farms though, were probably a good deal larger in Malacca than in most other parts of the Peninsula. The plots vary in size from less than half an acre (house-lots?) to around forty acres, with an average size of about ten acres, but though these were bottom lands it is not certain that rice was grown on them (Malacca P.W.D. Survey Department 1876–86).

In at least some of the Minangkabau areas, notably Sri Menanti, many holdings of rice land were sub-economic, i.e. smaller than one acre, as early as 1891 (NSSS unnumbered file). Much the same was true in parts of the Kuala Pilah district (Kuala Pilah MR 6/1895). For Rembau the evidence is equivocal, Hervey (1884, 256) merely suggesting that, 'The sâwah divisions ('jalor' or 'pêtak'. . .[were] a good deal smaller than those in our territory [Malacca]'). To what extent this smallness reflected intense sub-division as the result of inheritance or, alternatively, met the exigencies of water control in a situation where the valley gradients were fairly steep (as compared with the plain), is unknown. Both factors were doubtless present.

In the Minangkabau lands, the fields are frequently rectangular or irregular in shape, though in the former case, the ratio of length to breadth is rarely greater than two. This was presumably so in the past too. It is tempting to attribute this field pattern to the predominance of hand tillage but there is no conclusive evidence. The plains area now displays a wide range of field patterns but with strip-fields, in which the length to breadth ratio approaches ten, seemingly predominating in the older areas. Certainly the holdings were commonly of this shape, probably reflecting a desire to obtain the benefits of the varied ecological niches provided by river frontage, flood-plain, piedmont and hill-slope (see Malacca P.W.D. Survey Department 1876–86). Strip-fields undoubtedly speed ploughing and in a region of low gradients, a foot per mile or less being common, a close network of bunds for water-control was unnecessary though bunds invariably indicated lot boundaries (Cameron, 1865, 382).

SETTLEMENT PATTERNS

The two regions shared common settlement patterns in that in both of them two major types of settlements occurred, dispersed and agglomerated. In the vicinity of Malacca town, individual dwellings, some with coconut trees nearby, were scattered about the plain (Logan, 1887, 4, 8). Similarly in a Minangkabau area, the Muar valley upstream from Kuala Jempol, 'Large rice-fields, from a quarter to half a mile in width [were] studded with Malay huts and gardens. . . .' (Daly, 1882, 399). The same was true in the Terachi valley. At Parit, the '. . . highly-cultivated valley [was] studded all over with houses . . . .' and near 'Bandole' the 'open country' was studded all over with detached houses (D'Almeida, 1876, 375–6). Loose agglomerations of dwellings were set within the matrix of dispersed dwellings as for example at 'Bandole', 'a scattered village' (D'Almeida, 1876, 375).

The pattern of dwellings dispersed over flat land, with a thickening of settlement into a hamlet or village here and there was perhaps not as common as the sources indicate. A piedmont location, in modern times the invariable location, is suggested by those few sketch plans in the Malacca Survey Department field books in which houses are drawn (Malacca P.W.D. Survey Department 1876–86). In a single report, from Alor Gajah, a somewhat linear form is implied, '. . . a belt of fruit trees divided into several orchards, each surrounded by a fence and over-shadowing a house. This cultivated slope rests on an unusually broad paddy flat. . . .' (Logan, 1849, 26). Moreover, each house had adjacent to it a granary,

. . . a light and neat structure raised some feet from the ground, well-roofed and having its sides of narrow bambu [sic] placed . . . so as to allow a free passage to the air. The paddy is...stored in cylindrical receptacles about $2\frac{1}{2}$ feet high and 3 to 4 broad....

Logan, 1849, 26.

Similar structures, however, were not reported elsewhere.

TENURE

Just as areas of Minangkabau settlement can be distinguished (by the striking upturned roofs of the houses) so too can land tenure which was very different from that of Malacca or indeed any other part of the Peninsula. It was not so much that the rakyat had neither written title nor absolute ownership in the English sense (their absence was common enough) but that the disposition of land was usually a female, not a male, prerogative. By Minangkabau custom, land was vested in the tribal chiefs (*Undang-Undang*[1]). But family lands, *tanah pesaka*, were under the control of groups of matrilineally-related women and their families. Men were not allowed to own any of this 'redeemed land', *tanah tebusan*[2] (Alwee, 1967, 40), though in British times they certainly acquired land, presumably 'unredeemed land', *tanah waris*. Out of 560 lots of land in three Minangkabau villages in Malacca territory, only 15 per cent were owned by men. In contrast, of 220 lots in four Malaccan villages, 77 per cent were owned by men.[3] Data permit neither the division of landowners into the rakyat and other groups nor the analysis of size of holdings. It is clear, however, that chiefs of various ranks, through their womenfolk, controlled larger areas than rakyat (NSSS 354/93; 380/93).

It was judged shameful in the extreme for tanah pesaka to remain uncultivated or to pass out of the family or if perchance out of the family, then further than the *perut* or clan of which the family was a member. Further sanctions against slovenly work undoubtedly existed and where a family, by reason of misfortune, was unable to adequately till its lands, aid was given, usually by fellow members of the perut.

Prior to the irruption of British and Chinese interests, land bore no money value (Maxwell, 1884). Following the takeover, conflict arose only in Jelebu, which was partly depopulated, and in the Minangkabau areas of south-east Selangor and Sungei Ujong where tin and rice interests clashed (see p. 150). The tie between man and land was a strong one, leading to a stable economic system subject only to the vagaries of nature and politics.

The considerable variation of the area under rice in the Settlement of Malacca would suggest that there was less stability there than further inland. Certainly, in the Malacca plains lands, the almost mystical tie

---

[1]*Undang* also contains the meanings of law, statute and precept, indicating one function of a chief. Full descriptions of Minangkabau society, law and custom are to be found in Alwee (1967), Gullick (1958), Hooker (1968a, b), Wilkinson (1908) and Winstedt (1934).

[2]Tanah tebusan were lands acquired by the early settlers by nominal payments to the Undang. Lands not so redeemed belonged to the Undang and the *Suku Biduanda* (see Alwee, 1967, 40).

[3]Further details are given in Hill, 1973, 310.

between man and land was less strong than in the Minangkabau lands, though by no means completely lacking as is witnessed by the persistence of magico-religious observances pertaining to rice (Muhammed, 1897, 298, 301–2).

Lands in the Settlement were considered to have a monetary value, this undoubtedly a consequence of the introduction of written titles, transferable and mortgageable. As was noted earlier (p. 125), numbers of the rakyat were merely tenants of urban landowners. Others had mortgaged lands to money-lenders and others and some, being unable to meet their liabilities, had become landless as a result. Though some rakyats thus lost ownership of their land, there is little evidence that they were thrown off their lands by their new landlords in any number.[1] By the 1890s landlordism was officially described as 'rare' (Malacca AR 1892, 576).

Although landlordism was not absent from the largely Minangkabau lands of inland Malacca, there is no evidence that it existed in the Negri Sembilan. In the Settlement various landlord-tenant arrangements were in force in different places and 'customary rents' were more common than purely economic rents,

Thus in the 'Ulu Mukims' it is usual to divide the produce equally between the owner and the planter, an arrangement which bears much resemblance to the European 'Metayer' system, while in the villages near the sea, the owner gets a third of the produce, if he provides the seed only, or half if he also provides manure etc., the planter simply doing the work. Occasionally, however, a money rent is agreed upon, which of course tends to approximate to the economic rent of the land.

Malacca AR 1892, 576.

THE SPREAD OF CAPITALISM

The conferment upon land of a monetary value was but one symptom of the spread of new ways of valuing things. Money had, of course, long been used but extension of its use was officially encouraged by the commutation of quit-rents into money. More important was the development of strong demands for farm produce in Malacca, the tin lands of Sungei Ujong and parts of Jelebu and Kuala Lumpur. Prior to the establishment of British control in the Negri Sembilan and Selangor, the main selling point for rice, vegetables and livestock was Malacca town. Following British control and the burgeoning of non-foodstuff production, markets which had once been largely local with some export to Malacca, became linked to more distant parts.

In the Minangkabau areas, but not elsewhere, a two-tiered system of rice-pricing existed. Locally, since rice was grown by the Malays,

...primarily for own consumption, they were hardly at all concerned with its value in exchange....In fact it is customary here [Jasin] in the event of a good crop not to sell the surplus but to store it...and in certain of the [Minangkabau] villages of the interior it is...subject to a convention or customary price which is fixed, and is always lower than the price that could be got in an open competitive

[1] Dispossession by the Crown was perhaps commoner. See p. 124.

market. The market price of *padi* being 5 to 7 cents a gantang, the customary price
in the villages... is 3 cents only.

Malacca AR 1892, 575.

In the remoter parts of Negri Sembilan, money and the money economy
were largely lacking. Javanese coming to Jelebu, for example, '... remark
that the people of Jelebu so long as they have food are content' (Jelebu
MR 9/1890). Nevertheless the money economy spread, and swiftly as new
wants were created amongst the people. Cazalas, the acting District Officer
at Kuala Pilah was to remark that,

Ten years experience of the people here have demonstrated... that weakness for
fine clothes and for adorning themselves with gold and silver ornaments has
increased in proportion as facilities for procuring money has [*sic*] advanced... a
fondness for tweed suits, felt caps, smoking caps and even the 'sola topi' has been
creating [*sic*].

Kuala Pilah MR 3/1896.

The results of this process are difficult to establish. The cultivated area
continued to increase but this could be attributed as much to continued
population growth as to a demand for the things money could buy. Was
one result of accumulating money the application of increased capital to
rice-growing? There is no evidence of this in either Malacca or Negri
Sembilan, though in the Malacca plains region the adoption of modern
means of harvesting and threshing clearly indicate the spread of the view
that 'time is money'. Rather, the spread of an economy related to more
distant markets in all likelihood resulted in the diversion of the bulk of
such funds as were invested, into the production of crops other than rice.
It was not that local rice could not compete with imports from Kedah or
regions beyond the Peninsula, but rather that other products brought
more in the market. These included poultry, goats, buffaloes, and jungle
products, the trade in which was largely in Chinese hands (Negri Sembilan
AR 1892, 507). Other alternatives to padi existed. Fruit-growing was a
profitable enterprise but few local people undertook this activity which
remained largely in the hands of immigrant Malays (Jelebu AR 1891,
498). From about 1895, considerable numbers of hill small-holdings
ranging in size from three to fifteen acres were taken up for coffee and
coconut cultivation (Negri Sembilan AR 1896, 50).

The initial development of estates and the possibility of wage labour in
them or on government roads also aided the spread of money while
providing a useful stop-gap when harvests failed (Tampin MR 5/1897).
Another alternative source of income lay in either letting of hill lands to
Chinese for the growing of tapioca or engaging in wage-labour for them.
This was a major source of money in both states. In some cases rice land
was given over to tapioca, as at Paya Rumput and in the Ayer Pa'abas
district of Malacca (Negri Sembilan AR 1888, 1176). This phase was no
more than a flash in the pan since each plot occupied by tapioca could have
no more than two or, less commonly, three crops taken from it. The

tapioca boom likely resulted in some damage to rice fields because of silting following clearance of the hills, but this cannot be documented, and it must be concluded that no lasting harm was done, if equally, no lasting good.

It would seem therefore that by the 1890s, rice-growing on the Malacca plain was already partly commercialized and mostly had been so for a considerable period. The large size of the holdings and the techniques used and the narrow range of commodities produced—rice with a few coconuts and other fruits, possibly vegetables near the town—all suggest a fair degree of market specialization and commercialization. In the Minang-kabau lands the farms were smaller and though in some respects the techniques of cultivation were more sophisticated than those on the plain, the agricultural economy was less specialized and was commercially-oriented only to a limited degree. Rice-growing, however, was not abandoned in favour of more remunerative crops, as happened in Lower Perak; tradition was too strong for that. Moreover, as Lister noted (Negri Sembilan AR 1892, 12), rice-growing still repaid the cultivator for the time and labour he devoted to it. '. . .I find it may just do so connected as it is with his proprietorship of orchard garden and grass land and with the rearing of stock and poultry.'

8

The Marchlands

Kita orang kosong, orang miskin.

Che Elimit of Beneh, Pahang, 1890[1]

The Chinese working on [tin-]mining licences are the terror of Malays....

F.W. Nicholson, 1899[2]

BETWEEN the unsettled forests of the mountain ranges and the established areas of wet rice cultivation lay a large fringing zone. In these marchlands settlement was more or less permanent, except on the flanks of the ranges and in the south of the Peninsula, but the cultivation of rice was largely temporary. This is not to suggest that all rice was grown by shifting cultivation, but only that extensive areas of permanent rice-growing were lacking. Each settlement, whether more or less permanent Malay village or temporary cluster of aboriginal huts, was surrounded by its lands and these in turn were separated from neighbouring settlements and lands by intervening tracts of forest. It was, above all, a zone of colonization, though it contained some settlement nodes of long standing. In the local economies of the region rice-growing was rarely of prime or sole interest, even amongst aborigines whose economy was to a considerable degree self-sufficient.

The analysis of such a large region, comprising the bulk of the land area of the Peninsula, demands subdivision for the sake of clarity. The primary division adopted is first, those areas in which Malays were predominant. In these, rice-growing and settlements were largely permanent, or at least were developed with some idea of their being permanent. These areas included first, the stanniferous western piedmont lands extending in a strip from Kinta south to the vicinity of Lukut where this 'tin zone' reaches the coast, and second the Selangor coast lands, the two regions both being actively colonized from the 1870s onwards. The conflicts of rice and tin interests were important in the tin zone and these are considered subsequently. Another major region was Pahang, in places metalliferous, though conflicts of interest were of much less importance. The rest of the area, in which rice-growers were mainly Malays, comprises Johore

---

[1] 'We are the empty people, we are the poor', Kuantan AR 1890.

[2] Settlement Officer to CLR 29.4.1899, NSSS 1236/00.

and Singapore in which states, however, rice-growing was of minor importance.

In a second primary category may be placed those lands occupied largely by aboriginal tribespeople in which neither settlement nor cultivation were permanent, although each 'tribe' or band occupied its own clearly defined lands, usually a river-basin, within which cultivation proceeded on an irregular cyclic basis. In areal terms, the flanks of the ranges formed a region solidly aboriginal and from this core extended salients into Malay territory. To the south of a line in the vicinity of Tasek Bera, the ranges give way to a region in which isolated massifs, hills and valleys interdigitate. Here, forest, aboriginal and Malay lands and later Chinese-occupied lands were juxtaposed, though on the whole, Malay settlements tended to be located in coastal and in the lower though usually not estuarine areas, with aboriginal lands more commonly in the clear-water sections of river-basins. The areas occupied by aborigines were probably much more extensive than at present, or at least they were to be found much nearer the coast than nowadays.

THE COLONIZED LANDS

It is ironical that the number of sources for the reconstruction of the pattern of rice-growing is greater for this region in which rice was relatively unimportant in the overall economy than for regions in which rice was paramount. However, while it is not wholly true that the interior was a *terra incognita* prior to British protection as Mills (1966, 201) claimed, little enough is known of agriculture in the region prior to that time. Anderson (1824) at least provides some indication of settlement nodes, most of which were clustered along the lower reaches of the major rivers (see Fig. 14). Since these reaches were largely brackish or salt, it is certain that rice-growing was of minor importance in that environment. It was possibly of greater importance in the middle reaches of rivers such as the Selangor and Klang, though not the Bernam and the Langat which were but vast fresh-water swamps. In fact though, it seems likely that sago, not rice, was the main locally-produced staple (Swettenham, 1875, 3).

At a time when local chieftains kept a firm control of river-borne traffic, it may be conjectured that some attempt was made by the inhabitants of inland, largely mining centres, to render themselves less vulnerable to interruptions of their lines of communications. In the south, Sungei Ujong was a mining area of some note, having a population of some 1,400 in 1838. But although it was '. . . in some parts extremely rich in [tin] ore, . . . the quantity produced is very trifling owing to the interference of petty chiefs who object to the opening of new mines; the water from those already in operation. . . spoils their paddy sawahs. . .' (*SFPW* 8.2.1838).

Colonization by 'foreign' Malays was in progress during the 1850s when 'bold, fanatical and strong-handed' Rawa people were reported as establishing themselves in great numbers in the interior (*SFP* 24.12.1852;

3.6.1853). Rice growers in the Sumatran highlands, they presumably continued to be so in their new home.

The effects upon agriculture and settlement of the broils of the quarter century preceding British protection are easy to envisage but almost impossible to document. Certainly the burning of rice fields and villages was a standard tactic in war. The net result was that at the beginning of British control some of the regions were virtual *tabla rasa*, at least in terms of Malay agriculture and settlement.

PERAK INLAND

This region included the Kinta basin and the piedmont extending south to Tanjong Malim. For the most part cultivation was temporary and although in the northern part of Kinta in 1880 an active penghulu was busy '. . . in the formation of new and the reconstruction of old fields on the irrigation system', this was exceptional (Deane, 1880, 238). Around Ipoh and at Sungei Raia, Weld (in Lovat, 1914, 351–2) reported open padi land, across which, to save money, he proposed to build roads. But temporary cultivation was the rule, swamps and hills being treated alike in that the forest was cleared and the seed flung onto the soil, 'paddy turbuang'[1] as Murton (1878, 107) called it. Cleared areas were commonly linear in form, along the paths and elephant tracks as between Ipoh and Pengkalan Bahru or Ipoh and Gopeng (Murton, 1878, 107; Weld in Lovat, 1914, 352).

To the south lay the swamps of Bidor and Batang Padang margined on their inland side by low hills. In this area there were few Malays though some aborigines lived in '. . . comparatively permanent houses and to a great extent conforming to the customs and habits of the Malays' (Leech, 1879a, 32). Whether or not these customs included growing rice is unclear, and with almost all of the land subject to floods for five months of the year, rice may well have not been grown at all. Knaggs's list of crops included cassava, sugarcane and *sireh*, but not rice (Knaggs, 1875, 28). Towards the piedmont, however, the land was less subject to flooding and moreover, unlike that of Lower Perak, was for the most part irrigable (BPDO 116/89).

The great burst of land development in Perak in the 1880s did not significantly affect the Kinta district though in Batang Padang its effects were perhaps greater. In Kinta the cultivated land totalled only 9,000 acres and of this one-sixth was ladang, temporarily-cleared, land (Kinta AR 1888, 338–9). The few Malays who were agriculturalists preferred to grow bananas for sale to the Chinese miners, Brewster opining that there was '. . . not a really well-cultivated ten acres of rice in the whole district' (Kinta AR 1889, 190).

Nevertheless some little development of a more or less permanent nature did occur, though most people wished merely to obtain virgin forest land, *rimba*, for growing dry rice, in many cases attempting to avoid the govern-

---

[1]Malay, literally, 'thrown paddy'.

ment prohibition of this by claiming that they proposed to grow coffee, pepper or nutmeg (Kinta AR 1890, 763). Permanent development was largely by Sumatrans, who by 1894, outnumbered local Malays in the Kampar, Teja and Sungei Raia *mukims* (Kinta MR 4/1894, 203). Some worked for prominent Perak Malays such as Raja Mahmud, Imam Prang and Toh Mudah Wahab. Individual settlers took up particularly large blocks, blocks so large as to suggest that either the settler-owners employed wage-labour or worked in partnership, or, more likely, that they took up land as a speculation. At Gopeng, for instance, an area of about 355 acres of irrigated bendang land comprised only 34 holdings, of which the largest was 26 acres, the smallest 2 acres with a mean size of 10.5 acres (KLO 540/1900). The sources of income of the immigrants were particularly well-balanced, being derived partly from irrigated rice, from coffee and pepper grown on the hill slopes and from trading in and washing tin (Kinta AR 1891, 673; MR 11/1892, 12; 4/1893, 483; 6/1893, 626).

In the construction of irrigation works, Malay initiative was very much to the fore, though with varying success. Toh Muda Wahab spent $34,000 on a dam at Pinji and the Imam of Gopeng built another at Ulu Kampar where, as in all the smaller valleys, the water could be used for mining if padi-growing proved unsuccessful (Kinta AR 1896, 338; 1900, 7). Their common object was to become landlords in a big way, Abdul Wahab, for instance having forty or fifty tenants who paid him a tithe on their crop for water (KLO 397/96).

However, in many instances efforts at irrigation proved to be a waste of labour and money (BPDO 650/00). The only government-sponsored scheme in this sub-region was certainly a failure. This scheme, at Cheroh on the Cameron Highlands road, initially promised well.

The Mandelings [the settlers] are doing good work they have a large amount of jungle felled & burnt, the changkats to be planted with coffee etc. & the flat land turned into Bendangs....These people are all working together for the common good....They all live together in one square house, with little rooms all round the outside like a pigeon cote, & the mosque is upstairs in the centre of the building....

Batang Padang MR 7/1896.

Co-operative working and living were not enough, and within a year it was reported that nobody was using the irrigation system, which had cost the government $3,000 to build (BPDO 185/97). The Mandeling leader, claimed the District Engineer, had had the work built so that he could draw the $16 per month upkeep money (BPDO 221/98). Without accepting this imputation of base motives, several reasons for failure may be suggested. In the first place, Ingall, the original sponsor, was transferred and his successors took no interest in the scheme. Then the land itself did not yield a paying crop of rice and consequently was planted with coffee. In addition it may be surmised that the authority of Haji Ibrahim was inadequate to the task and the community seems to have broken up (BPDO 115/00). Similar stories could doubtless be told of other failures

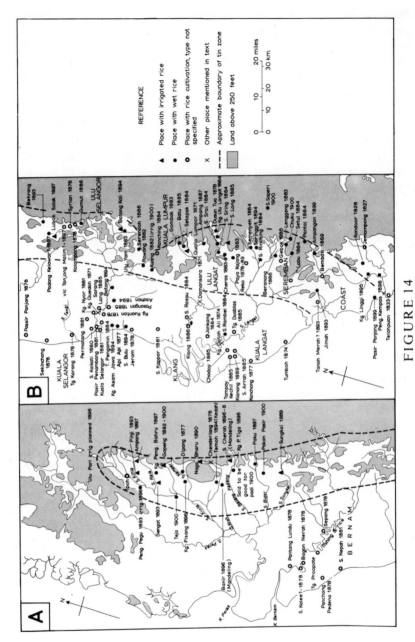

FIGURE 14

RICE-GROWING AND SETTLEMENT IN SOUTH-WEST PERAK, COASTAL SELANGOR AND THE TIN ZONE TO c.1900

REFERENCE

▲ Place with irrigated rice

● Place with wet rice

○ Place with rice cultivation, type not specified

✕ Other place mentioned in text

▬ ▬ Approximate boundary of tin zone

▓ Land above 250 feet

0   10   20 miles
0   10   20   30 km.

right down to the present, but all would share one common feature, that failure was the result of a complex of reasons, not least of which were purely personal ones.

But even where rice-growing was successful, much of the land was stanniferous and it took only the collapse of a dam or damage to the bendangs by tin-tailings from upstream or the decision to realize a newly-discovered asset, to trigger off the change from rice-growing to mining (KLO 540/1900). Even where the land was not provenly tin-bearing, tailings, especially from *lampan* workings, were an ever-present danger (Kinta MR 8/1898, 709). Yet no matter how carefully the land was farmed, in the short run, at least, tin was worth more than any crop and whilst it might have been expected that established agricultural areas would have been protected by legislation, neither established agricultural areas nor protection existed.

SELANGOR INLAND

In the inland parts of the state several agricultural regions can be recognized. In Ulu Selangor wet rice cultivation was of small significance, consisting of a few discrete centres in a number of small valleys flanking the Ranges. To the south, around Kuala Lumpur, the Setapak, Ampang and Gombak valleys were well-cultivated, but it was in the south-eastern corner of the state, on the line Cheras-Kajang-Reko, and more important-ly in the Beranang basin that cultivation was at all extensive. Only in Beranang was cultivation long-lived, that being the location of five-sixths of the tiny total of 8,000 acres existing by 1905 (Selangor AR 1905, 47). Between these nodes of permanent cultivation, shifting cultivation was the rule and this form of culture, in which hill rice was one crop amongst others, occupied a considerable proportion of the total cultivated area. This, by 1884, totalled only some 14,000 acres for the whole state, of which half was in the inland districts: Ulu Selangor, 837 acres, Kuala Lumpur, 4,492 acres and Ulu Langat, 1,500 acres (Selangor Lands Dept. AR 1883; 1884; Selangor AR 1884, 1004).

In Ulu Selangor, settlement and agriculture were patchy, mining being of predominant interest and as early as 1882 it was reported that agricul-ture was nearly abandoned in favour of mining which was more remunera-tive. At Kuang, for instance, the people had fields of maize and rice but also worked at lampans or burnt charcoal for the miners at Rawang, nearby (Turney, 1894, 30). Elsewhere, the only places at which cultivation lasted more than a year or two were Batang Kali, Yen and Kerling, but by 1890 only at Ulu Bernam were there fields of good quality, the work of a vigorous penghulu (Ulu Selangor MR 7/1890, 467).

In the intervening period, however, especially in 1884, attempts were made to finance the immigration of settlers from Sumatra and from Perak. Their plans were sound enough:

...they wish to build homes, remain permanently on the land & open up the country for Padi, Coconut, Tobacco, & other plantations, as well as the Durians,

Mangoosterns etc. When their homes are completed they intend calling over their relatives from Menang Kabau.

SSS unnumbered/84.

But although various prominent persons were granted sums ranging between $150 and $500, they had very little to show on the ground for their expenditure (e.g. SSS 249/84; 1794/84; 1516/86). Despite aid to develop land and to buy buffaloes, by 1890 so little padi was cultivated that prices were at famine levels (Selangor Lands Dept. AR 1889, 245). Subsequent developments were a mixed success. Small-scale irrigation succeeded at Batang Kali (Anon., 1894, 203). Large-scale irrigation failed at Kuang as did Mr. Loke Yew's grandiose scheme for growing rice on a 20,000-acre concession at Ulu Bernam (Selangor AR 1900, 48; 1902, 45; Ulu Selangor AR 1900, 4).

TABLE 15

KUALA LUMPUR DISTRICT: RICE AND OTHER HOLDINGS BY SIZE CLASSES, 1879

Size Class acres	190 Rice Farms %	83 Other Farms %
< 1.0	15	10
1.0– 1.9	27	13
2.0– 2.9	18	13
3.0– 3.9	8	7
4.0– 4.9	10	7
5.0– 6.9	11	11
7.0– 9.9	6	14
10.0–19.9	5	21
20.0–29.9	–	4
Total	100	100
Mean	3.4 acres	7.0 acres
Median	2.4 acres	4.9 acres
Standard deviation	5.1 ± 0.4 acres	8.5 ± 0.6 acres

Source: Kuala Lumpur District Land Statistics 1879.

In the vicinity of Kuala Lumpur, lands now a waste of tin-tailings were widely cultivated, to the extent that the whole of the Ampang valley above Kuala Lumpur was under padi (Gullick, 1955, 59). By 1884 large tracts were being opened 'everywhere'. Much of the Setapak valley was planted up by several hundred Sumatrans under Datoh Sati. These men were well acquainted with irrigated cultivation, having cut a channel from the river for that purpose. Gombak was under cultivation and lands at Petaling to the south of the town and Batu to the north were being opened up (Selangor Lands Dept. AR 1883; 1884). But although in the 1880s there was more land under cultivation in the Kuala Lumpur district than in any other, by 1893 only 4,560 acres were cultivated, of which rice accounted for some 1,170 acres, little advance on 1,155 acres in 1888, and the people were beginning to turn to the cultivation of coffee (Selangor Lands Dept. AR 1888; Selangor AR 1893, 17). No further record of rice in this district has been found and the rice lands were eventually destroyed by mining.

Surviving records, however, permit some useful comparisons with regions elsewhere to be drawn. In the area, the rice farms (total recorded 190) were on the whole smaller than farms growing other crops (total number 83). Compared with farms in other parts of Malaya, however, the Kuala Lumpur farms were slightly larger on the whole and there was a greater spread of size as measured by the standard deviation. These features are shown in Table 15.

In the district 47 per cent of the holdings recorded were held by people who may be broadly denoted a 'middle' class,[1] 49 per cent by the rakyat and 4 per cent by non-Malays. Unlike other areas for which farm size data have been presented, in Kuala Lumpur there was no significant difference in farm sizes as between the rakyat and the 'middle' class, though amongst the latter there was a tendency towards a rather greater spread of farm sizes.

TABLE 16
KUALA LUMPUR DISTRICT: SIZE OF HOLDINGS
(RICE AND OTHER LANDS) BY SOCIAL CLASS OF OWNERS, 1879

Size Class acres	Rakyat %	'Middle' Class %
< 1.0	12	11
1.0– 1.9	24	24
2.0– 2.9	18	16
3.0– 3.9	7	9
4.0– 4.9	7	11
5.0– 6.9	12	10
7.0– 9.9	10	8
10.0–19.9	10	10
20.0–29.9	1	2
Total	101	101
Mean	4.6 acres	4.7 acres
Median	2.8 acres	2.9 acres
Standard deviation	7.8 ± 0.6 acres	10.0 ± 0.7 acres

Source: Kuala Lumpur District Land Statistics 1879.

[1]Those whose names included the following were considered to form the 'middle' class: raja, tunku, engku, baginda, panglima, dato, malim, khatib, sheik, penghulu, nakhoda, haji, lebai, imam, bilal, orangkaya, pandita. There is the strong possibility that the 'sample' was biased in favour of the literate who would tend to take out title documents.

The analysis of the relationship between farm size and total farm yield provides insight into the nature of production. Since the farms were on the whole notably large, it might be surmised that production was largely for the Kuala Lumpur market nearby. Assuming that the average annual requirement for subsistence was 400 gantangs of padi per family, production greater than this would have been available for sale or kept as a reserve stock. Data from seventy-nine farms are plotted in Figure 15 on which the line A–A indicates the single family subsistence threshold. Of the seventy-nine farms, twenty-five were below the threshold and fifty-four above it. Two-thirds of the farms had a sufficient surplus to market. Of this number, fifteen farms produced sufficient to support two families (line B–B).

Since the maximum area which could be satisfactorily worked by a single family was about 4 acres, it must be concluded that most farms were only partly planted. This is confirmed by correlating size and yield. Had holdings been fully cultivated, these two variables would not be significantly correlated. In fact the value for r was –0.60, which is significant at better than 0.1 per cent, indicating that farms were not fully planted.

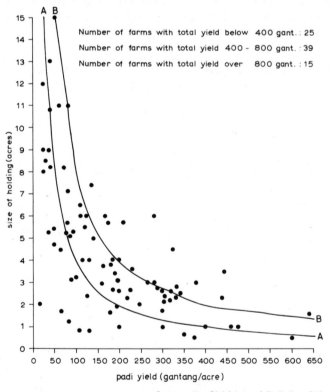

FIGURE 15
RICE YIELDS AND SIZE OF HOLDINGS IN THE
KUALA LUMPUR DISTRICT, 1879

Thus many farms had a reserve of land which could absorb at least one further family. Whether owners of these large farms later put tenants on their land or sold off a portion for profit is not known. But the potential for the evolution of landlord and tenant classes existed nevertheless.

Another question which arises is, did immigrant Malays take up larger or smaller holdings than other folk? Unfortunately only forty-seven holders of land on which rice was grown could be recognized as coming from Java or Sumatra, but of these all but five from Jambi and another five from elsewhere in Sumatra held 5 acres or more, whilst no fewer than thirteen held 10 acres or more. Thus of the immigrants, three-quarters had more than 5 acres whereas amongst the others only one-sixth had an equivalent area. The immigrants would thus seem to have taken up as much land as they could reasonably lay hold of.

In the south-east corner of the state, rice was cultivated more extensively and more permanently than anywhere else in Selangor. By 1905 the total area of rice was about 8,000 acres, of which five-sixths was in the Beranang and adjoining valleys. Earlier, however, cultivation was focused at Paya Kajang with a linear extension along the road to Cheras, and another southwards to Reko. Flanking these cultivated swamp lands were extensive areas of ladangs, occupied by Kampar and Mandeling men, but these quickly moved off when, in 1882, they came to be required to pay an increased quit-rent (Selangor AR 1883, 260; SSS 220/83; 537/83; Ulu Langat MR 12/1883). Later, from around 1886, the Beranang valley was opened.

The reason why rice-growing in this area was fairly stable seems related to the class of people there. Whereas the Sumatrans in these parts were in Syers's words, 'merely ladang men'[1] permanent settlers were Minangkabau folk mainly from Sungei Ujong, Jelebu and Rembau, as well as some direct migrants from Sumatra, the earliest of whom had moved in during the mid-1870s (SSS 273/77; 537/83; Ulu Langat MR 5, 6, 7, 9, 10/1883). These people were skilled agriculturalists and although they initially complained of lack of irrigation water, their leaders quickly set about providing it as at Kajang, Cheras, Kampong Bukit and Sungei Sring (Ulu Langat MR 6, 7/1883; 1, 4/1884; 2, 4/1886). Development was well-balanced. On the hills, after an initial catch-crop of dry rice, coconuts, coffee, tobacco and gambier were planted to provide a cash income beyond what rice might bring whilst a certain amount of tin-mining was undertaken on the side. Rice was looked upon not merely as a means of subsistence, but was grown with an eye to the market amongst Chinese miners in the neighbourhood (Ulu Langat MR 5/1883). Such was the boom in land development along the Cheras-Kajang-Reko axis during the three years from 1883, a boom aided by government grants, that by 1886 no further suitable land was available (Ulu Langat MR 2/1886).

As in Lower Perak (p. 102) a start was made with Tamil settlement, at

---

[1]Instability of Malay settlement is also suggested by migration figures for October and November 1886. During each month around 650 Malays entered the district and 370 left it (Ulu Langat MR 10, 11/1886).

least to the extent of granting loans for the purpose (SSS 2240/86; 2259/86). The Cheras-Kajang-Reko area was not further reported upon after 1894, by which time the area under rice had contracted to Paya Kajang alone where a mere 150 acres was still cultivated (Anon., 1894, 344). At the same period the total rice area of the state had shrunk to about 1,500 acres and this shrinkage was ascribed to the high profits obtainable from Liberian coffee '. . .as compared with the laborious operations, followed by smaller profits, involved in the cultivation of rice. . .' (Selangor AR 1893, 23). After this short-lived boom, however, rice again increased in importance, reaching about 6,500 acres by 1905 (Selangor AR 1905, 47).

Between the various centres of permanent *paya* and *sawah* cultivation, a good deal of land was under shifting cultivation, but the extent of this is impossible to establish. No estimate can be made for Ulu Selangor, but in the Kuala Lumpur district it was quite extensive. Most of the land under cultivation in 1883 was planted with hill rice, tapioca, bananas, maize and sugarcane, a typical dry-land crop assemblage (Hornaday, 1879, 127; Selangor Lands Dept. AR 1883). This was partially confirmed by Ridley (1896, 445-6) who noted that such forest as was left was chiefly of secondary growth, though much rimba had presumably been felled for firewood and industrial timber. The same authority also noted much evidence of secondary forest in Ulu Langat where its origin must have largely been the result of cultivation.

NEGRI SEMBILAN TIN LANDS

The progress of colonization of these lands is virtually impossible to document beyond the bare fact that rice was being grown at the places shown in Figure 14 at the times stated. The main area of cultivation was in the vicinity of Seremban where some 2,570 acres out of 3,500 acres alienated for rice were actually cultivated (Sungei Ujong and Jelebu AR 1893, 5). Elsewhere the main areas of cultivation were, in 1891, Lenggeng with 812 acres, Labu with 504 acres, and Pantai with 400 acres. If the average size of holdings is any criterion, the earliest-settled area was Pantai, average holding 2.0 acres, followed by Lenggeng, 3.2 acres and Labu, 4.2 acres (Sungei Ujong AR 1890, 1380).

It was in these lands that conflict of rice and tin interests came to a head, the areas now being largely a mass of tin-tailings. Although the actual area involved was much greater elsewhere, it is for Lenggeng that adequate documentation survives and this may be taken as a model for other areas. Potential conflict of rice and tin interests, the former of course being Malay and the latter Chinese, was present in a number of parts of the region but precisely how far these potentialities were realized during the period is difficult to document though spoilation of rice fields by tin-working existed as early as 1837 (*SFPW* 8.2.1838). Conflict arose at two points, one being the physical destruction of fields by mining, the other being the abandonment of rice-growing in the face of the greater short-term gains furnished by mining.

If agriculturalists took up the land first, they were deemed to have a prior claim, but in many instances the miners made a start at the very heads of the valleys and in the hills surrounding the lower lands, themselves often tin-bearing, which were already occupied by rice-fields. Where lampan mining occurred on the hill slopes, the bendangs below inevitably suffered as a result of the deposition of debris in the valley floor. Where hydraulicking was practised, streams were tapped in their upper courses so as to supply the requisite water, thus depriving the bendangs of irrigation water. The escape of tailings from such operations was only partly controlled and smothering of the rice-fields with slimy effluent frequently occurred.

The attitude of government towards such encroachment upon rice land by tin-miners was crucial. Until late in the 1890s the policy enunciated by successive local British officers was followed.

In places where the padi land is poor, and where for several years padi has not been planted, there is no difficulty as the surface occupier is rather better off by the appropriation of his land for mining purposes, but where it comes hardest is on the cultivators in [long-settled] districts like Pantai, where even the largest compensation benefits him only a short time. The Malay is naturally improvident, and although he may get $30 an acre for his land, which would be ample for him to open fresh sawahs elsewhere, . . . he spends the money and finds himself without either that or the land.

Sungei Ujong AR 1892, 514.

But it was not really a case of improvidence since the whole territorial basis of life was destroyed even though abundant land might exist elsewhere. As Bland pointed out, 'Under local custom land is looked-upon as the family inheritance (*Tanah Pesaka*), and a thing to be religiously preserved, and hence the Malay occupier generally objects most strongly, not only to mining it himself, but to allowing anyone else to do so'. Yet it was the same official's view that economic forces should have free play. 'I see no reason for refusing the right to mine to Chinese provided that proper compensation is paid, and subject to proper regulation. It is quite certain that if tin is to be found there, these rice fields will be mined sooner or later' (Sungei Ujong and Jelebu AR 1893, 22). By the end of the century the position had changed and although Malay squatters were not to be provided with any legal protection, those holding titles to their lands were protected from encroachment. 'I am much opposed', minuted the Commissioner of Lands, 'to allowing any agricultural land under cultivation to be annexed' (NSSS 3109/00).

The manner in which conflicts arose and were resolved is exemplified by proceedings in the Lenggeng valley, north of Seremban. This valley had been settled by migrants from Minangkabau in the 1860s and settlement was thus hardly 'comparatively new' as claimed by Bathurst, the Commissioner of Lands (Negri Sembilan AR 1897, 46; NSSS 1344/97). Mining began in 1895 though in most cases the lands involved were still held by the Chinese purchasers under agricultural, not mining titles, and such lands as were not yet being mined were rented back to their former

Malay owners. Chinese owners, who had bought the lands in the unful-
filled expectation of being permitted to mine all their lands, petitioned
government to allow them to realize their investment. The penghulu of
Lenggeng, on the other hand, complained of 'extremely large' damage to
'a great many Malays', Nicholson, the Settlement Officer, playing a
supporting role in suggesting that if nothing were done for the Malays
they would soon be compelled to abandon their land (NSSS 4396/99;
1236/00). In the event, mining was stopped and the rice lands survived.

What are particularly revealing in this affair in which the Datoh Dagang
himself was involved, are the reasons given by the people for selling their
lands. Of the dozen people concerned each held on the average nearly
5 acres and received an average of about $40 per acre. Four had had their
former lands mined out, five still planted them, paying rent to the towkay.
Of the group, two admitted that they had squandered the money, four had
performed the *haj* and the rest made no statement regarding the matter
(NSSS 1344/97). Another result, not obvious in this affair but clear
elsewhere, was the divisive effect of land sales for mining. Under British
law, owners had every right to dispose of their lands as they wished but
that they should do this to the obvious detriment of the whole community
violated every tradition. Thus the penghulu at Ampangan was strongly
opposed to the sale of sawah to Chinese for mining because this would
affect adjoining lands. Nevertheless the sale was made. The Chinese
purchased the land, the Malay sellers received $40 per acre, the Govern-
ment received $10 per acre premium and presumably everyone, except the
penghulu and the sellers' neighbours, was happy (NSSS 1965/99).

While a good case for Malay rice-growing interests can be made out,
it must largely rest upon humanitarian and very long-term economic
considerations. In states lacking any form of modern infrastructure it was
to be expected that the relatively quick and large returns of mining should
be partly invested in providing such an infrastructure. Twenty-five cents
per acre per year from quit-rents on rice land was not going to go far in
financing government, let alone providing general development capital.

SELANGOR COAST

Whereas in the inland parts of the tin zone there was considerable
justification for attempting a modest degree of self-sufficiency, in the
coastal areas there was little, even if alternative means of subsistence were
available. This was not always the case, even in British times, and spasmodic efforts were made to develop the coastlands. The coast was of two
types—a mangrove coast, especially in the Bernam, Klang and Langat
estuaries, and a sand-ridge coast, as northwards from Kuala Selangor,
where it was backed by the peat and muck soils of fresh-water swamps.
Only in the Selangor delta proper were soils, the Selangor series, thoroughly suited to rice, but these were only marginally developed during the
period.

In the mid-1850s a considerable block of rice fields extended from Telok
Penyamun on the Selangor river as far as Kampong Kedah. This area

continued to be worked, using buffaloes, until around 1860 when a severe rinderpest epidemic carried off this means of traction. As Raja Bot noted, 'Sultan Abdul Samad was not powerful enough to insist on the work being continued for though he himself liked padi planting, he could not enforce it upon the raiats of the country' (Raja Bot, 1902, 3). Further factors in the decline of rice-growing were the ease with which money could be made by trading in the Lukut, Klang and Kuala Lumpur tin-fields, and finally civil war lasting until the establishment of British control. War affected the Kuala Selangor rice fields especially severely. J.W.W. Birch, writing in 1874, somewhat overstating matters, said, 'Now not a soul was to be seen. The houses had fallen down...and the coconut and fruit trees are covered with...creepers; even the padi fields now are overgrown...' (Birch, 1892, 26).[1]

In the Kuala Langat district there were no sawahs, shifting cultivation in the swamp-forest being the rule, in a strip along the river for ten or twelve miles (Braddell, 1874, 819; Raja Bot, 1902, 2). But at Bernam, above the estuarine tract, it was reported in 1817 that, 'the population is considerable; the houses have an air of comfort, and the plantations of fruit-trees and paddy-fields appear to be well tended and cultivated' (D'Almeida, 1876, 368).

Following the establishment of British control, a considerable influx of population took place. The new administration was naturally anxious to redevelop the land, but in an orderly manner, though one Malay leader, Sheik Mahomet Ali, suggested that government insistence upon orderliness, involving documentation and proper sale of land, was making the people afraid to come into the state. But as Robinson (to CO 21.1.1878, CO 273/93) stated, 'These new arrivals wish land for nothing [but] to keep it forever without paying rent, taxes or anything...they scrape the ground in cultivating a few plantains or a little paddy and bearly [sic] live.' The migratory habits of the ladang-makers had two positive values; they sorted out good land from the bad and the economic activities from the uneconomic, though only at the cost of destroying large tracts of forest, the preservation of which was a peculiarly European desideratum.

In the following half century, three foci of cultivation came into existence. On the Bernam was a cluster of villages margined by the fishing *bagans* of the estuary downstream and extensive fresh-water swamps upstream. Inland from Kuala Selangor the quantum of development was rather greater than on the Bernam but along the Selangor river both settlement and agriculture were discontinuous and the solid block of rice land of the 1850s was not reconstituted. From Kuala Selangor north to the Bernam mangroves was a string of coastal settlements, in most of which some attempt at rice cultivation was made, though without much to show as a result. In the Klang valley, rice cultivation amounted to very little though it was the scene of several abortive attempts at large-scale development. At Langat was a cluster of villages on the plains

---

[1]There were in fact still people about, though not growing rice, in 1871. See D'Almeida, 1876, 371.

around the royal estates at Jugra and along the coast but these too were not surrounded by rice lands of any extent.

The lower Bernam valley contained fifteen small villages and hamlets with a total population of just over a thousand in 1879. Eighty per cent of the people were Malay and of the 552 economically active persons, 85 per cent were returned as 'planters', though it is highly likely that many supplemented their incomes by fishing and collecting rattan (Bernam MR 11/1877). As might be expected in a pioneer community, the dependency ratio was strikingly low, at 0.8 dependants per economically active person. This, of course, was one reason for the quiet prosperity of the area. But much of the area was swampy and newcomers experienced some difficulty in obtaining lands free from inundation, and as in Ulu Selangor the small patches of rice were much subject to the depredations of elephants and other wild animals (Bernam MR 2, 3/1878).

The coastal strip southwards to Kuala Selangor was uninhabited between Panchang Pedena and Sekinchang, except for fishermen's huts, in 1877. In the following year the strip received an influx of eight or nine hundred people from Langat who were in search of better rice land, and these took up lands at many of the points at which rivers broke through the sand ridges bordering the fresh-water swamps inland. But the area was topographically of marginal suitability, though reckoned to be 'all good Paddy land' (Kuala Selangor MR 11/1877). In periods of extended rain the water level in the swamp would rise and submerge the crops in acid swamp water (Bernam MR 5/1878). During dry spells, on the other hand, water-levels fell so far as to result in crop failure and this could only have been avoided by a system of irrigation (Selangor AR 1891, 426). Preliminary survey showed that this was feasible but a scheme for irrigating 5,000 acres foundered on economic grounds, it being held that a net revenue of 2 per cent was insufficient return upon government capital (Selangor AR 1895, 5; 1896, 42). Although there were subsequent references to a large-scale drainage-cum-irrigation scheme in the Tanjong Karang section of the swamps little was done until post-Independence times (Selangor AR 1899, 40; 1901, 45). Nevertheless minor drainage works near existing foci of settlement resulted in some extension of the cultivated area, but at no time did this amount to more than about 1,200 acres (Kuala Selangor AR 1882). If much of the coastal strip was environmentally marginal, some was also economically marginal, and from the mid-1880s people began to drift away. For example, half the people of Panchang Padena moved to villages on the Selangor river, leaving the rest to fish and make atap since 'they lose money by paddy cultivation' (Kuala Selangor MR 6/1885).

As a whole the Kuala Selangor district had a population three times larger than Bernam, having, in 1881, a population of about 3,200, of which number, 92 per cent were Malays. Of the economically active, 42 per cent were padi farmers, and of the eighteen locations listed in a return of population, all but four had some padi farmers (SSS 273/81). Rice-growing, however, was far from the farmers' sole interest. Most villages produced

poultry, sago, sugarcane, areca and coconut whilst other agricultural produce included 'kinds of yam, plantains...Indian corn [maize], arrowroot
and a species of rye [millet?]' (Kuala Selangor MR 3/1884). Non-
agricultural products included salt fish, *blachan* and atap (SSS 1538/83)
giving a fairly well-balanced local economy.

The people themselves were of varied origins. The S. Kelekati and S.
Kanang people came from Perak and were thus familiar with the coastal
swamp environment (Kuala Selangor MR 3, 10/1878; 7/1884). Bugis
settled at Bukit Jerom (Kuala Selangor MR 5/1878), people of Kedah
origin were to be brought in from Krian together with the odd family
from Penang (SSS 115/81; 1935/85). Interestingly, there is not a single
report of Rawa, Mandeling, Kampar or Minangkabau people taking up
these coastlands, confirming the preference of these highlanders for the
narrow, irrigable valleys of the interior rather than the broad expanses of
coastal swamps. But although the coastlands continued to be developed
in the late 1880s, more new rice land being opened in Kuala Selangor than
in any other district of the state in 1888, this trend was quickly reversed
and by 1900 the cultivation of rice was practically given up (Selangor
Lands Dept. AR 1888; Kuala Selangor AR 1900, 2).

The affairs of Klang can be considered in brief space. Notable was the
Selangor Sago and Padi Company fiasco. The Company was managed by
a former Selangor government official, Syed Zin in the role of 'Ali' and
two Chinese, Yap Shak and Teck Yong in the role of 'Baba'. The Company
took up 6,000 acres in 1883 but initially succeeded in planting only a few
tens of acres, though by 1890 it had actually cleared and planted about
350 acres (Selangor Lands Dept. AR 1883; SSS 693/84; 1501/84; 2102/86;
Selangor AR 1890, 1365).

Equally unsuccessful were the speculations of Tunku Dia Udin who
took up 2,000 acres at Sungei Rasau for irrigated rice and, of all things,
teak, and the speculations of Tamby Abdullah, an Indian, who was
granted 1,000 acres on which to settle his countrymen (Selangor Lands
Dept. AR 1883; SSS 1813/84; 1832/86). Another briefly successful enterprise was that of the Dato Dagang whose 600-acre areca and rice plantation was worked with Javanese labour (Selangor AR 1886, 568). By 1888
the cultivation of rice showed a serious falling off in Klang, as elsewhere
in Selangor, because cash could come more easily than by growing rice
(Selangor AR 1888, 1050).

The Langat district had a population of 2,800 in 1879 and of this number
87 per cent were Malay. The greater portion, 68 per cent, was returned as
'gardeners' thus giving little indication of the extent of rice cultivation
(Selangor Census 1879). Until the mid-1880s, '...the men in Langat have
hitherto collected two or three klamins [families] together and gone away
into the jungle & thrown down the paddy & left it to come up as best it
may...' (Langat MR 4/1884). A report of 1883 suggested that only 48
acres were under padi[1] though here and there, especially near Jugra, were

---

[1]This tiny total possibly referred to permanently-cultivated rice fields.

evidences of former cultivation (Langat MR 10/1883; SSS 1863/83). By 1889 there was some improvement, Javanese settlers succeeding in taking two crops in a year from their land (Selangor AR 1889, 1522).

Interest lies rather in the role of the royalty in land development. This initiative took two forms, assistance to settlers and large-scale, plantation-style working. Settlers at Kanchong, Tampoi Kechil and S. Ara received aid from the Sultans' privy purse (Langat MR 3/1885). In 1892 advances totalled $3,000 (Selangor AR 1892, 11). In addition the royal demesne was extended, involving the large-scale cultivation of pineapples at Jugra (Langat MR 3/1884), and of rice, coconut, areca and bananas at Jelutong, where Javanese coolies were employed (Langat MR 6/1884). Later, plans were made to open up a large area for rice at Tanjong Duablas but these never came to fruition (FMS Lands Dept. AR 1898, 26; Selangor AR 1898, 43; 1899, 40).

Other members of the royalty were also active. The Raja Muda planned to open 800 acres at S. Rambei but this was for sugar, not rice, though individual settlers there were allowed to grow it as a catch-crop in an efficiently organized programme of development (SSS 2370/86; Langat MR 5, 6/1884).

He [the Raja Muda] first allows anyone who wishes it to make a clearing and plant padi. The following year this padi ladang is prepared for the sugarcane by Javanese labour while the padi planter moves off further into the jungle & clears a new patch of country which in its turn is planted with sugarcane so on till a very large area is cleared.

SSS 2370/86.

But throughout the coast of Selangor, despite the considerable efforts of the royalty, district chiefs and penghulus, the facts were that much of the land was marginal for rice under circumstances other than that of a large integrated scheme of colonization, and rice-growing was thoroughly uneconomic to boot. At the end of the period, permanent cultivation on anything but a minor scale was still half a century in the future.

PAHANG

If Pahang were an unknown land in the eighteenth century, it remained that way until after the establishment of British control in 1888. Although it was the largest state in the Peninsula, its population was small. One estimate for 1837 was 40,000, and another 50,000 (SFP 26.1.1837; Malcom, 1839, 121). Only the coastal areas and the mining areas inland were reported upon before about 1885. Medhurst (1830, 149) visited 'Pahang', i.e. Pekan, in 1828 but made no comment on agriculture. Abdullah bin Abdul Kadir noted that at Kuala Pahang, coconuts, areca, bananas and tubers were grown, but failed to mention rice. Raising livestock was the chief source of income, a feature of the agricultural economy long retained (Coope, 1949, 8). In the south-east part of the state, part of the Endau basin had been settled by Malays growing rice and maize (SFP 6.7.1837) but as late as 1890 this region was still largely unoccupied, except by a scattering of aborigines (Swinney, n.d., 7). The state as a whole would seem to have been rice-deficient[1] though apart from Pekan and the mining areas of the interior, local self-sufficiency probably prevailed. However, to judge from a report of 1885, self-sufficiency was barely achieved (Tenison-Woods, n.d., 153).

Rice deficiency or at best, bare sufficiency, prevailed for several reasons. One was the relative ease with which other sources of income could be tapped. Along the coast, sea-fishing was the prime interest, especially among immigrants from Kemaman and Trengganu. Other alternatives were the collection of gutta and rattan which were especially attractive following the abolition of the royal monopoly in 1889. These forms of activity were sufficiently remunerative for rice-growing to be of comparatively minor importance in the Kuantan district and other thinly-peopled parts of the State (Pahang AR 1894, 4; KDO 650/99). Mining was also an attractive alternative or supplement to rice-growing. In Kuantan, boat-work on the river was important and this was doubtless equally important on the Pahang. In the Pahang basin, mining was undertaken by Malays, men from Chenor, for example, regularly going off to the mines after planting the rice and returning in time to harvest it (Temerloh MR 10/1896).

Another major concern in Pahang was the intensity of flooding which was accompanied by loss of life, of livestock and other fixed capital. In 1896, again in 1897, as in 1926, severe floods occurred such that in one place people were picking their crop out of trees where it had stuck (Temerloh MR 12/1896; Pahang AR 1896, 63). In December 1896,

Vast areas in Pahang have since early in the month been submerged by a flood the magnitude of which is altogether without parallel in the last 20 years. The rice crop from K. Lipis to the mouth of the Pahang, a distance of 200 miles, & far and wide thro' the Coast Dist. has been utterly destroyed.

TDO 125/97.

Such losses were aggravated by the popular habit of planting without regard to the seasons, many Malays thinking that rice should be planted at the same relative distance of time from the conclusion of fasting month (Pahang AR 1898, 62). One result of such calamities was that, 'many people borrowed money...to tide over the scarcity of rice, & are now unable to meet their creditors without selling the land' (TDO 304/98). The rich thus got richer and the poor poorer. Another result was the decimation of buffaloes by the floods themselves and by subsequent starvation through lack of feed (Temerloh MR 12/1897).

But flood and famine were not the only killers; pestilence was at least as important since to most farmers, buffaloes were vitally necessary. Rinderpest was a major killer and its effects in the Lipis valley have been described by Clifford (Pahang AR 1900, 78).

[1]The deficiency was presumably made good by imports by sea channelled up the Pahang, though this is difficult to document, the sole reference found being to the piracy of a vessel with rice from Singapore (SCCR 1.7.1830).

The immediate result of this destruction of their cattle [i.e. buffaloes], has been to reduce the natives of the hitherto most prosperous villages in Ulu Pahang to very great straits. Their padi fields are abandoned, overgrown with jungle and a large number of men have had to quit their ordinary avocations, and seek a means of livelihood by obtaining work in the mining camps.

THE REGIONAL PATTERN

The location of places in which rice was grown is a matter of considerable difficulty, though Figure 16 is an attempt to show this. In most cases, little beyond the fact that rice was grown at a certain place and a certain time can be suggested. Nevertheless some attempt at a regional subdivision can be made.

In the western hill country, in the narrow valleys of Jelai, Raub, Bentong and Semantan, rice was grown largely by people of Minangkabau origin who had moved into the state from the west perhaps in the fifteenth century, though later, in 1644, partly withdrawing (Sircom, 1920, 151). In this region, the valleys were cultivated under two different systems. The commoner system, here and elsewhere in Pahang, was a form of dry cultivation in which river terraces were ploughed up without irrigation and a crop taken for four or five years, following which the land was fallowed for a similar period. This was termed the tenggala system. Thus as in Ulu Jelai, '. . . the whole country is an open plain, and where not cut up into padi fields, is covered with fine grass, and studded with low shrubs. . . .This plain forms the grazing ground of large herds of buffaloes' (Clifford, 1887).

Permanent cultivation, without grass fallow, was also carried out with the aid of irrigation as at Gali which had a small 'run-of-the-river' system (Pahang AR 1892, 2), or, as on the Lipis, where Swettenham (1885, 17) reported a 'gigantic water-wheel', obviously a Minangkabau kinchir ayer.

A second region comprised the Pahang valley from the vicinity of Kuala Tembeling to the seaward limit of rice cultivation somewhat upstream of Pekan.

The general character of the country bordering the [Pahang] river up as far as Kuala Tembeling is pretty much the same. Along the river bank, is a strip of jungle, 100 to 200 yards wide, with frequent small villages and plantations of coco-nut, banana and mangosteen trees. Inside of this lies a tract of open grass or swampy land, varying from 100 yards to half-a-mile in width, and beyond comes the jungle proper. The tract of open land is in places ploughed and cultivated by the natives, who use rude wooden ploughs, which, however, do the work required of them fairly well. The draught animal is the water-buffalo. . . .

Kelsall, 1894, 35.

This was, of course, tenggala cultivation, and it is significant to note that rice was not the only crop cultivated in this way: maize and Italian millet (*Setaria italica*) was also being grown in a like manner (Kelsall, 1894, 55). In the low-lying lands, permanent cultivation of wet rice was, expectably, the rule.

The third region was centred upon the Kuantan basin. This region

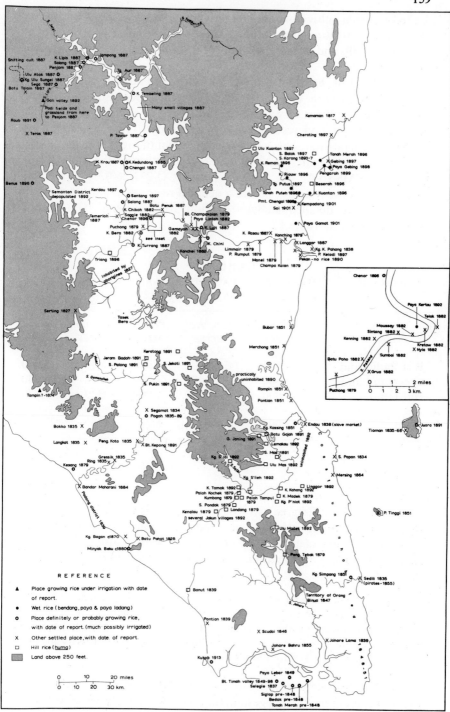

FIGURE 16
RICE-GROWING AND SETTLEMENT IN PAHANG, THE INLAND PORTIONS OF SOUTHERN MALAYA AND SINGAPORE

lacked tenggala cultivation and the only two major classes of cultivation were paya cultivation and shifting cultivation, the latter being practised both on the hills and in swamps. Many of the cultivators were Kelantanese (KDO 650/99).

For the rest of the state shifting cultivation was undoubtedly the rule, being practised both by Malays and aborigines. Because much of the northern part of the state was still unknown even in 1910, it is likely that its incidence was underestimated in Wise's report (1901), and that his Malay informants were correct in suggesting that the area of *tanah ladang* annually brought under cultivation exceeded either of the other forms (Res. Gen. FMS to Ag. HC FMS 30.1.1900, CO 273/260).

Although sources do not permit a detailed regional treatment, they do permit a more detailed analysis of cultivation systems. The overall pattern is given in Table 17.

TABLE 17

PAHANG: ESTIMATES OF AREA UNDER VARIOUS SYSTEMS OF
CULTIVATION BY DISTRICT, 1901

	Ulu Pahang acres	*Temerloh* acres	*Pekan* acres	*Kuantan* acres	*Total* acres
Wet Padi Land	5,500	8,200	1,700	440	15,840
Tenggala Land	3,500	40	2,600	–	6,140
Hill Land	4,000	200	900	320	5,420
Total	13,000	8,440	5,200	760	27,400

Source: Wise, 1901, 1.

PERMANENT WET CULTIVATION

The authorities disagree as to the extent of this form. Wise (1901, 1) suggested that about half of the rice land was under wet rice, disagreeing with the estimates of his Malay informants. There is also disagreement as to the incidence of irrigation. Rodger (Pahang AR 1891, 523) claimed that,

In some parts of Pahang the swamps utilized for rice planting are natural, but for the most part they are irrigated by artificial means, a combination of owners being formed to defray the expenses of the operation.... Malays from the neighbouring State of Kelantan are often hired...to do the necessary manual labour of digging trenches, for purposes of irrigation.

Wise, on the other hand, held that unirrigated swamp, paya, cultivation was more common, also suggesting that bunded fields, *bendang berbatas*, accompanied irrigation, whereas in paya cultivation, water was regulated merely by a single embankment at the lower boundary of the swamp (Wise, 1901, 1). It was also commonly held that the Pahang folk were too lazy to construct their own small irrigation works, since in many cases they were too poor to pay Kelantanese who were skilled in their construction, but in reality, ignorance of the methods of laying out levels for tali ayer rather than indolence was the cause (Pahang AR 1891, 523; 1897, 61).

Two features common to all permanent wet rice cultivation systems were the method of soil preparation and transplanting. Unlike Negri Sembilan, where the soil was usually tilled with a heavy hoe, the changkol, or Selangor and Krian where the implement employed was the tajak, or Malacca, Kedah and Province Wellesley where the buffalo-drawn plough was used, in Pahang a small herd of buffaloes was tethered in the wet field to churn the soil about, a process termed *melanyak*. Padi grown on land prepared in this way was termed *padi lanyak*. Transplanting, as elsewhere, was termed *chedong*, but whereas in other states any suitable plot, wet or dry, was selected for the nursery, in Pahang a dry plot under heavy secondary growth was selected (Abdul Rahman, 1920, 176).

Three distinct types of permanent wet rice cultivation can thus be recognized.

1. *Bendang berbatas.*
   a. flat land with tali ayer irrigation; melanyak soil preparation; chedongan, transplanting;—a common system.
   b. flat land with kinchir ayer irrigation, probably by heavy hoe; chedongan;—confined to Minangkabau areas of W. Pahang.
2. *Paya chedong.*
   a. swamp, no irrigation, some water-level control where possible; melanyak soil preparation; chedongan;—a common system.
   b. swamp, no irrigation; slash-and-burn only, no soil preparation; chedongan;—common only in Kuantan district.
3. *Bendang berbatas.* Flat land, no irrigation, entrapment only; various methods of soil preparation; chedongan;—not reported but unlikely not to have existed.

PERMANENT DRY CULTIVATION WITH FALLOW

Whether the tenggala system should be considered a permanent system of cultivation with grass/scrub fallow, or a short-cycle system of shifting cultivation is moot. The former is perhaps to be preferred since owners probably held prescriptive rights of dominion over their lands and not usufruct rights only. The same piece of land is always cultivated by the same holder. This was probably true in the past.

The system has been vividly described by Swettenham (1885, 21),

It was a curious sight [for a Briton] to see in the Malay Peninsula buffaloes ploughing the slightly undulating plain of dry but not hard soil and more strange still to be told that the rice grain is then sown as wheat is in the West, the ground harrowed and no irrigation done whatever, the harvest depending simply upon the rain. These fields when fallow seem to grow no weeds, only a sparse short grass and they are ploughed across and across like a chess-board several times before the wooden plough gets deep enough, then sown, harrowed and nothing more is required till the time of harvest.

These fields have for many years yielded crop after crop under these conditions, and the only renewal or manuring of the soil is the small annual flood, which rises over even these high banks. . . .

In fact continuous cultivation was not usual, a fallow of three to five years usually following three to five years' cropping, though in a few cases cropping took place in alternate years (Wise, 1901, 2; Coombs, 1917–18. 324–6). The system was also used to pioneer new land, in which case the felled timber was either burnt and then removed or vice versa (Abdul Rahman, 1920, 177). There do not seem to have been any variations of the tenggala system.

4. *Tenggala*. Flat or undulating alluvial terrace land; no water control; tenggala, plough, soil preparation; seed sown broadcast.

TEMPORARY SYSTEMS OF CULTIVATION

These were probably the most widespread of all systems in Pahang and were by no means confined to hill lands as in most other parts of the Peninsula. Certain of the systems were clearly intermediate between permanent cultivation and long-cycle bush-fallowing. In no case, however, did the Malay systems involve shifting of the settlements which was a feature confined to aboriginal bush-fallowing, discussed on pp. 165 et seq. Two swampland systems were described by the Kuantan District Officer in 1899.

. . .there are parts of them [swamps] which after three consecutive crops require to lie fallow three years to recover. . . .[The] land [is] not drained & is so low-lying that any attempt to drain it would result in an influx of sea-water. Nurseries are planted in June or July & after 40 days, determined by the progress made in the partial clearing and burning of the swamps, the plants are transplanted in the ordinary way. . . . No weeding or attention of any kind except to keep off vermin is attempted. . . .The above applies to 'payah chedong' padi & differs somewhat from the method used in the 'payah tabor'. The swamps are cleared and burnt as in the 'chedong' cases during the dry weather and the seed is scattered immediately the fire is cold so that it may sink in the light ash before rain or dew has fallen; if this be not done the exposed seed will be carried off by birds etc & no crop result. When the young padi sprouts it is pulled where the seed has fallen too thick & replanted where thin. Nine months is the period this form usually ripens in.

Closely akin to these systems was the *tugal* system.

. . .the land is cleared, burnt off and after a short interval to allow the rain to carry the ash into the earth, the seed is dropped into holes made with a pointed stick. This padi ripens [illegible] five to six months. . . . Riverside slopes are usually chosen & they are much subject to flood & the ravages of elephants and vermin. Most of the hill land can only be planted once & is never fit for use again if lalang follows the rice, but in one or two localities. . .some swelling ground is so exceptionally good that it will carry hill padi for three consecutive years & be fit again after abandonment for three years if brush-wood springs up—lalang spoils this land forever also. The hill fields are usually planted about the same time as the swamp nurseries are put down.

DO Kuantan to BR Pahang 25.11.1899, KDO 650/99.

This last system is synonymous with huma cultivation, though it is pertinent to note that tugal planting was not confined to hill swiddens, whereas simple broadcasting was not reported except in swamps (Kuantan MR 12/1898).

5. *Padi paya chedong.* As 2b but with three years' bush fallow after three years of planting.
6. *Padi paya tabor.* Swamp, no water control; slash-and-burn only, no soil preparation; seed broadcast;—Kuantan and other coastal swamps.
7. *Padi tugal (huma).* All classes of land except saline and excessively steep slopes; no water control; slash-and-burn only, no soil preparation; seed dibbled.

Attempts by government to prevent shifting cultivation or even to gain revenue from ladangs were a very mixed success in Pahang. In one case, near Kuantan, the people simply moved off when asked to pay for land, and although 'ladang licences' were issued, for a fee, in the Temerloh district, the matter was not treated seriously because little or no virgin forest was affected. Controlling legislation was not enacted until 1900, by which time 'ladang cultivation' was becoming yearly less popular (Pahang AR 1900, 78).

JOHORE AND SINGAPORE

JOHORE

Other than that cultivated by aborigines in the interior of Johore, rice was of very minor importance in the south of the Peninsula, being confined to a few minor areas mostly near river mouths. In 1834 the total population was estimated at 25,000 (*SFP* 26.1.1837). About one-tenth of this number occupied Muar, mainly the Ulu, the economy of which consisted, '. . . of a little rice,[1] sago, ivory, ebony, gold dust, tin, wax, aloe-wood, gum benzoin, camphor . . . rattans' (*SFP* 5.1.1837). Elsewhere, along the coasts, was a scattering of settlements. The east coast settlements, by mid-century, were mainly centres for fishing, exporting timber, gutta and rattan, together with a little piracy on the side[2] (Thomson, 1851; Maharajah Johore to Secy. Gov. SS 4.4.1864, MJLB). Rice-growing was insignificant. On the south coast, near Johore Lama, only shifting cultivation was reported in 1826 ('Viator', 1837, 267), whilst Scudai was the only settled place within fifteen miles of Gunong Pulai (*SFP* 28.5.1846).

On the west coast, settlements existed at Kesang on the Malacca frontier and at the mouths of the Muar, Padang, Batu Pahat, Benut and Pontian rivers (*PRM* 6.8.1828; Newbold, 1839, 2, 41–3). Of these places,

[1]Grown by shifting cultivation (Newbold, 1837b, 73; Lake, 1894, 293).

[2]The coast and islands were well-frequented by local, Ilanun (Mindanao) and Brunei pirates. See *SCCR* 25.8.1831; 15.11.1832, 4.4.1835; *SFP* 12.7.1855; 2.10.1856; Logan, 1848.

rice was reportedly grown at Kesang (*Singapore and Straits Directory 1901*, 318) but not at Muar (Lake, 1894, 293), at Batu Pahat (Burridge, 1956, 160) and, by aborigines, at Benut (Favre, 1849a, 58). Rice-growing was considered extremely difficult and as migrants developed the western coastlands, bananas, tubers and tapioca rather than rice were grown for subsistence and occasional sale, together with fruits, coconuts, copra and areca as cash crops for the Singapore market (Burridge, 1956, 160, 193; Husin Ali, 1964, 29). Gutta, to be found in the remoter areas of the State, commanded good prices, prices so good that at times cultivation was abandoned in favour of its collection (Winstedt, 1932, 91–2).

Yet like Selangor and southern Perak, Johore was considered to have great potential for rice production. In 1879, Laurie, a Ceylon planter, secured a tract of some ten square miles for large-scale rice production (*ST* 10.3.1879), but like many a similar proposal, plans remained plans. Nevertheless some expansion of the rice area seems to have taken place, and by 1912 rice was reported as being 'grown in some quantity in the districts of Muar, Batu Pahat and Kukob [Kukup]' (Johore AR 1912, 3).

SINGAPORE

The quantity of Rice produced on the Island is so small that it can hardly be taken into account. This deficiency will always, since there is but a very small extent of good rice land available, prevent any large number of Malayan [i.e. Malay] agriculturalists from settling here. . . . Some hill rice is produced at wide inter-vals. . . .

SFP 11.11.1841.

In fact, much of what little rice was grown grew in the swamps of the Bukit Timah valley, Siglap, Selegie, Kallang, Tanah Merah and Paya Lebar (Moor, 1837, frontis.; Little, 1848, 469–70, 481; Thomson, 1849, 746, 751; Wheatley, 1954). Nevertheless there was some concern in the 1830s that an interruption to trade might seriously threaten the food supply, and it was claimed that in fact considerable areas were suited to the crop.

The greatest part of the land to the north-east of the town is covered with extensive arable marshes. . .[and] narrow sand banks at an elevation of a few feet above the level of the marsh. Those banks afford dry situations for roads and cottages, and the ground between them possesses every advantage that can be required to render the cultivation of rice both easy and profitable. . . . Of its productive qualities, the abundant crops yielded by the scattered patches now under cultivation give sufficient proof. The aggregate quantity of rice culture now occupies between four and five hundred acres. . . .

SCCR 17.2.1831.

The same commentator went on to suggest that the rice growers, who lived at Kampong Glam, lacked title to their land and consequently, 'If any of those poor people cultivate a lot of ground, as soon as it becomes productive it is sure to be claimed by some retainer of the native chiefs. . .

[and thus] there can be little left for the encouragement of industry on the part of the cultivator....'

But the vision of fertile fields full of grain remained a vision and these lands now grow houses, flats and factories. Just when rice ceased to be grown in Singapore cannot be established but the last report found mentioned the harvest at the third milestone Bukit Timah road (*SFP* 21.11.1898).

RICE-GROWING BEYOND TANAH MELAYU[1]

Any consideration of the affairs of the aborigines during the nineteenth century must inevitably be rather biased as to area. The Temiar and Senoi groups living in the hills of eastern Perak and Selangor were comparatively well known because of contacts with successive exploring parties. In Malacca, the 'Mantera'[2] lived at no great distance from settled places whilst in Johore and south-east Pahang, the explorations of Lake and Kelsall brought to light a good deal concerning the Jakun. But even in 1910 little was known of aborigines in most parts of Pahang, Trengganu and Kelantan.

Concerning agriculture, reports are depressing in their sameness. So far as the techniques of cultivation are concerned, there is no reason to suggest that these failed to conform to Crawfurd's model of shifting cultivation (p. 37) in any major respect, except that the use of the hoe was not reported. The use of the dibble was reported in but two instances, one amongst the 'Binua' of Johore and one amongst the 'Pô-Klô'[3] (Logan, 1847, 255; Annandale and Robinson, 1903, 26).

In one respect, however, aboriginal shifting cultivation differed from that of the Malays. Settlements were not only rather smaller, the usual being two or three houses often grouped around a ladang, but less permanent, not because rice or any other crop exhausted the soil more rapidly under aboriginal methods of cultivation than Malay methods, but because, unlike the Malays, the aborigines very generally moved house following a death (see for example Leech, 1879a, 29; Blagden, 1892, 178–9).

The aborigines occupied discontinuous areas from sea-level to around two thousand feet. The coastal-dwellers, the *orang laut*, however, were said to be, '...ignorant of the culture of rice, and plant very few roots, neither do they cultivate the cocoa nut.... The plantain or *banana*...is the great object of their attention' (Crawfurd 1828, 82). On the other hand a report written at Kuala Langat in 1886 suggested that, 'The Orang Laut plant padi, bananas, kaladi [*Colocasia* spp.] etc., to a very great extent... [whereas] the Orang Bukit plant tapioca and a little rice, but depend mostly

---

[1] *Tanah Melayu* is here taken in its literal sense, 'lands of the Malays', not in its modern sense, 'Malaya'.

[2] These people would nowadays be referred to as Temuan or Belandas.

[3] 'Pô-Klô' is a complete misnomer, the term meaning 'brother-sister'. The group was almost certainly the Temiar. 'Binua', correctly *benua*, is Malay for a large country or 'mainland' as against 'island'. The people were certainly Jakuns (Proto-Malays).

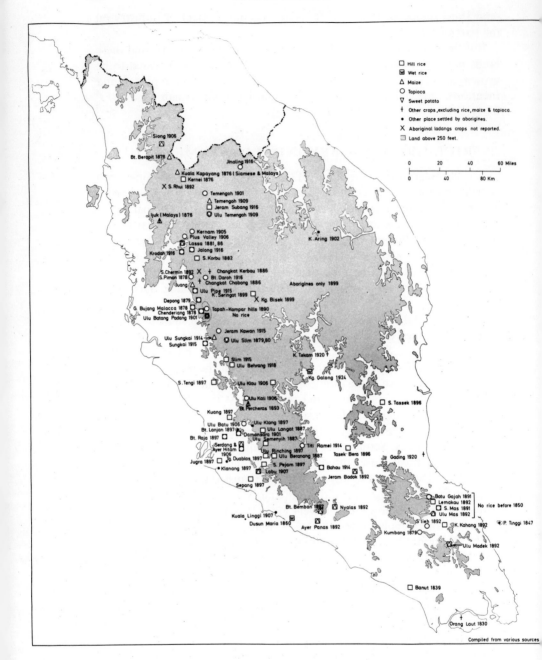

FIGURE 17
ABORIGINAL SETTLEMENT AND AGRICULTURE
IN MALAYA TO c.1915

on their fishspears or sumpitans (blowpipes) for their daily food.' (Bellamy, 1895, 229).

But the main concentration was not coastal but montane though within the mountain zone, marginal rather than interior (see Fig. 17). The best known concentration extended from the eastern mountains of Upper Perak to the Tapah hills with another smaller concentration at Slim.[1] Around Gunong Bujang Melaka, for instance, Leech (1878, 225–7) reported that,

From where we stood [on the summit] we could see the opposite side of the valley below us to the east [i.e. the Chenderiang] almost completely covered by old Sakei ladangs, which quite bears out...[the fact] that there are fully 700 people living there.

I again noticed a fact which attracted my attention when up the Kinta valley... that the Sakei cultivation appears limited to a height of between 300 or 400 feet up to 2,000 feet. Above this height they scarcely ever appear to go. Possibly this is the limit at which *padi* will thrive.

Leech may have been correct in his surmise, though now the upper limit is a good 1,000 feet higher than this in Malaya, and more than double that figure in northern Luzon.

Because this area was relatively accessible, introduced crops—rice, maize, tapioca and tobacco—were cultivated, but in some of the remoter areas to the north and south this was not the case. De Morgan, on his journey from Ulu Kinta to Kelantan, made numerous mentions of crops, including sugarcane, tubers of all types, of which tapioca had but recently been introduced, maize, various gourds, 'saffron', bananas and millet, the last probably *Coix* rather than *Setaria*. Nowhere was rice mentioned (De Morgan, 1886, 8–66). At Laseh, on the Plus river, cereals were not grown at all, only tubers, *Colocasia, Dioscorea* and *Manihot* (Brau de St. Pol Lias, 1883, 279–80). Near Temengor in Upper Perak, millet, *Coix* not *Setaria*, tapioca and banana were reportedly grown by the Temiar. 'The Malays make great fun of them, because they [the Temiar] say that rice makes them sick and therefore they refuse to eat it' (Annandale and Robinson, 1903, 26). To the south, aborigines in the headwaters of the Slim grew tapioca, sugarcane, bananas and 'sweet potatoes',[2] but not rice (Leech, 1879b, 42; Swettenham, 1880a, 59). South again, in the Endau basin, rice was reported as having been introduced to the aborigines by the Malays around 1850 (Hervey, 1881, 122), and it was but one of a list of 'foreign' crops which later also included tapioca, pineapples and tobacco (Lake and Kelsall, 1894, 9).

These evidences could be multiplied, but all point in the same direction, that rice was a recent newcomer to the aboriginal economy. This is not to suggest that it was unknown both to people exhibiting an avoidance

[1]Swettenham (1880a, 59) has made population estimates, giving 10,000 for the hills of Slim, Batang Padang and Bidor, including 3,000 at Slim.

[2]Almost certainly these were the greater yam, *Dioscorea alata*, rather than the American sweet potato, *Ipomoea batatas*. Malays tend to use *keledek* indiscriminately for both.

reaction and to others (a majority?) for whom it was regarded as a much-desired luxury. For the aboriginal agriculturalist who had no acquaintance with cereals, the step from tuber-cultivation to cereal-growing was a considerable one. Amongst those who already grew cereals, notably *Coix* millet, there was little need to add another. As Benjamin has pointed out in a personal communication, the Temiar, and one might add, possibly others, regarded rice as a Malay crop and appropriate only to the lands of the Malays and not to the lands of the hill peoples.

9

Pattern and Process

...you will find in the good earth and fields a sure refuge from dangerous materialism.

Pope John XXIII, 1959.

But these men compose the great mass of life which sustains all civilisations and bears their burdens. They are content barely to live....

Rabindranath Tagore.

Kalau tiada padi, sa-barang kerja ta' jadi.[1]

Malay proverb.

RICE GROWERS, whether Malay or aboriginal, by no means uniformly benefited from changes during the period in which imperial control became established. Change would seem to have by-passed remote areas almost entirely. Had the population of such regions increased, and even this cannot be established, a slow extension of the cultivated area presumably ensued; but the economy remained subsistence and local in orientation. For 'foreign' Malays, it is likely that life was materially easier in the Peninsula than it had been in their homeland. Why else would they have migrated? Yet for some, the toil of the rice fields, for relatively little return, was unattractive and they turned to growing coconuts, as in Lower Perak and western Johore, to coffee as in Selangor and increasingly after 1910, to rubber.

For the Peninsular Malays it is impossible to make a single generalization that will apply justly to all regions. In the north-east there can be little doubt that for the Kelantanese there was a modicum of quiet prosperity so long as land suitable for rice-growing and cattle-rearing remained abundant; but by about 1910, intensification of peasant production had begun as fallows were reduced. Although there was as yet no evidence of a fall in income levels, the lack of development in the commercial sector of the economy boded ill for the future. The transformation of Kelantan from one of the richest states in Malaya to one of the poorest took place under a half-century of British guidance. In nearby Trengganu, however, the collapse came prior to direct British interference. The well-developed craft and commercial sectors of the state economy declined

[1]Briefly, 'No rice, no work'.

between 1890 and 1910. The result was an increase in the proportion of agriculturalists and fishermen (see p. 69).

In the north-west, the craft sector was less important than in Trengganu and its destruction was less keenly felt, being compensated for by a spectacular development of commercialized rice cultivation stimulated by the presence of the Penang market and controlled by a commercially-minded Malay aristocracy. By 1910, from the ashes of war, Kedah had once again regained its ancient pre-eminence in rice production, though methods and the organizational basis of production remained essentially peasant in nature. The same was true in Province Wellesley and the Krian district of Perak, which also lay within the hinterland of Penang. In these areas, however, 'top management' was imperial rather than indigenous though at middle levels Malay entrepreneurs were by no means lacking. Moreover, in Province Wellesley a good proportion of the production was skimmed off by landlords and rich peasants and this class may have also existed in Kedah and in Krian.

In the south-west, the rice economy of the Minangkabau lands, except perhaps Naning and Rembau, was essentially self-contained, though this isolation was being broken down by 'foreign' Malays, especially in Jelebu. Minangkabau farmers were highly skilled, and as in Kelantan, the picture was one of quiet stability and prosperity as the effects of political broils diminished. The Malacca plain was in many respects similar in economy and size to Province Wellesley though less productive.

Elsewhere, rice-growing was of marginal importance in the overall economy, at best providing a sufficiency to those who opted out of the drudgery and repetitiveness of wage labour. Not only in states being developed for plantation agriculture or mining, were there '. . . thousands of Malays. . . who feel no shame in planting padi and do not find the work irksome, who would decline absolutely to do a day's work as a labourer' (B.R. Perak to Gov. SS 16.3.1893, CO 273/46). Yet by clinging to the only occupation they knew, the great majority ensured that they would remain at the bottom of the economic heap. In this they received every encouragement from government.

In the Federated Malay States from 1874 until 1895 it is clear that

. . . the establishment of a large self-employed agricultural population (as distinct from plantation labour) was also considered desirable and the encouragement of Malay agriculture and settlement had a place, though a minor one, in the plans and allocations of the state governments.

Sadka, 1968, 351.

The development of rice agriculture had been steadily promoted by Swettenham but by the end of the century a Residential instruction that no further irrigation works were to be undertaken without detailed estimates of expenditure and expected revenue was not only a matter of financial prudence but also an indication of increasing official disinterest. Stanley Arden, a government agronomist, was of the opinion that native agriculture was 'in lamentable condition' and that the generally-held view, namely that this was because of 'the indolence of the natives', could not be sustained. The problem, according to Arden, was that the Malay agriculturalist was rarely able to sell his product to his best advantage. The remedy was for government to set up marketing machinery (Arden, 1903, 399–400). Yet nothing was done and the matter did not receive serious attention until after Independence though a guaranteed price was introduced in 1939 (Ooi, 1963, 227). By 1909, official indifference was complete, the FMS Director of Agriculture himself being presumed by a District Officer 'not to...consider rice a crop of sufficient importance to justify much attention being given to it' (Larut & Krian AR 1909, 4).

THE SPATIAL PATTERN AND ITS EVOLUTION

One measure of official disinterest in rice cultivation is the lack of Malaya-wide accounts and statistics prior to the 1920s. The only continuous series of figures for area under rice cultivation before that time are those for the Straits Settlements—Singapore, Malacca, Penang and Province Wellesley. For each Settlement, the relevant *Blue Book* figures are somewhat suspect. Not only do they vary widely without apparent reason but the same figure may be given for several years running. Nevertheless it is worth giving a selection of figures not only from the *Blue Book* data, but also from data for other states (see Table 18).

In most areas there was clearly an expansion of rice lands in step with the expanding population. This expansion was maintained until 1910, though in Kelantan some decrease in the rice area had begun by 1904 when some rice fields were converted into coconut plantations (Kelantan AR 1904–5, 14). A similar change of land use cannot be documented for any other major region down to 1910. The marked fall of the rice area in Penang and Province Wellesley between 1910 and 1919–20 is more apparent than real (see Table 19).

Neither of the two sources available for the reconstruction of the spatial pattern *c*.1910 are wholly reliable (Raja Mahmud, 1920; Jack, 1923a). Jack's map (Fig. 18) must be taken as showing those areas which were actually under rice together with those considered to be potential rice lands, both lumped together and exaggerated in extent by the cartographer. It is possible that in some of these areas, a few crops of rice were taken during the First World War, either by shifting cultivation or as catch-crops in the establishment of permanent tree-crops (Lr Perak MR 9/1898, 764; Pears, 1901; Coombs, 1917–18). But the areas shown on Jack's map certainly cannot be regarded as those under permanent cultivation.

The data of Raja Mahmud are somewhat more reliable though the rounded figures given for some of the Unfederated Malay States indicate some uncertainty. With the exception of those given for Penang and Province Wellesley, the figures accord reasonably well with those of Jack (1923b, 104) and are sufficiently accurate to permit the extrapolation of areal data for the states for which those data do not exist, namely all

TABLE 18

MALAYA: SELECTED DATA FOR AREA OF RICE TO 1911

Date	Penang acres	Prov. Wellesley acres	Malacca acres	Perak acres	Dindings acres	Krian acres	Selangor[5] acres	Pahang[6] acres
1861		40,000[1]						
1871		63,100	52,000					
1877		63,444	51,000					
1883	9,000	45,000	18,745					
1887	9,000	45,000	21,738					
1891–2	7,935	40,150	31,630	69,075[2]	300	40,000[3]		
1899	7,783	45,700	34,826		2,198	30,000[4]		
1901	7,700	48,085	31,686					
1905	7,660	49,368	37,229		2,310		8,000	
1911	6,129	45,200	40,410		10			27,400

Source: SS *Blue Books* for the years stated (except where otherwise noted).

[1]Guthrie et al., 1861, 6.
[2]Perak AR 1891, 417.
[3]B.R. Perak to Col. Sec. 5.4.1892 CO 275/46. But Perak AR 1892, 399, has 37,000 ac. whilst Anon. (1892, 1101) has 60,000 ac.
[4]Out of 46,000 ac. alienated for rice (FMS Lands Dept AR 1899, 3).
[5]Selangor AR 1905, 47.
[6]Wise, 1901, 1.

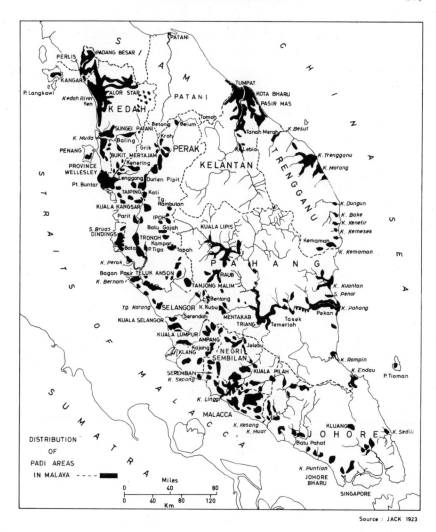

Source : JACK 1923

FIGURE 18
PADI AREAS IN MALAYA ACCORDING TO JACK

regions except Penang, Province Wellesley and Malacca (Table 19). Only the actual data for 1919–20 have been mapped (Fig. 19).

The north-western region was and remains clearly dominant, with the Kedah-Perlis plain accounting for roughly a third of the total. To the east, Kelantan and Trengganu accounted for another quarter of the total area, though there the high proportion of 'dry' cultivation, mainly tenggala and related systems, would have ensured that production was proportionately lower than in the north-west region. In Perak, except the Krian and Kuala Kangsar districts, and in coastal Selangor, the proportion of 'dry' cultivation was also high, doubtless because of the high

TABLE 19
MALAYA: ESTIMATED RICE AREA 1911–12 AND 1919–20
BY REGION AND STATE

	1911–12[1]				1919–20[2]			
	acres	acres	%	%	acres	acres	%	%
North-west	381,470		60		364,887		58	
Kedah		185,265		29		193,668		31
Perlis		16,258		3		20,400		3
Penang		6,129		1		135		4
Prov. Wellesley		45,200		7		26,238		
Perak		128,618		20		124,426		20
(incl. Dindings)								
North-east	141,984		23		152,830		25	
Kelantan		131,137		21		142,000		23
Trengganu		10,847		2		10,830		2
South	66,960		10		56,904		9	
Malacca		40,410		6		27,265		4
Negri Sembilan		26,550		4		29,639		5
'Marchlands'	44,672		7		53,310		8	
Selangor		7,877		1		11,441		2
Pahang		30,123		5		32,869		5
Johore		6,672		1		9,000		1
Total	635,086		100		627,931		100	

[1]Figures for Penang, Province Wellesley and Malacca are from the Straits Settlements *Blue Book* for 1911. That for Negri Sembilan is from Far Eastern Geographical Establishment (1917, 14) and is for 1912. The remaining figures are the writer's estimates based upon the ratio of rice growers, 1921, to area under rice, 1919–20, extrapolated for 1911 using Census data for that year (Marriott, 1911a; 1911b; Cavendish, 1911; Pountney, 1911). The Far Eastern Geographical Establishment (1917, 14) also gives the following figures: Perak, 84,550 acres, Selangor, 4,438 acres, Pahang, 7,213 acres. Accepting the 1919–20 figures as reasonably accurate, it is clear that these values are too low. It is stretching the imagination to suggest that areas increased by 47, 158 and 356 per cent respectively between 1912 and 1919–20. The Far Eastern Geographical Establishment figures almost certainly refer to lands for which titles had been issued, not to total area. The estimates given correspond reasonably well with other data, notably Jack (1923b, 104).
[2]Raja Mahmud, 1920. The value given for Penang is far too low. The *Blue Book* for 1919 has 5,879 acres while Jack (1923b, 104) gave the area as 6,030 acres. That given for Province Wellesley is not confirmed by the Straits Settlements *Blue Book* for 1919, and is also suspiciously low, since the *Blue Book* for that year has 44,481 acres. Jack (1923b, 104) gave an area of 33,500 acres.

incidence of catch-cropping of rice as tree-crop plantations were established.

NORTHERN DOMINANCE

Some explanation of this dominance of the northern states is clearly called for. In part the reasons are meteorological: three or four wet months

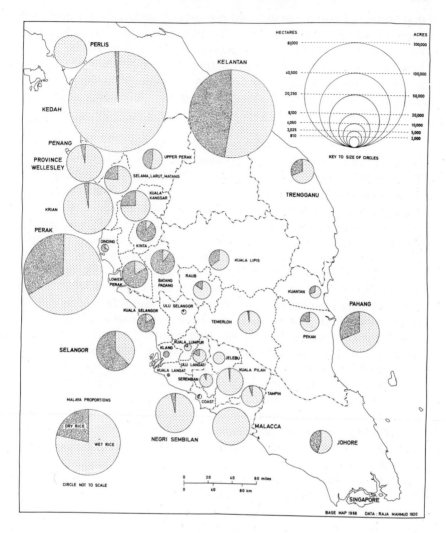

FIGURE 19

MALAYA: RICE AREAS BY STATE AND DISTRICT, 1919–20

are followed by at least two or three dry months in which clear skies prevail, thus promoting satisfactory growth and ripening of the crop. In part the reasons are topographical: in the north are extensive plains where the soils are youthful, reasonably fertile, fairly readily drained, and not peaty. In the south, the plains of the Perak, Bernam, Selangor, Langat, and Pahang rivers and those of Johore are either limited in extent, are peaty or muck soils, or are of very low gradients, making drainage very difficult.

But these are only partial explanations and other reasons for the dominance of the north lie deeply embedded in history, much of which still defies anything beyond imprecise formulations. Were it to be established that Malayan Hoabinhian included rice as a collected grain, as a protected grain, or even as a cultivated grain, northern dominance would be established as existing at a very early period. Bronze- and iron-using groups were more southerly in their distribution, but rice-growing by any pre-historic group in Malaya has not been established, though elsewhere culturally-allied groups are known to have been rice growers. In early historical times, it is likely that rice was known probably as one crop amongst many others.

As time went by populations slowly grew both by natural increase and as a result of a centuries-long southward drift from the Isthmian region. Though the evidence is exiguous, some of the newcomers probably used the technique of flooding fields and may also have introduced the plough. The significance of bunded wet field cultivation is that it provides a controlled environment which raises yields and improves their reliability, though the lower end of the yield curve for wet fields intersects the upper end of the yield curve for dry fields. The extent of wet fields would seem to have grown slowly and to have been accompanied by a steady growth in dependence upon rice, since the environment of the wet fields is one which militates against the simultaneous cultivation of rice and other crops, though such promiscuous cultivation is characteristic of dry fields.

But whence came the bunded wet field tradition, or rather traditions, since there are two, one in the north marked by the term bendang and one in the south denoted by the Javanese term sawah? Malay tradition in the north has it that the techniques of flooding fields (and also ploughing) were introduced from Thailand in the fifteenth century (Ooi, 1963, 224: Zaharah, 1968, 42). That one introduction was from the north need not be challenged. What may be questioned is whether or not it was a Thai tradition (Ooi makes no judgement here) and whether the fifteenth century is of the correct order of time. The evidence is extremely scanty, largely because the Isthmian region is almost unknown archaeologically. But on the balance of probabilities it is likely that a Mon rather than a Thai origin is indicated. Concerning the timing, a much earlier date may be surmised, possibly as early as the sixth century, contemporaneous with the kingdom of Dvaravati (see p. 20). Concerning the origins of the southern tradition of wet fields there is little more certainty. While it is just possible that in both Malacca and Johore the technique was known, it is more likely that such rice as was produced was grown only in natural swamps. Bunded wet fields are almost certainly the introduction of the Minangkabau though just how and when the Javanese term sawah came to apply to the fields remains a puzzle.

The spread of the plough is very difficult to document satisfactorily. It seems reasonable to suppose that early Kedah farmers used it, since linguistic and perhaps archaeological evidences point in this direction. The ultimate origin would thus be Indian. The tradition of a fifteenth-century introduction of the plough from Thailand points to a much later, possibly a second introduction. But it was not an introduction by ethnic Thai. Bowring (1857, 1, 201) noted that,

In many parts of Siam, the land is prepared during the rainy season by turning in herds of buffaloes to trample down the weeds and move the soil, which is afterwards harrowed . . . . The seed is then broadcast upon the surface. But wherever the Chinese are established, they introduce their native usages and improvements [i.e. ploughs].

This form of tillage is the exact equivalent of Malay melanyak and it seems likely that this form of soil preparation, but not ploughing, is derived from a Thai or an earlier Mon practice. Was the plough thus an introduction ultimately from a Chinese source via the Thai? If so, how did it acquire an Indian name, tenggala? Were a Thai-Chinese source to be accepted, the fifteenth century would be of the correct order of period.

A Malthusian would seize upon the spread of these new techniques, and would argue that an increase in population would have been triggered off. Such an argument would be pure surmise. There would seem to be no reason to suggest that the replacement of melanyak tillage by the plough would result in higher yields per unit area. The converse is more likely since the input of dung would be reduced. On the other hand, the adoption of the plough by increasing the tilling capacity of the animals would have led to the possibility of increasing the cultivated area and the population. The population, and hence the cultivated area, did in fact expand in peacetime and in the absence of natural disasters. Conversely, population and area contracted through war, as during the assault by Acheen upon Kedah in the seventeenth century, by the Siamese upon Kedah in the nineteenth century, or during typhoon, famine and pestilence as in Kelantan in the 1880s. The imposition of peace by the British upon the region led to marked increases of the Malay population, both naturally and by immigration, mainly from Sumatra but also from Java and Borneo. Whereas the population of Malaya totalled roughly 425,000 in 1834,[1] by 1911 it reached 2,644,000 of which the Malay, hence largely agricultural, component was about 1,410,000 or 53 per cent (*SFP* 26.1.1837; Newbold, 1839; Ooi, 1963, 113, 120). Although it is possible that intensification of use and higher yields slowed the expansion of the rice area somewhat, the rice area roughly trebled between the 1830s and the 1910s. Some of this expansion took place in the south, but most of it resulted from expansion first in Province Wellesley, then in Krian and Kedah under the stimulus of the Penang and subsequently other West Coast markets. To this must be added undocumented expansion in Kelantan and Trengganu. It was largely from pre-existing nodes that expansion took place. Thus 'ink-blot' growth was rather more important than 'leap-frog' colonization.

In some areas this was a movement from inland along the middle reaches of rivers towards the richer but less readily-worked soils of the coast. Kedah is a case in point. But it would be incorrect to conclude that expansion was in this direction throughout Malaya. In Kelantan it seems to have been the reverse. In Perak the coastlands were not colonized from

[1]This estimate is very much above that given by Ooi for 1835–6, namely a total of 280,680.

old-established centres of cultivation inland, but by foreginers from
abroad or from the coastlands of Province Wellesley. In the narrow valleys
of Upper Perak there was some upstream movement of settlers from the
Kuala Kangsar core area though the predominant direction was downstream from across the Siam border. Upstream colonization also occurred
in Negri Sembilan and Malacca, the Jelebu and Ulu Serting and Ulu
Kesang areas being examples. In yet other cases, colonization proceeded
from the main valleys up tributary valleys as is suggested by the dates of
reports of cultivation in the villages (see for example Figures 11 and 13).
In the lands occupied by aborigines, rice-growing spread slowly and
unevenly from the Malay-occupied piedmont into the hills, but this was
the spread of a crop, not colonization. Apart from a general southward
thrust in the north-west region, there was no general direction of movement from established areas in the Peninsula. This contrasts with 'leap-
frog' colonization by foreign Malays which was exclusively western in
focus. The eastern coastlands from the Pahang to Ujong Tanah (Ramunia
Point) in south-east Johore remained essentially uncolonized.

INITIATIVES IN THE EXPANSION OF THE CULTIVATED AREA

In the expansion of the cultivated lands during the nineteenth and early
twentieth centuries, two forms of initiatives may be distinguished, large-
scale and small-scale. The former involved large areas, many people and
the resources of government or at least the very wealthy, for both governments and individuals were involved. The latter involved small areas and
relatively few people, a few hundred at the most. In these, the entrepreneurial role was usually taken by private individuals though sometimes
by minor governmental functionaries, with government assisting in some
cases and not in others.

LARGE-SCALE DEVELOPMENT: MALAY INITIATIVES

Apart from a single major scheme of irrigation and drainage, the Krian
scheme, large-scale development lay exclusively in the Malay domain.
But this development was not greatly different, except in scale, from small-
scale developments which were to be found throughout Malaya. Whether
'big' man or 'small' man, the Malay entrepreneur generally had above-
average means and was almost invariably a person of some status in
society. The big men had interests close to the royal court or were themselves members of royalty; the Sultan of Kedah and several of his
ministers, Datoh Muda Abdul Wahab and Raja Mahmud in Perak, and
the Raja Muda of Selangor are examples. The small men were village
headmen, government clerks, and leaders of immigrant bands from
abroad. All saw in the pioneer situation an opportunity to make their
fortunes. All used their social status, personal influence and power to
control the investment of such labour and capital as they could muster.
Where the difference lay among the entrepreneurs was in the amount

of land they could lay claim to and the resources they had at their disposal. Thus although colonization of the Kedah-Perlis swamplands was achieved by means of several large-scale schemes of drainage and settlement, it would be dangerous to argue that those lands could only have been successfully settled by large-scale schemes. The swamplands of Province Wellesley were successfully colonized by many individuals without large-scale works, as was Krian, at least marginally.

The nature of developmental initiatives cannot be documented for Kelantan and Trengganu, but doubtless, as in Kedah and Perlis, no real distinction can be made between private and governmental enterpreneurial roles. Just as rulers made no distinction between state funds and their private fortunes, the big enterpreneurs, the Sultan of Kedah himself, his ministers Wan Mat Saman and Syed Abdullah and others, made no distinction between their role in government and their role as investors. For them public interest was private interest and private interest was public. Locally they were the government, and their power was of major significance in mobilizing capital and labour.

The extent to which the big entrepreneurs used feudal rights of krah for developmental purposes is difficult to establish, but before foreign wage-labour became available, in Kedah in the 1880s, krah had a basic economic function. Although forced labour had been feared and, by flight avoided when Kedah was under direct Siamese rule, there is little evidence that the rakyat objected to its deployment on capital works the rakyat themselves considered productive. Once Province Wellesley became a refuge from krah, however, it became increasingly difficult to insist on it in Kedah. Late in the nineteenth century in Kedah and Perlis, though not in Kelantan and Trengganu, the deployment of labour in a capitalistic manner began to replace insistence upon feudal rights. This change required a much larger capital input than previously. Whereas formerly a feudary required merely sufficient rice to feed the rakyat working out their krah obligation, now cash was required to pay wage-labour. The sources of this development capital are extremely difficult to document. In Kedah and Perlis the profits of trade and taxes on rice, vegetables and livestock exports to Penang were likely sources and to these may be added revenues from tin-mining, though these were not large, and briefly from duties on tapioca and sago (Sharom, 1970). It may also be reasonably surmised that the financiers of Penang provided loan capital for Kedah entrepreneurs as they certainly did in Krian and Selama. In Kelantan, if large-scale development existed at all, it was presumably locally-financed.

LARGE-SCALE DEVELOPMENT: BRITISH INITIATIVES

Compared with the great expansion of rice lands under Malay initiative, both large- and small-scale, the sole major developmental project, Krian, is insignificant. As was noted earlier, this was as much a scheme for improvement as for development. Moreover, it benefited the capitalist sugar grower at least as much as the rice-growing peasant.

One question that arises is, were schemes of drainage and irrigation such as that actually constructed in Krian, and such as those proposed for Lower Perak and for the Selangor coastlands, essential to successful colonization of coastal plains? Krian, Lower Perak, Selangor and indeed. Malacca, were all coastal plains with notably gentle gradients, with pronounced tendencies to turn into inland seas during wet spells and to lack adequate water at other times. The example of Krian would suggest that unless reasonably adequate drainage was provided, fluctuations in the level of the water-table were such that the crop was always in danger of drowning were run-off to overtax the natural water-channels. Thus although colonization was possible without artificial drainage, production levels would have been low and annual fluctuations of production would often have been unacceptably high, as they were indeed in Krian. The accompanying problem, lack of water at crucial periods of the cropping cycle, was rarely acute in the north except in Krian, though it would have been a problem in the Lower Perak and Selangor coastal plains had these been colonized by rice growers on any scale. Thus it can be argued that the successful utilization of the coastal plains from Krian south depended upon large-scale, hence governmental, initiative. This initiative was, with minor exceptions, lacking until the late 1930s when a whole series of schemes were proposed, most of which were not implemented until the late 1950s and 1960s. From the 1910s until the late 1930s, with the exception of the later years of the First World War, no major government plans for providing rice-growing were realized. Krian alone remained as a major monument to Swettenham's land colonization policies. But even the Krian Irrigation Scheme was a mixed success in the establishment of a large self-employed agricultural population. Nor were efforts to establish non-Malay rice growers any more successful. Though Swettenham pushed the idea of non-Malay colonies of rice planters, and though attempts were made both in Perak and Selangor to bring in South Indians and in Perak to bring in Chinese, nothing of substance was achieved.

SMALL-SCALE DEVELOPMENT

Rather greater, but still mixed, success attended attempts by governments to support the efforts of what may be termed 'small' entrepreneurs. Malays almost exclusively, who had the means, the force of character or the social position to induce a few tens of followers to colonize new lands. Many of these entrepreneurs were foreign Malays, some from Sumatra including Minangkabau, Rawa and Mandeling men, Banjarese from Borneo, and in western Johore, a scattering of Javanese. Others were from 'out-of-state', Kedah people being particularly noteworthy in this category. Many of the 'foreign' Malays set up colonies spatially separated from already developed areas. Notable were colonies of Rawas at Selama and Mandelings at Cheroh and Slim, all in Perak. Others joined planned developments such as Krian where the government undertook settlement work. 'Out-of-state' Malays, and in the north mixed Siamese-Malay groups, seem to have also set themselves up in distinct communities. For example, people from states under Siamese dominion settled in Upper

Perak, at Sungei Patani and in the Trans-Krian district, and Minangkabau folk from Sungei Ujong settled at Beranang, Selangor. Besides these migrant groups were others, especially in the pioneer fringe areas of the marchlands, in which the initiative lay with the local nobility who mustered foreign migrants to aid the opening of land as in Selangor and in the Kinta district of Perak and especially Kelantanese refugees in Kedah.

In addition to these groups whose leadership and composition may readily be documented, there must have been others concerning whom little is known. Some were doubtless active village headmen, others men of some status, hajis, minor nobility and the like, whose power, influence and wealth could not fail to be boosted by a vigorous programme of expansion which would not only cater to 'their people' but might attract others. In many parts of the Peninsula, especially during the broils that preceded and sometimes accompanied the imposition of *pax Britannica*, and also at other times of natural disasters and small-pox epidemics, there were good numbers of people moving about looking for peace and stability. Since status and wealth devolved from the control of people and only secondarily from land, the ambitious man was prompted to actively promote land development in the hope of attracting people, and by bettering their lot, thereby gain power, prestige and wealth.

In development, the role of government varied from region to region. In the Siamese-controlled northern states government aid was personal aid since government was personal. Amongst the functions of government were construction and maintenance of irrigation, drainage and water communications networks, the registration of land, and the collection of feudal dues and religious taxes. In the Straits Settlements the role of government was less prominent. The main function was to give out land and to register titles, though in Malacca, the latter was opposed by the people for a long period. The lack of opposition to this in Province Wellesley doubtless stems from the fact that the people were initially almost all refugees. Only in the later part of the nineteenth century did government assist with the stabilization and intensification of rice-growing by undertaking minor works of drainage, irrigation and flood control.

In what became the Federated Malay States, government expenditure upon the development of rice land was never lavish except in Krian, and became less so as time went by. Down to the late 1890s moneys were advanced for development *ab initio*, as well as for assisting settlers who had already made a start, to construct irrigation works. By 1900, loans and grants for colonization had virtually ceased though a small irrigation scheme on unoccupied land was under construction in Ulu Selangor and the Krian Scheme was still unfinished. Government aid was a mixed success. In some cases no permanent good resulted. This was especially true of sums expended in the tin zone of Perak and Selangor. Support of Toh Mudah Wahab and Imam Prang in the Kinta valley or Haji Ibrahim at Cheroh are examples. In Selangor in the 1880s it is clear that sums given to individual small entrepreneurs for the support of their followers failed to achieve anything substantial and in many cases such loans ultimately had to be written off. There is no doubt that the economies of Perak, Selangor and Negri Sembilan could bear this very minor extravagance and it could be argued that it was harmless foolishness to lend money without the assurance of it producing the required result, namely a prosperous, self-sufficient peasantry. Further, it could be argued that in the very long run, and that was what was important, any expenditure on land development would ultimately bring a return merely because people had been brought into the state. Such arguments have some merit but there were dangers in reliance upon government hand-outs.

In the first place the mobilization of peasant capital or its substitution by labour were to some degree discouraged. The tradition of *gotong-royong*, community self-help, was attacked. The very understandable desire of government to control the expenditure of its funds may also have inhibited applications for development funds, especially since many small entrepreneurs seem to have had inadequate control over their followers and ended up in the situation of having spent government money and having neither funds nor followers nor much to show for their efforts. Even more important was the fact that the traditional large entrepreneurs, members of royalty and others close to the royal courts had, if they possessed capital, more profitable investment opportunities in the modern, colonial sector of the economy than in developing rice land. If they did not have capital they were content to lead a comfortable life as government pensioners. To be fair though, some devoted themselves to development using their future pensions as security for government loans as numerous letters preserved in the Selangor and Negri Sembilan State Secretariat archives testify. But the nub of the matter is that the big entrepreneurs, who alone could undertake large projects, who could control the rakyat and use their labour for the common good as well as the furtherance of their own interests, had their power broken by British rule, not because they were big entrepreneurs but because they were bases of political power and hence potential threats to imperial interests.

A TYPOLOGY AND ITS EVOLUTION

The construction of an evolutionary model of types of rice-growing in Malaya is fraught with difficulty since much of the evolution would seem to lie in a period for which evidences are few and often open to more than one interpretation. Nevertheless it is possible to proceed on the assumption that simple preceded complex, here referring to techniques and to the structure of societies using them. The various types recognized should be considered 'levels' rather than stages since 'stages' tend to imply that change was a one-way street. It was not. There is abundant evidence of halts and regressions. Furthermore, it should be recognized that change was of three types—purely autochthonous; second, that resulting from dispersal of ideas unaccompanied by migrations of peoples on any significant scale; and, finally, that resulting from foreign colonization. With some exceptions, it is not possible to attribute change to any one of these three sources without equivocation.

A major question concerning the spread of rice cultivation in Malaya is whether or not there was a single ancestral form of cultivation which then evolved into a wide but recently narrowing range of types (Hill. 1970). It is usually suggested that this ancestral type was a form of un-irrigated, forest-clearing cultivation (Ooi, 1963, 224) or that shifting cultivation such as that now practised by aboriginal peoples was the prototype (Lim, 1967, 153). There is no direct evidence of a single ancestral type in Malaya: there may well have been several, if the profusion of recognizable types is any indication.

Nevertheless, in the scheme which follows, a single South-East Asian ancestral type is suggested. In broad outline the model probably has chronological reality but at the detailed level this may not be true.

AN EVOLUTIONARY TYPOLOGICAL MODEL (WITH REGIONAL EXAMPLES)

A. Ancestral South-East Asian type: semi-permanent cultivation. implying permanent settlement with fields used at close intervals but not annually, slash-and-burn; probably 2–3 years crop followed by 2–3 years fallow; no fallow-period use; rice one crop of many. This falls into the short-fallow system of Boserup (1965, 16).

B. 1. Temporary: hill-slope cultivation: slash or slash-and-burn: 1–2 years crop, at least 8 years regenerating forest fallow; little or no fallow-period use; rice one crop of many. Common aboriginal system, huma. This and the following system fall into the forest- or bush-fallow categories of Boserup (1965, 15).

2. Temporary: hill-slope cultivation usual but also flat land and swamps; rice the major crop; remainder as B.1 above. Common Malay system, huma.

Variants: a. without dibble, padi terbuang, common; b. with dibble, padi tugalan. Kuantan.

C. 1. Semi-permanent, derived directly from A: swamp cultivation: slash or slash-and-burn; 2–3 years crop, 2–3 years fallow; no fallow-period use; rice major crop. All the semi-permanent systems fall into Boserup's short-fallow category.

Variants: a. without dibble, paya tabor. Coastal Kuantan, Kuala Langat.
  b. with dibble. Modern survival, Trengganu.
  c. with melanyak. Coastal Kuantan.
  d. with hoe. Modern survivals in many remote areas.
  e. with transplanting. Coastal Perak, coastal Selangor.
  f. with hoe or melanyak and transplanting, padi paya chedong. Coastal Kuantan.

2. Semi-permanent: flat land, not swamp; minor clearing with parang or later, tajak; 1–2 years crop, 1–2 years fallow; fallow-period grazing; rice major crop. Many survivals in remote areas; formerly widespread in Patani, Kelantan, Trengganu, Pahang, Perak valley, inland Kedah.

Variants: a. hoe ('scratch-hoe', *keri*, only)
      i. unbunded fields—broadcast sowing
              —dibble
              —transplanting
      ii. bunded fields, sawah, bendang
              —broadcast sowing
              —dibble
              —transplanting.
      b. melanyak, with variants above. Probably more common in the north-east and Pahang than elsewhere.
      c. plough, with variants above. Variant with bunded fields and transplanting probably by far the most common of all.

    3. Semi-permanent: flat or gently rolling land; clearing unnecessary except where pioneering new land; 3–5 years crop, 3–5 years grass fallow; fallow-period grazing; plough (tenggala); closely related to C.2c above.

Variants: a. with broadcast sowing, seed harrowed in Pahang.
      b. with dibbling of seed. Modern survival in Trengganu.

    D. Permanent, annual cropping (Boserup 1965, 16): flat land; minor clearing with parang and from nineteenth century tajak in some areas; one crop per year; bunded fields; no off-season crop, grazing only; transplanting usual though dibble and broadcast seeding also found.

Variants as C.2 above with the addition of the following:
      a. with off-season vegetable-growing. Malacca Chinese. This was probably the only system of multi-cropping in the Peninsula.
      b. hoe, transplanting, gravity or kinchir irrigation. Kelantan, Krian, Minangkabau areas, Chinese in Province Wellesley.
      c. tajak, transplanting, gravity irrigation. Krian.
      d. plough, transplanting, gravity irrigation. Kelantan, Perak valley, small areas in the inland parts of Kedah, the tin-zone, Malacca.
      e. with sickle-harvesting replacing tuai, Kedah and Malacca plain.
      f. with animal threshing, Kedah only.

Sources: based in part upon field-work, in part upon Hill (1964; 1966a; 1970), with minor additions from Baker (1940) and Great Britain, War Office (1891).

EVOLVING SYSTEMS AND THE BOSERUP HYPOTHESIS

The scheme outlined above indicates something of a progression from extensive to successively more intensive systems of rice cultivation (Boserup, 1965, 17). However, the primal system, probably practised by tribal bands, involved the moderately intensive use of small areas. This is because no band would deliberately cut itself off from favoured areas in which a supply of protein-rich food could readily and enjoyably be obtained. Such areas included the sea-shore (except the mangrove), lake margins and rivers. So long as population densities remained low, permanent settlement was possible, but as pressure upon protein sources increased, and as agriculture became more important in the group economy, dispersion into hitherto less attractive unoccupied areas began. Forest- or bush-fallowing became more general.

Initially, individual forest-clearings were small since tubers give a much higher calorific yield per unit of area than do cereals. With the adoption of rice, a process still in progress amongst aboriginal communities in 1910, larger individual clearings were necessary. To this extent, the change from tuber-based to cereal-based cultivation represents intensification of aboriginal long-fallow agriculture. The only other, and very minor example of intensification of aboriginal agriculture was in Malacca where French Roman Catholic missionaries at Dusun Maria attempted to stabilize settlement and to teach the aborigines how to grow wet rice.

Intensification of Malay long-fallow agriculture is less easy to document. That long-fallow cultivation was widespread is certain. It was practised in the piedmont zones of most regions except in the Straits Settlements. Only in the Federated Malay States was official action taken against it, though in Pahang relevant legislation was largely unenforced and unenforceable. The result of action to prevent ladang cultivation was a direct leap to annual wet rice cultivation in most areas, though in parts of inland Selangor permanent tree-crop cultivation replaced long-fallow cultivation.

One question which arises is, why did long-fallow cultivation persist for so long, to some extent despite attempts at government control? Nowhere were there social or legal controls until the 1880s and then only in some areas. The reason was surely not ignorance of methods of wet cultivation, though ignorance of irrigation as distinct from wet cultivation can certainly be documented, as in Pahang. One reason may well have been a preference for the hill-grown product which is superior in smell and in keeping qualities to lowland rice. Another reason was economic. Though no precise data can be produced, it is clear that less labour was required to produce a measure of rice by ladang cultivation than by wet methods. At around 300–350 gantangs per acre in the first year of production with perhaps 100–150 less in the subsequent year, yields were as high, if not higher than in some sawahs, certainly higher than in pioneer sawahs such as those of inland Selangor. Any comparative advantage of sawahs was delayed until yields rose above the 300–350 gantang per acre threshold and there was seemingly, no way of knowing beforehand whether such yields would be attained. If there were comparative advantages, why were so many attempts at opening sawahs failures? Moreover, since more labour was required in the sawah than in the ladang, why bother if self-sufficiency could be achieved anyway? This seems to have been the situation in the Perak valley and probably elsewhere.

Boserup (1965, Chapter 1) has argued that the conventional sequence of intensification is from forest- or scrub-fallow (in Malaya the two were not distinguished) through a grass-fallow of 1–3 years, to annual cropping and multiple cropping. She has argued that as the fallow is reduced and grass replaces scrub, the need for a plough for successful clearing of the grass, fire no longer availing, is so compelling that cultivators usually avoid the stage of short-fallow if they are unable to use ploughs (Boserup, 1965, 25). Though this is doubtless correct where grasses are rhizomous, stoloniferous or sod-forming, it is not true in Malaya. Though it is true that the plough formed a part of the grass-fallow tenggala system of Pahang and other north-eastern regions, modern survivals, as in Ulu Trengganu, would suggest that the use of the plough was usual rather than essential (Hill, 1964). The use of the changkul to turn over the soil has been neither observed nor documented in grass-fallow systems, and though the use of the short-handled *keri* or 'scratch hoe' survives, it is not an implement which can be satisfactorily used to truly till the soil.

The great advantage of grass-fallow cultivation was that it permitted true mixed farming. Animal dung was a major source, in most cases the only source, of fertilizer. Though milk was not customarily consumed, and buffaloes produce little enough, it seems a reasonable surmise that red meat played a larger part in the diet in mixed farming regions than in regions of annual cropping. Moreover, cattle were a source of cash income and the survival into the nineteenth century of major droving routes into Kedah, Upper Perak and Ulu Selangor, as well as the supplying of the Penang and Singapore markets with beasts from the north-eastern region especially, testify to the sound economic sense of this form of mixed farming.

Boserup (1965, 32) has also suggested that unless a peasant keeps a large herd of cattle and laboriously spreads dung on the fields, the yields obtained per unit area will be much lower under grass-fallow than under forest-fallow. This cannot be documented for Malaya where the shift from forest- or bush-fallow to grass-fallow, where it occurred, would seem to have involved a shift from hill slopes to alluvial lands. Nevertheless Boserup's supposition may well be correct for lands not subject to annual flooding and slope-wash.

How then did this grass-fallow system arise? Two main possibilities exist. One is that it represents a stage in the Boserup sequence, i.e. it arose from a reduction of fallow. As this change took place, the hoe or dibble were replaced slowly and unevenly by the plough. The other possibility is that it represents a transference of swamp cultivation techniques to a flat or gently-sloping environment. There is no evidence either way. It is certain, however, that the presence of cattle in some numbers is essential to the maintenance of the grass sward as well as providing a source of traction. The very existence of melanyak tillage would seem to suggest that cattle pre-dated the plough. When this might have been is difficult to establish. The fact that Selangor farmers of the late nineteenth century lacked both cattle and the plough, and that Minangkabau farmers eschewed the implement, suggest a very late introduction. On the other hand, the word tenggala points to a much earlier introduction. Though two types of buffalo were domesticated, one in India *c*.2500 B.C. and the other in China about 1,000 years later, their spread in South-East Asia has not yet been documented (Cockrill, 1967). The same is true of oxen.

Annual cropping, in one form or another, was undoubtedly the most widespread form of cultivation by 1910. Although nowadays the use of the plough is widespread, the plough is not essential to annual cropping. The same is true of transplanting. What is invariable is tillage in some form whether by melanyak, plough or true hoe (changkol) and of course tillage is essential to transplanting.

The shift from grass-fallow cultivation to annual cropping may have been initiated when a critical density of population was reached in accord with the Boserup hypothesis (1965, 41). In the century or so from $c.1800$, the agricultural populations of the various states would seem to have increased between five- and tenfold, but to provide full support for the Boserup hypothesis it would have to be demonstrated that the cultivated area failed to expand sufficiently rapidly for the grass-fallow system to remain. That the grass-fallow system failed to remain is evident. The facts that in 1891 Patani was still a region of pasture as much as of rice, the contrast between Abdullah's description of coastal Kelantan in 1838 and that region in 1910, the survivals of grass-fallowing to the present, the continuance of grass-fallowing in the peripheral areas of Kedah, all point to recent change. But to suggest that the reason for change was simply rapid population growth smacks dangerously of single-factor causation and circular reasoning. The processes of commercialization, especially in the Penang market region, and agrarianization, as in Trengganu and to a lesser degree in Kedah, may equally be invoked. Moreover, since a fair proportion of the population increase consisted of immigrants, it was to be expected that they would continue the annual-cropping traditions of their homelands.

One major problem associated with the shift to annual cropping was that of the livestock. They were essential to thorough tillage and to adequate soil fertilization in most areas. The area an animal could till with the simple type of Malay plough was smaller than the area needed to feed it on natural grazing. The problem was how to feed the animals adequately when most of the land was occupied by rice for up to ten months of the year. One solution would have been fodder-cropping but this lay far in the future. Another would have been to allow poorer classes of land formerly under grass-fallow to become permanent pasture. This may have happened but cannot be documented. A further solution was transhumance, and the survival to this day of this practice in Trengganu and Kelantan suggests that this may have been a common one. The other possibility was a reduction in the number of livestock. It is possible that this was associated with a change from melanyak tillage which would seem to have required more animals per unit of area than were required for ploughing. In Kedah/Perlis especially, where guano fertilizer was available, and in Penang where cattle were in strong demand, some reduction of stock numbers or the ratio of stock to land may have taken place. Moreover there is the distinct likelihood that epidemics of cattle disease, probably rinderpest, such as occurred in Kelantan in the 1880s, forced a change from melanyak to plough and in some cases to hoe tillage. In other words hoe tillage may well be regressive from the standpoint of technical evolution as well as regressive in requiring a large increase in labour input for little or no return by way of increased production.

There can be little doubt that intensification of rice agriculture had far-reaching results, the major one being large increases in production, though only in one case, Kedah/Perlis, did these result in the establishment of a lasting export trade. Elsewhere the great bulk of production was consumed locally. Another result of intensification may well have been changes in the nature of the work-load. Boserup (1965, 53) has suggested that intensification generally leads to the annual work-load developing marked peaks at the periods of planting and harvesting with lows at other times marking seasonal unemployment. While this may have been true for workers in areas of large-scale rice monoculture such as Kedah, in most regions seasonal off-farm employment opportunities existed in fishing, in the collection of jungle produce, in mines or on paid or unpaid public works. Of these, paid work for the public good decreased as governments organized full-time work-gangs, krah was abolished by fiat and mining fell into the hands of the Chinese who employed their own full-time labour. Seasonal underemployment, therefore, was only partly the result of agricultural intensification. It was equally a result of economic specialization.

THE REGIONAL PATTERN OF ECONOMIC PROCESSES

Specialization was a concomitant of modernization of the whole economy of Malaya. More correctly, one may speak of the economies of the various regions within which local economic regions may be further distinguished. Until the early nineteenth century when the economy of Penang began to expand and to provide a market for agricultural products, the economy of Malaya was relatively self-contained. To be sure there had long been a flourishing export trade in a wide range of commodities including tin, a wide range of forest products and rice, but the greater portion of the labour-force was only marginally involved in such production. A larger portion was involved in the production of commodities for intra-regional trade. Dried fish, salt and atap produced along the coast were undoubtedly exchanged for rice grown inland. Some further regional specialization is exemplified by the shipping, metal-working and textile craft industries of Trengganu and to some degree, Kedah. Coinage was in at least partial use. The basis of production was the peasant family. But the bulk of the labour-force was engaged in rice-growing for subsistence.

SPECIALIZATION

With the development of the Penang market some degree of regional specialization emerged, first in Kedah, then following the Siamese invasion of 1821, in Province Wellesley and later still in Krian, yet later in Kedah and Perlis once more. Their role was the supply of rice and, in Krian and the Province, sugar. The market orientation thus changed from an internal to an external orientation. The results were far-reaching in some respects but not in others. It would seem a reasonable guess that this change of market orientation aided or perhaps even triggered off intensification of

TABLE 20

MALAYA: OCCUPATIONAL GROUPS BY REGION AND STATE, 1911

	Rice-growing	All Agriculture[1]	Econ. Active Persons	Rice-growing as % of All Agriculture	Rice-growing as % of Econ. Active Persons	Agriculture as % of Econ. Active Persons
North-west						
Kedah	102,925	115,740	145,033	89	71	80
Perlis	17,672	17,841	20,241	99	87	88
Penang and Prov. Wellesley	34,736[3]	46,539	143,705	74	24	32
Perak (incl. Dindings)[2]	57,936	136,798	342,393	42	17	40
North-east						
Kelantan	118,141[3]	137,440[3]	164,596[3]	86	72	84
Trengganu	41,722[3]	48,440[3]	80,965[3]	86	52	60
South						
Malacca	23,588	15,456	62,555	61	15	25
Negri Sembilan[2]	22,861	56,165	89,127	41	26	63
'Marchlands'						
Selangor	5,251	86,163	221,435	6	2	39
Pahang[2]	33,846	39,396	72,279	86	47	55
Johore	850[4]	17,686	143,971	5	0.6	12
Malaya	459,528	717.664	1,486,290	64	31	48

Sources: Calculated from Cavendish, 1911; Marriott, 1911a; 1911b; Pountney, 1911; Nathan, 1922.

[1] Excluding stock-rearing *per se*.

[2] Following Hose, 1919, half of the totals for the categories 'kampong owner' and 'planter unspecified' have been added to the Census category 'padi planters'. Number of rice growers in Dindings is not available but agriculturalists totalled 1,557.

[3] An estimate, assuming that proportion of rice growers, etc., in the population in 1911 was the same as in 1921.

[4] This value seems to be low by a whole order of magnitude in view of the return of 11,324 persons as rice growers in the 1921 Census.

rice agriculture in Kedah. The remainder of the suitable lands within easy reach of Penang were brought into its market catchment by active colonization. A commercial superstructure thus came to be erected, but its roots lay not with the producer but with the merchants, the new landlord class and the entrepreneurs. The basis of production, the peasant family, remained. The surplus would seem often to have been appropriated by others. Though specialization in rice-growing for market was considerable, commercialization was only partial and ultimately a developmental dead-end. As Higgins (1959, 257) has noted, 'The very essence of economic development is a fall in the ratio of agricultural employment to total employment'. In the Kedah/Perlis plain, the Province, Krian and also in the small rural area around Malacca town, so far as can be judged, the ratio did not fall (see Table 20). Indeed there is evidence that the proportion of agriculturalists in some parts of both the north-west and the north-east, namely Kedah and Trengganu, rose.

In both states some degree of agrarianization occurred. In Kedah it accompanied specialization and commercially-oriented production, whereas in Trengganu it accompanied a shift to agriculturally-specialized production which, however, remained essentially non-commercial. Concerning Kedah, Hart (Kedah AR 1906–8, 3) noted that

During the ninety years that followed [Raffles' comments upon the need to prevent economic domination by the Chinese] the native population of Kedah have practically abandoned every useful trade that formerly existed with the exception of paddy planting. Cloth and silk are no longer woven, as sarongs and cotton piece goods can be far more cheaply obtained from Birmingham and India, carpentry and brick-laying are almost entirely in the hands of the Chinese, Malay blacksmiths and potters still exist, but iron-mongery is now usually imported as are the earthenware pots and cooking utensils. . . .

For Trengganu the case was similar. In the 1890s, Trengganu was unique in Malaya in having a well-developed industrial craft sector as well as a considerable merchant marine (Clifford, 1897). By 1910, Scott (Trengganu AR 1910) reported that sarong-weaving still existed, and fishing would continue to thrive, but noted that metal-working, ship-building and transportation in sailing vessels were doomed. The result was probably not so much that people were thrown out of work but that their sons, and especially Malay entrepreneurs, saw no future for them in the old activities now increasingly pre-empted by foreigners. The upshot was that the land, in general, and rice-growing, in particular, even on marginally-productive lands, were increasingly resorted to as population pressures increased. However, Trengganu and Kedah were special cases. For other areas, an increase in the proportion of rice growers and agriculturalists cannot be documented.

Elsewhere, production was less specialized and market orientation was local or, as amongst shifting cultivators, almost non-existent. It would seem reasonable to surmise that amongst Malay wet rice growers, a small and erratically-produced surplus found its way into local markets. This

was true in the Perak valley, especially amongst the Siamese in Upper
Perak, in Kelantan and Trengganu, in Negri Sembilan and, though full
documentation is lacking, in Pahang, Selangor and Johore. In these regions
though rice-growing was still of major significance as a form of employment (see Table 20), production was for self-subsistence and the existence
of a surplus, except where this was required by authority as in Naning,
was more or less accidental and incidental. Within this group of states,
however, a major division existed. Whereas in Kelantan, Trengganu and
Pahang 86 per cent of the agriculturalists were rice growers, in the remaining states, the proportion ranged from 42 per cent in Perak down to 5
per cent in Johore.

By 1910 a clear pattern had emerged. Perlis, Kedah, Kelantan and, to a
lesser degree, Trengganu and Pahang, had relatively specialized economies, the speciality being the least lucrative of all, rice-growing. In
these states the ratio of rice growers to the total work-force ranged from
87 per cent in Perlis to 47 per cent in Pahang. In the others, although regions of both commercial and non-commercial rice production existed,
diversification and genuine development of the states' economies had
taken place as is evidenced by ratios of rice growers to total work-force
of 15 to 26 per cent in Penang and Province Wellesley, Perak and Malacca.

PROCESSES AND ECONOMIC ZONES

Cutting across this pattern of economic specialization was another
pattern and this can be defined in terms of the regional variation of
processes. In the north-east on the plains of Kedah and Perlis, commercialization and possibly intensification of production had barely begun
before they were interrupted by war. Not until the 1880s could production
be said to be commercialized and intensive once more as a very large
expansion of the cultivated area began. To the south, the colonized lands
of Province Wellesley and Krian were the scene of intensive commercialized production, virtual rice monocultures from the beginning of large-scale
settlement—in the former from about 1820 and in the latter from the
mid-1870s. Throughout this region the basis of production remained the
peasant family, but the basis of appropriation was commercialized
though retaining traditional elements. Flanking this zone of intensive,
commercial production was a second zone of less commercialized, less
intensive, and less specialized agriculture. This zone lay beyond the rice
market catchment of Penang, though it still lay within the Penang livestock
market hinterland. Rice-growing was for subsistence or for local markets.
Beyond this second zone again lay a third zone, largely one of shifting
cultivation, in which all agricultural production was for self-consumption.
Thus a von Thünen-like series of economic zones existed. In each of these
zones, rice played some part. This is indicated in the scheme below.

In the north-east centres of Kelantan and Trengganu the pattern of
zonation cannot be readily reconstructed though a similar zonation, at
least in the two main valleys, doubtless existed. In these two states commercialization of rice-growing cannot be adequately documented, and it

	Town	George Town
Increasing distance from town	A. Fruit and Vegetable Zone: some rice but not important	Peniagre Plain
	B. Intensive Agricultural Zone: commercialized rice monoculture, minor production of fruit, vegetables, livestock	Balik Pulau (Penang) Kedah/Perlis plain, Province Wellesley, Krian
	C. Extensive Agricultural Zone: subsistence rice with grass fallow, livestock	North and eastern margins of Kedah/Perlis/Province Wellesley plain, Perak valley
	D. Shifting Cultivation Zone: rice one of many crops, no livestock, no market orientation except jungle products	Margins of the ranges

is highly probable that production was mainly for subsistence, with some local market in the main towns of Kota Bharu and Kuala Trengganu. It seems clear that in the course of the nineteenth century a fair degree of intensification of production took place resulting in the extension of annual cropping at the expense of grass fallow.

In the south the economic zone model applied, as in Penang, though not as clearly. Around the town of Malacca lay a small zone of fruit and vegetable cultivation with which rice was intermingled (Zone A). On the plains beyond lay a zone of commercial rice monoculture (Zone B). Further inland, in the Minangkabau areas, rice was still grown by intensive methods but not primarily for market (Zone C). As in the lands margining the Kedah/Perlis/Province Wellesley plain, rice was but one element in a diversified economy, but in the Minangkabau lands intensive, annual cultivation, not extensive, triennial cultivation was the rule because the amount of flat land available was limited to narrow valleys. Intermingled with this indigenous agriculture were the estates of European and Chinese industrial crop producers. Beyond this zone again lay small patches occupied by shifting cultivators (Zone D).

The 'marchlands' fit the model less well and zonations were ephemeral. For example, around Kuala Lumpur in the early 1880s, zones A, B and D could be clearly recognized, with zone C represented by Jelebu. But this was ephemeral in the face of mining activities. In the pioneer lands of southern and inland Perak, Selangor and Sungei Ujong, large-scale, intensive production for commercial purposes was frequently intended but nowhere achieved. Small-scale, intensive but non-commercial production had some slight success. Pahang, however, was a slightly different case. In the Minangkabau areas of the west, production was intensive but not commercialized. Elsewhere extensive, subsistence production was the rule and the state as a whole did not conform to the model.

The process of commercialization and its resultant processes of intensification and extension of the cultivated area may be encompassed within a further simple model.

Subsistence Production	Commercial Production	Suitable Land Available	Suitable Land not Available	Result
X		X		Extension
X			X	Intensification
	X	X		Extension
	X		X	Intensification

In the first case it would seem reasonable to suppose that with continued slow growth of the population, perhaps with moderate immigration of other subsistence farmers, a slow extension of the cultivated area would ensue. The archetype here was the Perak valley prior to the legislative prohibition of shifting cultivation which resulted in a sudden 'jump' to intensive methods. Other examples were Kedah prior to the growth of Penang, Kelantan until late in the nineteenth century, and small, stable centres of rice-growing such as the Lebir valley of Kelantan or Ulu Selama in Perak.

Where further suitable land was not available, it might be supposed that in order to maintain levels of food production, more intensive methods would be adopted. Lands under grass fallow would be brought under annual cultivation, rain-rice lands would be irrigated and so forth. One example of this case would seem to be Kelantan from around the turn of the century by which time a full recovery from the disasters of the 1880s had been made, though the evidence is suggestive rather than conclusive. It is possible that the technically sophisticated farming methods of the Minangkabau were a response to the spatial limitations of the valleys they occupied. Though the growing of hill rice was capable of almost infinite expansion, its usefulness in supplementing lowland production was reduced by its vulnerability to drought. Crop reliability, it could be argued, had thus to be ensured by adopting sophisticated cultivation techniques in the lowlands. There is, however, not a shred of evidence that this was the case. It is possible that intensification resulting from lack of land took place at an unknown, early period but on balance this seems unlikely. The Minangkabau appear in the record with a technically-developed form of cultivation that owes much to Minangkabau cultural antecedents and little to spatial limitations in their adopted homeland. In other areas of limited availability of land, in Ulu Perak and Ulu Selama, for instance, intensification took place at the behest of administrators who wished to curtail shifting cultivation so as to protect forests. The rakyat would doubtless have continued to make up any short-fall in lowland production by growing hill rice. In areas where land suitable for wet cultivation came to be lacking as the population grew, the answer in a number of cases would seem to have been extension into the hills rather than intensification in the lowlands, Kelantan alone being a likely exception.

The third and fourth cases may be discussed together. With a change from a subsistence and local market orientation to a more distant and commercial market orientation, two things could happen, depending upon the availability of land. If no land were available, intensification would result. Where land was available, the area would be extended. In the north-western region, abundant land was available, yet when it came to be developed, it was developed using relatively intensive methods. At the same time it seems probable that some of the older areas of grass-fallow cultivation were brought into annual cultivation. Intensification and extension thus proceeded simultaneously and this demands some explanation.

Down to the time of the Siamese invasion no great expansion took place, at least none was reported, and it may be surmised that some degree of intensification of cultivation took place in Kedah as the Penang market grew. But it would seem likely that a fair proportion of the farms were grass-fallow farms on which livestock were an important element. When Province Wellesley was developed, methods were fairly intensive right from the beginning and annual cultivation was the rule. The question arises as to why this was the case and why did extensive farming not precede intensive, annual cropping? One likely reason was that, at least initially, plough animals were few. In other words, buffaloes were of greater value as traction than as meat. But much more important was the urgent need to supply Penang with the staple and in so doing to make money to satisfy newly-aroused needs for the products of Western industry. This continued to be true within the Penang 'rice catchment' as production resumed in Kedah and Perlis. In the Kedah/Perlis plains region the economic interests of large-scale entrepreneurs were reinforced by their high status which derived from traditional sources within Malay society. But everywhere in this north-western region the twin drives of obtaining land to call one's own and of satisfying needs which could only be satisfied in a commercial context, motivated both expansion and intensification.

RICE GROWERS IN A CHANGING SOCIETY

One need not be an economic determinist of the Marxist variety to observe that large economic changes result in as well as result from social transformations.[1] Rice production in a good number of areas, especially in the north-west, came to be at least partly commercialized by 1910, and

[1]Lefebvre (1968, 14) is surely incorrect in suggesting that Marx himself championed the universalist idea that the development of productive forces automatically determined the forms and relationships of society. The whole tenor of Marx's argument is quite the opposite. See Avineri, 1968, 151–2, 155–7.

now it only remains to examine the social changes which accompanied and were intimately linked with the process of commercialization. At this point the caveat must be entered that commercialization took place in the context of pioneering and that social change is inextricably bound up with both. Nor is it possible to present any 'final answer' as to the precise factors responsible for change. It would be all too easy to argue that in the north-west region, the existence of the Penang market, and later, markets in the Perak, Selangor and Negri Sembilan tin-lands resulted in a fair degree of commercialization of agriculture, in the establishment of the idea of land as property and in the emergence not only of an entrepreneurial class but also in the appearance of a 'rich peasant' group of petty landowners.

There can be little doubt that in the 1880s the Kedah aristocracy played a major role in expanding the cultivated area and in stimulating change to a commercialized but still peasant-based form of production. But the motivations of these entrepreneurs lie beyond reconstruction. Certainly though, the aristocratic entrepreneurs of Kedah were very far from being the disaffected characters that Barnett (Vogt, 1968, 555) would suggest are typical of innovators. Rather, their role was completely in keeping with the Malay notion that leaders should be fathers to their people. Certainly too, the entrepreneurs, with a few minor exceptions such as Francis Light and James Low, were not true capitalists. In Malacca, the tithe-impropriators of the Dutch regime were 'capitalists' only in the sense that they gained an income merely by virtue of 'owning' (if indeed they did 'own') land, but there, any trend to capitalism was quickly reversed by their expropriation by the British. Nowhere could it be said that labour was separated in any significant degree from the means of production, namely land. The only point at which labour came to be separated from land derived from the abolition of krah which resulted in the deployment of (foreign) wage-labour on capital works.

Nevertheless Malay society changed. Though its essence, in Firth's terminology, the social structure, was little affected by commercialization, by agrarianization, or by such relatively minor matters as the disappearance of bondsmen (*hamba*) and slaves, social organization was modified. The entrepreneurial role of the aristocracy is proof enough of this but the aristocracy was never any the less the aristocracy for undertaking this transformative role. Amongst the rakyat change was more radical. Though rakyats remained rakyats, some were more 'rakyat' than others. The fact that some peasants were able to obtain land suitable for developing into holdings capable of producing far more than was needful for subsistence, was a potent factor in the emergence of a new rich peasant group. This new group was as much property-based as status-based, though this is something of a 'chicken-and-egg' question. No doubt there had always been some individual rakyats who by energy and good fortune had accumulated property, but pioneering in a colonialistic milieu had the effect of enhancing the rewards of personal ability. This was especially the case where governments did not hesitate to direct aid into channels other than those of traditional authority, especially in those cases where traditional authority was content to lead a comfortably sybaritic life.

A necessary concomitant of the emergence of a class of rich peasant landowners was the growth of a tenant class. Presumably by no means were all the tenants landless. At present a significant proportion of rice farmers own some land and rent more.[1] Tenants may well have had at least as much land at their disposal as those farmers who owned their own land. This is true at the present time (Hill, 1967, 102). However, their total farm income was probably much less since even as early as the 1830s in Province Wellesley, tenants were surrendering as much as half of their crop to their landlords.[2] The incidence of tenancy during the period is exceedingly difficult to establish. At present, tenants and owner-tenants together account for two-thirds of all rice farms in Penang, Province Wellesley and Kedah (Hill, 1967, 106). One study (Wilson in Hill, 1967, 106) showed that in the course of twenty-five years about a quarter of the pioneer farms in a Perak irrigation scheme became occupied by tenants. Obviously this rate cannot be satisfactorily extrapolated backwards in time since to do so would suggest that by now all long-occupied farms are now worked by tenants which is not so.

Paralleling these changes in social organization was a change in attitudes towards land. No longer was land 'owned' by God whose trustee was the raja. It now became real property and by 1910 a market in rice land had developed in most regions except those occupied by Minangkabau. Rice land, even with tenants on it, was bought and sold. The tenant was a source of income. The rakyat had always been a source of income for the rajas, but in a sense more people, all the landlords, had become 'rajas' without being rajas in social status and social responsibility. Thus conflicts arose between those who saw land in a capitalistic way as a realizable asset and those who retained the traditional view of land as a common good upon which he who was entitled could draw at will.

CONCLUDING DISCUSSION

Rice-growing in Malaya thus underwent a major expansion and intensification during the colonial period. Unlike Burma[3], Thailand and Vietnam however, expansion was stimulated not by growing export markets but by an expanding internal market and also by colonization which was not necessarily directly linked to that market. The dominance of the northern production areas was merely re-emphasized during the colonial period when 60 per cent of the total rice area was to be found in the north-west (including Perak) with another 23 per cent in the north-east.

[1] In 1960, 15 per cent of the rice farmers were owner-tenants (see Hill, 1967, 101).

[2] In such cases it cannot be concluded that the income of tenants was half that of those who owned their own land since in modern times production per unit area on tenant farms is consistently higher than on owner farms.

[3] For studies of the Burmese rice industry see Cheng, 1968, and Adas, 1974.

This northern dominance can be partly explained in terms of favourable environmental elements: adequate water in most years for the beginning of the cycle of cultivation; except in Krian, adequate drainage; warm sunny weather for ripening; in some areas, availability of manure. But at least as important as these factors was tradition. Although, for lack of conclusive evidence, rice-growing cannot be fully established for prehistoric times, it is nevertheless clear that a relatively sophisticated technique existed in the north in fairly early times. The introduction of the partly-controlled micro-environment represented by wet, bunded fields may have been as early as the sixth century. But until the advent of local export markets, bunded fields, which necessitate monoculture, were not the only sort in which rice was grown in the lowlands. More extensive forms of cultivation were equally if not more important.

There is no evidence that the widespread adoption of techniques which tended to produce a surplus, namely ploughing, transplanting, bunded fields and irrigation, removed Malthusian checks upon food supply. Certainly the population grew but the area cultivated expanded at least in step with population growth and possibly ahead of it. In some areas the areal pattern of expansion was from inland areas towards the coast. This was true in Kedah and parts of Province Wellesley where movement was from relatively free-draining soils of the middle reaches of the rivers to heavy but higher-producing soils nearer the coast. In Trengganu the move was in the same direction but onto the acidic mucks lying between the coastal *permatangs*. In Kelantan, colonization was upstream and the same was true in Malacca and Negri Sembilan. The main valleys were occupied first with the side valleys being settled subsequently.

Initiatives in nineteenth-century expansion were of several sorts. On the Kedah/Perlis plain, the activities of men with royal connexions and of royalty itself were of major significance in mobilizing development capital and in using traditional labour sources for the public good. Even the loss of traditional labour involved in the abolition of krah failed to hinder these large-scale operations. Unlike Krian, however, large-scale working was fortunately not essential to successful colonization. British initiatives were insignificant beside Malay achievements. Krian was a mixed success though it showed that only large-scale development would fully succeed in the difficult environment of low-gradient coastal plains. In the Federated Malay States small government-aided schemes for settlement and irrigation were a little more successful. Until 1890 loans were given for both purposes, but after that time only for the latter. But failures were frequent, both by government and by entrepreneurs. Some eventual, indirect return to government doubtless resulted from the encouragement of immigration but government aid led to dependency. The tradition of gotong royong was weakened and the same thing happened to the entrepreneurial role of royalty, some members of which were content to lead an easy life as government pensioners.

Since entrepreneurs stood to gain personally from their success in contributing to expansion of the cultivated area and increased production, it would seem probable that they would have actively promoted the intensification of cropping. At the same time, intensification involved the widespread adoption of one major system of cropping, namely an annual rain-fed (rarely irrigated) system based upon animal tillage. This, however, was the end result of a lengthy period of evolution stretching back into remote periods.

The primal system in South-East Asia was probably relatively intensive, intensive enough to lead to the replacement of swamp forest by swamp grasses and shrubs. It was probably 'anchored' to coastal and riverine locations by the fact that these were habitats where protein foods, mainly fish, could easily be obtained. This form of cultivation, in which rice was but one crop amongst many, evolved in two directions, one towards long-fallow systems of shifting cultivation, mainly on slopes, and the other towards rather shorter scrub or grass-fallow systems of the swamps and lowlands. The second of these ultimately led to the ubiquitous forms of annual cultivation. But even as late as the early twentieth century, less intensive forms remained. Long-term forest-fallow persisted, at least as a supplementary form, because it gave a superior product, required less labour and yielded better than pioneer wet fields.

Short-term grass-fallow was significant because it represented a form of mixed farming which probably had major advantages both from the point of diet and income. It provided income from the periodical sale of livestock which were a more or less permanent realizable asset. Moreover, though vulnerable to epidemic disease, livestock were less vulnerable than crops to bad seasons and furthermore did not deteriorate rapidly with age. At the same time soil fertility was maintained, especially since a crop was harvested from the same land only one year in three or four.

In a sense therefore, the shift to annual cultivation was regressive, though annual cultivation no doubt increased total production and income. This shift necessarily implied a reduction in the ratio of animals to land, since with the fields being occupied with a crop for eight to ten months of the year, provision of grazing was difficult. Only enough remained to feed tractive animals, not herd animals and this is indicated by the virtual cessation of melanyak tillage. One answer to this problem was the provision of grazing in areas marginal to the intensively cropped area, as in Kelantan and Trengganu. In the Kedah/Perlis plain the use of guano was an answer to loss of valuable animal manure, but elsewhere this was unavailable. The result was probably some decline in soil fertility, a decline aggravated by the common practice of stubble-burning.

Boserup, Geertz and others have suggested that intensification in these circumstances may be triggered off by rising population and the failure of extension of the cultivated area to keep pace with such growth. While this may be true of regions with economies in which trade in the staple is largely lacking, it is not true elsewhere. In Malaya, for example, Kelantan offers an example of intensification arising largely from population growth though even there the fact that some rice land came to be given over to the cultivation of coconuts suggests compensatory intensification or extension elsewhere. In Malaya, intensification must be attributed to two additional processes. One is commercialization and the other is agrarianization.

Of these two the former was rather more important. In pre-colonial times the agrarian economy of Malaya was largely self-contained, the major exceptions being Kedah, which produced pepper, rice and livestock for export, and Trengganu, a major pepper-producer. With the development of the Penang market and, later, markets elsewhere in the Peninsula, production in the north-west became specialized in three commodities, spices in the hands of the Europeans, sugar in the hands of the Chinese, and rice in the hands of the Malays. The production of rice came to be market-oriented and in most accessible areas the size of holdings and yields were great enough to ensure a surplus. However, the unit of production remained unchanged, and since amongst the Malays there was no fall in the ratio of agricultural workers to total workers, true economic development did not follow.

Agrarianization also contributed to the push towards more intensive farming. As Malay traditional crafts, notably in Kedah and in Trengganu, came into competition with imported industrial goods and as steamers, began to compete with traditional forms of coastwise transportation, these sectors declined. One result was the intensification and the extension of rice-growing.

From these processes stemmed distinct economic zones. Near the urban market, cultivation was intensive. Some land was in annually-grown rice, some under vegetables or fruit-trees for market. This was a rather limited zone since the urban markets were not large. The market for the staple was larger and so was the specialized production-zone around it. Here annual-cropping and marketing of the surplus were characteristic. Further out again, production was less intensive, grass-fallow rather than annual cropping, and less commercialized, the staple rarely coming to market though livestock might. Beyond again, extensive, shifting cultivation was the rule and market orientation was lacking.

This spatial model would seem to apply fairly generally, though in many cases there were enclaves of one zone within another. Kedah/Perlis in relation to Penang as a centre fits well, but in the north-east data are too scanty to be certain. In the south, a similar zonation existed centred upon Malacca, and briefly, upon Kuala Lumpur. Most other urban centres were either very small or were developed in a period of relatively easy transportation and so the concentric zone pattern was lacking.

The processes themselves can also be incorporated into a simple model. Given the situation in which the population was increasing, under subsistence production, intensification would result when land was not easily available, and extension would result when land was available. The evidence would support this general proposition. A change to commercial production might be expected to result in a swing to intensive methods where sufficient land was not available or to result in extension of the cultivated area if it was. The actual result was that both processes proceeded simultaneously. The area was extended, but under intensive annual cultivation, not under extensive methods. In part this was accidental. Province Wellesley was colonized by refugees who necessarily adopted annual cropping as a matter of personal urgency as well as to supply a market suddenly cut off from its usual supply. In the south Kedah plain and in Krian, the nature of the market provided reason enough for annual cropping. Elsewhere these factors were scarcely operative. In the Federated Malay States, especially in Perak, intensification was a result of government fiat. Amongst the Minangkabau, by way of contrast, intensive working had been an accomplished fact since early times. Even apart from those regions in which a clear commercial orientation developed during the course of the nineteenth century, it would seem very likely that either intensification or extension took place in order to satisfy newly-developed 'needs'.[1]

It is a truism to suggest that large economic changes result in social change. Pioneering, and in some areas commercialization, were large changes by any measure. Amongst the higher echelons, these processes in some cases served to reinforce members' places in society. Thus the Kedah notables ensured for themselves a continuance of their economic role in society as well as of their social role. Though they used their already established position in society partly for capitalistic ends, the means were traditional. In most other areas, however, the highest ranks played only a minor part in developing land for rice, though they were by no means inactive in other fields. At the other end of the scale, the abolition of slavery and debt bondage was completely without economic motivation and had little economic effect. Nevertheless amongst the rakyat a new group of rich peasants emerged. Their status accompanied the possession of more than average amounts of land and this reinforced status in other fields especially in religion. In the course of the nineteenth century attitudes to land changed. Land, once developed, acquired monetary value and, except amongst the Minangkabau, freely entered into commercial transactions. The range of products which could be transformed into money also increased, and rice was one major example. Nevertheless market forces did not yet have full play in the countryside. Conditions of tenancy, indebtedness and fixed prices still prevailed.

The peasant was thus not a petty capitalist on the Western pattern and the spread of new social and economic orientations failed to bring him benefits equalling those of other segments of the broader community. Even if he were materially better off than his grandfather had been, he was still at the bottom of the socio-economic heap. It was his lot to be 'content barely to live' and to 'find in the good earth and fields a sure refuge from materialism'. *Kalau tiada padi, sa-barang kerja ta' jadi*—and the opposite is even more true.

---

[1]Brookfield (1972) has a particularly valuable discussion of the effects of changing need systems upon agriculture.

Glossary

Malay terms appearing in the text have been freely anglicized, especially in the plural for which the Malay forms seem either clumsy or pedantic in an English text. Nineteenth-century spellings have been retained.

Ali Baba:	used to refer to a business arrangement in which Malay (Ali) participation is mere window-dressing for Chinese (Baba) financing and control
Ani-ani (Javanese):	see *tuai*
Atap, attap:	palm thatch, usually made from *Nipah*
Baba:	male Chinese, usually one of local birth or long residence who has adopted Malay customs to some degree, also used collectively
Bagan:	lit. platform for drying fish; by extension, a fishing village
Baginda:	king, ruler, prince
Balukar:	see *belukar*
Batas (sing. and pl.):	low bund of earth separating wet rice fields
Beliong:	axe, traditionally made with a flexible handle of *rotan*
Belukar, balukar, blukar:	secondary forest
Bendang:	northern Malay equivalent of *sawah*
Bendang berbatas:	bunded wet rice fields
Benua:	large country, continent, inland as distinct from coast
Bilal:	muezzin
Blachan:	a pungent paste made from prawns or fish
Blukar:	see *belukar*
Bras, beras:	rice grain not yet prepared by cooking
Budak raja:	lit. raja's children, see *kawan*
Campong:	see *kampung*

Changkol, changkul:	heavy, long-handled hoe
Chedong, chedongan:	see *padi chedongan*
Chetty, chitty:	Chettiar money-lender
Copang, kupang:	tin coin of small and variable value
Coyan, koyan:	in modern times a measure of 40 *pikul* weight, but formerly a volumetric measure of variable size. Some authorities give a coyan (of rice) as equivalent to 1,250 *gantangs*, others give 800 *gantangs*
Dammer, damar:	resin
Dato, datuk:	lit. grandfather but frequently the title of a distinguished (male) person, usually not of royal blood
Dusun:	orchard
Engku:	a person of high rank, usually, but not invariably, of royal blood
Gantang:	a variable measure of approximately one Imperial gallon. Since the 1880s it has been officially exactly equal to an Imperial gallon
Haj:	the pilgrimage to Mecca
Haji:	Muslim male who has completed the pilgrimage to Mecca
Hamba:	lit. slave, but more usually bondsman, servant, as distinct from *rakyat*
Huma, padi huma:	clearing on hill land; rice grown in such a clearing
Imam:	chief official of a mosque
Kajang:	waterproof mat used especially on boats
Kampung, kampong, campong:	hamlet, village, homestead
Kawan:	friend, follower, following (n.)
Kayu gharu:	garu wood, camphor wood
Kebun, keboon:	garden
Keladi:	*Colocasia* spp., see *keledek*
Kelamin:	see *klamin*
Keledek:	yam, *Dioscorea alata*; sweet potato, *Ipomoea batatas*. Not to be confused with *keladi* which refers to taro (cocoyam), *Colocasia* spp.
Keri, kri:	a short-handled hoe (see Kitching, 1930)

Keris:	see *kris*
Khatib:	mosque official ranking below *imam*
Kinchir ayer:	current-driven, undershot water-wheel used for raising water from a river
Klamin, kelamin:	married couple, family
Koyan:	see *coyan*
Krah:	forced labour, corvée
Kri:	see *keri*
Kris, keris (sing. and pl.):	wavy-bladed dagger or short sword
Ksatriya (Sanscrit):	warrior, member of warrior caste
Kuala:	mouth of a river
Kupang:	see *copang*
Ladang:	forest clearing cultivated with food crops; modern meaning extended to any clearing, estate
Lalang:	coarse grass of the genus *Imperata*
Lampan:	lit. wooden tray or bowl for washing tin; by extension, working tin in this manner
Lanyak, melanyak:	to churn the soil by means of cattle penned upon it
Lebai:	mosque official, layman renowned for piety
Lesong, lesong batu:	mortar for husking grain; stone mortar
Malim:	learned person, esp. in religion
Maulud:	lit. birthday
Melanyak:	see *lanyak*
Mukim:	minor administrative unit roughly corresponding to a parish
Munshi:	teacher of languages, scholar
Nagara, negara:	nation, chief of state
Nakhoda:	ship's captain
Nibong:	palm of the genus *Oncosperma*
Nipah, nipa:	*Nipah frutescens*, a common palm of brackish water. The fronds are widely used for the making of *atap* thatch
Nonya, nonia:	female Chinese, usually one of local birth or long residence who has adopted Malay customs to some degree

Orang bukit (sing. and pl.):	lit. hill person, hill people, usually aborigines
Orang kaya:	lit. rich man, also a title
Orang laut (sing. and pl.):	lit. sea person, sea people, coast-dwelling aborigines
Orlong:	see *relong*
Padi, paddy:	strictly, rice plant, but frequently used by Europeans as equivalent to both *padi* and *beras*. The modern American use of 'paddy' as meaning a wet rice field is unknown in Malay and Malayan English
Padi berat:	lit. heavy rice; a rice variety which is slow-growing but heavy-yielding
Padi chedongan:	transplanted rice
Padi huma:	see *huma*
Padi ringan:	a rice variety which is quick-growing but light-yielding
Padi terbuang:	padi thrown down in a roughly-cleared spot and left to come up as it may
Padi tugalan:	rice sown directly into dibbled holes
Pandita:	learned man, teacher, pundit
Pangara:	rake, harrow
Panglima:	ruler's 'right-hand man', esp. military leader
Parang:	heavy knife, machete
Pawang:	traditional Malay doctor, wise man, magician
Paya:	swamp
Paya chedong:	swamp used for transplanting rice
Paya tabor:	swamp used for broadcast rice
Penghulu:	district headman. Often incorrectly used for village headman who is correctly termed *ketua kampong*
Permatang:	sand ridge marking present or past shore-line
Perut:	lit. belly, womb. In Minangkabau, clan
Pinang, penang:	*Areca* tree or its nut
Pulut:	sticky rice commonly used for cake-making or brewing
Raja:	prince, ruler

Rakyat (sing. and pl.), *raayat, raiat:*	a commoner, peasant; the common people, peasantry
Rapai:	a tax on cultivators
Ratan, rattan, rotan:	rattan; woody, armed climbers mainly of the genera *Calamus* and *Daemonorops*
Relong:	as a linear measurement, 10 *jumba* or 240 feet; as a square measure, officially 1 1/3 acres in Penang and the Province, 7/10 acre in Kedah though these are modern equivalents, cf. *orlong*
Rimba:	mature lowland rainforest
Rotan:	see *ratan*
Sagu:	sago, cf. *segu, sega* meaning rice in east and central Java
Sali:	millet, *Coix lachryma-jobi.* Interestingly the word also means 'strength' or 'power'
Sam Sam, Samsam:	Siamese-speaking Malay
Sarong:	a broad loop of cloth, customary lower garment of Malays of both sexes
Sawah:	a levelled wet rice field, not necessarily irrigated, surrounded by and divided by low bunds (batas). By origin probably Javanese
Segu, sega (Javanese):	cooked rice, sago (see also *sagu*)
Semai, semai tuah, semai penegah, semai muda:	Rice nursery, nursery for long-term varieties, for medium-term varieties, for short-term varieties
Semangat padi:	an anthropomorphic term for rice soul; essential spirit of the rice
Serang:	helmsman, shipmaster
Shaik(h), sheik(h):	an Arab, usually much venerated by Malays
Sireh:	betel, *Piper betle*
Suku Biduanda:	lit. tribes of the original inhabitants (Minangkabau)
Sultan:	ruler. Not in common use until late in the nineteenth century
Sungei, sungei korok:	river; large drain or river cut
Surat, surat putus:	letter; sultan's letter granting title
Syed:	male descendant of the Prophet Muhammed
Tabor, taboran:	broadcast seed

Tajak:	a form of bill-hook
Tali ayer:	drain, water-channel
Tanah chedong:	land into which rice seedlings could be transplanted
Tanah hidup:	lit. living land
Tanah Melayu:	land of the Malays
Tanah mati:	lit. dead land
Tanah pesaka:	family property, lands under the control of matrilineally-related women (Minangkabau)
Tanah tebusan:	in Minangkabau, 'redeemed' lands, acquired by payment to the *Undang*
Tanah tugalan:	land into which seed rice could be dibbled
Tanah waris:	lit. inherited land; in Minangkabau, unredeemed lands (see *tanah tebusan*)
Tebbas, menebbas (tebas, menebas):	to cut brushwood; cf. *tebang, menebang*, to cut trees
Tenggala:	plough
Towkay (Chinese):	rich Chinese, entrepreneur
Tuai:	a somewhat annular-bladed reaping-knife of ancient origin in common use in Malay lands, cf. *ani-ani*
Tugal, menugal:	dibble, to dibble
Tulang mawas:	lit. apes' bones. Common name for ancient sickle-shaped tools of iron found in parts of the Peninsula
Tunku, tengku:	member of royalty, usually not the ruler
Ulu:	upper portion of a river valley, the interior country
Undang-Undang:	in Minangkabau, tribal chiefs. Also law, statute
Ungku:	member of royalty, not the ruler
Wan:	descendant of a great chief

Bibliography

Abbreviations are listed on page xvi ff. Entries marked* are not specifically referred to in the text.

UNPUBLISHED MATERIALS

These are located in the National Archives, Kuala Lumpur, unless otherwise indicated.

Batang Padang District Office, MS files.

Batang Padang Monthly Report, 7–1896 (BPDO 315/96).

Bernam Monthly Reports, 11–1877 (SSS 8/78); 2–1878 (SSS 107/78); 3–1878 (SSS 143/78); 5–1878 (SSS 161/78).

Bonney, R., 1967, 'Kedah: 1771–1821, the Search for Security and Independence', M.A. thesis, University of Malaya, Kuala Lumpur.

Clifford, H., 1887, 'Journal of Mr. H. Clifford's Mission to Pahang', MS, CO 273/144.

Dyce, C.A. 1847, 'Sketches in the Straits', holograph MSS in Art Museum, University of Singapore.

East India Company, Board's Collections, see Great Britain, East India Company.

Forrest, T., 1784, 'Letter to Hon. Warren Hastings', 15.9.1784, MS, British Museum additional MSS 29, 166.

Great Britain, Colonial Office, MSS in Public Records Office, London, series CO 273; series CO 275.

Great Britain, East India Company, Board's Collections, MSS in India Office Library, London (selections on microfilm in University of Singapore Library).

Great Britain, India Office Library, London, Documents relating to Penang, Home Miscellaneous, vol. 434.

Hill, H.C., 1900, 'Report on the present system of forest conservancy in the Straits Settlements with suggestions for future management', CO 273/258 (with map in CO 273/357).

Hill, R.D., 1973, 'Rice in Malaya, a Study in Historical Geography', Ph.D. thesis, University of Singapore.

Jackson, J.C., 1965, 'Chinese and European Agricultural Enterprise in Malaya, 1786–1921', Ph.D. thesis, University of Malaya.

Jelebu Annual Report, 1894, NSSS 1497/95.

Jelebu Monthly Report, 9–1890, NSSS 1485/90.

Kelantan Land Office Records, Duplicate Grants.

Khoo Hock Cheng, 1959, 'The Trade of Penang, 1786–1823', B.A. academic exercise, University of Malaya, Singapore.

Khoo Kay Kim, 1967, 'The Western Malay States 1861–1873', M.A. thesis, University of Malaya, Kuala Lumpur.

Kinta Land Office, MS files.

Kuala Lumpur District Land Statistics 1879, SSS 299/79.

Kuala Pilah Monthly Reports, 6–1895 (NSSS 1482/95); 3–1896 (NSSS 826/96).

Kuala Selangor Annual Report, 1882 (SSS 148/83).

Kuala Selangor Monthly Reports, 11–1877 (SSS 8/78); 3–1878 (SSS 94/78); 5–1878 (SSS 188/78); 10–1878 (SSS 235/78, 439/78); 3–1884 (633/84); 7–1884 (SSS 1434/84); 6–1885 (SSS 1037/85).

Kuantan Annual Report, 1890, KDO 43/91.

Kuantan District Office, MS files.

Kuantan Monthly Report, 12–1898, KDO 614/98.

Langat Monthly Reports, 10–1883 (SSS 1682/83); 3–1884 (SSS 636/84); 4–1884 (SSS 886/84); 5–1884 (SSS 1059/84); 6–1884 (SSS 1272/84); 3–1885 (SSS 558/85).

Lee Chye Hooi, 1957, 'The Penang Land Problem, 1786–1841', B.A. academic exercise, University of Malaya, Singapore.

Light, F., 1787, 'Description of living conditions, commerce and policies in Penang and a brief report of the surrounding countries', MS letter to Hon. Sir A. Campbell, 2.2.1787 (microfilm in University of Singapore Library, original in Edinburgh).

Lim Teck Ghee, 1968, 'Perak, Aspects of British Land and Agricultural Policy 1874–92', M.A. thesis, University of Malaya, Kuala Lumpur.

Low, H., 1877, Diary, MS.

MacGregor, A., 1886, 'Proposal [sic] scheme for Indian immigrants to Teluk Anson', SSS 970/86.

Maharajah and Temenggong of Johore, Letter Book, MSS on microfilm, University of Singapore Library.

Malacca Public Works Department, Survey Department, 1876–1886, MS field books, Nos 1–117.

Negri Sembilan State Secretariat files, 1888–1900.

Ong, M.T. Seok-Keow, 1958, 'Population Trends in Kelantan, 1909–1957', B.A. academic exercise, University of Malaya, Singapore.

Penang Land Office Records, 1829–1833, duplicates of grants, bound volumes in Penang Land Office, George Town.

Perak Census, 1891, MS.

Raja Bot, 1902, 'Translation of a letter by Raja Bot giving his view on the subject of extending the area of rice cultivation to Sultan of Selangor & Resident-General F.M.S.', 22.8.1902, typescript, CO 273/284 (publ. in *Agr. Bull. FMS*, 1, 582–6).

Resident's Diary, Malacca, 1827–8, Straits Settlements Government Records, ser. O, MSS in National Library, Singapore.

Selangor Census, 1879, SSS 339/79.

Selangor, Lands Department Annual Reports, 1883 (SSS 334/84); 1884 (SSS 204/85); 1888 (SSS 442/89).

Selangor, State Secretariat files, 1877–1900.

Shamsul Bahrin, 1964, 'Indonesians in Malaya', M.A. thesis, University of Sheffield.

Sharom Ahmat, 1969, 'Transition and Change in a Malay State, a Study of the Economic and Political Development of Kedah, 1879–1923', Ph.D. thesis, University of London.

Smith, Sir C.C., 1891, 'Report on a visit of inspection to Malacca and Negri Sembilan', CO 273/173.

Stubbs-Brown, M., 1963, 'A History of Penang 1805–1819', M.A. thesis, University of Malaya, Kuala Lumpur.

Tampin Monthly Reports, 10/12–1887 (NSSS 9/88); 5–1897 (NSSS 1940/97); 7–1898 (NSSS 2498/98).

Temerloh District Office, MS files.

Temerloh Monthly Reports, 10–1896 (TDO 369/96); 12–1896 (TDO 8/97); 12–1897 (TDO 7/98).

Tregonning, K.G., 1958, 'The Founding and Development of Penang, 1786–1826', Ph.D. thesis, University of Malaya, Singapore.

Ulu Langat Monthly Reports, 5–1883 (SSS 790/83); 6–1883 (SSS 946/83); 7–1883 (SSS 1133/83); 9–1883 (SSS 1541/83); 10–1883 (SSS 1689/83); 12–1883 (SSS 82/84); 1–1884 (SSS 235/84); 4–1884 (SSS 921/84); 2–1886 (SSS 614/86); 4–1886 (SSS 1109/86); 10–1886 (SSS 2574/86); 11–1886 (SSS 2609/86).

OFFICIAL AND SEMI-OFFICIAL PUBLICATIONS

Abdul Rahman, Syed, 1920, 'Padi cultivation in Pahang', *Agr. Bull. FMS*, 8, 176–8.

Anonymous, 1892, Notes [of a journey by the Acting British Resident] *PGG*, 5, 1101–4.

——, 1894, 'Notes of the Resident's visits to districts in Selangor, 1894', *Selangor J.*, 2, 201–6, 255–9, 342–6.

——, 1906, 'Opening of the Krian irrigation canal', *Agr. Bull. Straits FMS*, 5, 283–6.

*——, 1940, 'The development of rice cultivation in Malaya', *Malay. agr. J.*, 28, 472–8.

Arden, S., 1903, 'Encouragement of agriculture among the natives', *Agr. Bull. Straits FMS*, 2, 399–402 (with comments by Ridley, H.N., 402–5).

Birch, E.W., 1896, 'Report by the Secretary to the Government of a visit to Ulu Bruas', *PGG*, 9, 779–85.

Birch, J.W.W., 1875, 'Report of H.B.M.'s Resident at Perak', *SSGG*, 1875, 375–84.

Blue Books, see Straits Settlements *Blue Books.*

Braddell, T., 1874, 'Continuation of report on proceedings of the government relating to the Native States in the Malay Peninsula', Great Britain, *Accounts & Papers*, 1874.

Brewster, E.J., 1896, 'Report of inspection of the Lower Perak District by the District Magistrate', *PGG*, 9, 395–8.

Cavendish, A., 1911, *Report on the Census of Kedah and Perlis A.H. 1329 (A.D. 1911)*, Penang.

Coombs, G.E., 1917–18, 'Notes on the production of dry-land rice', *Agr. Bull. Straits FMS*, 6, 321–7.

Federated Malay States, 'Conference of Chiefs (minutes of a), 1903', *PGG*, 9.10.1903, suppl.

Federated Malay States, Lands Department Annual Reports, 1898, (*PGG*, 9.6.1899, suppl.); 1899 (*PGG* 8.6.1900 suppl.).

Hose, E.S., 1919, 'Memorandum on the figures of Malay population in the Federated Malay States in relation to padi cultivation', *Agr. Bull. FMS*, 7, 5, 320–2.

Jack, H.W., 1923a, *Rice in Malaya*, FMS & SS, Department of Agriculture, Bull. 35, Kuala Lumpur.

——, 1923b, 'Rice in Malaya', *Malay. agr. J.*, 11, 103–19, 139–69, 168 [*sic*] –212.

Jelebu Annual Reports, 1891, (*SSAR*, 1891, 497–500); 1892, (*SSAR*, 1892, 523–37).

Johore Annual Report 1912, 1913, Singapore (actual title, *Johore in 1912*).

Kedah Annual Reports, 1905–6, (Calcutta, microfilm in University of Singapore Library); 1906–8 (Bangkok); 1909, (Kuala Lumpur).

Kelantan Annual Reports, 1903–4, (microfilm in University of Singapore Library); 1904–5 (Bangkok).

Kinta Annual Reports, 1888 (*PGG*, 2, 333–49); 1889 (*PGG*, 3, 189–93); 1890 (*PGG*, 4, 762–8); 1891 (*PGG*, 5, 672–7); 1896 (*PGG*, 10, 336–45); 1900 (*PGG*, 14, 5.6.1901 suppl.).

Kinta Monthly Reports, 11–1892 (*PGG*, 6, 11–12); 4–1893 (*PGG*, 6, 483–4); 6–1893 (*PGG*, 6, 625–6); 4–1894 (*PGG*, 7, 203–4); 8–1898 (*PGG*, 11, 709–10).

Krian Annual Reports, 1888 (*PGG*, 2, 63–92); 1889 (*PGG*, 3, 223–4); 1894 (*PGG*, 8, 404–12).

Krian Monthly Reports, 5–1889 (*PGG*, 2, 572–3); 9–1890 (*PGG*, 3, 615–16); 1–1891 (*PGG*, 4, 99); 10–1893 (*PGG*, 6, 946); 6–1894 (*PGG*, 8, 394–5).

Kuala Kangsar Annual Reports, 1888 (*PGG*, 2, 350–3); 1891 (*PGG*, 5, 807–14); 1896 (*PGG*, 10, 136–8); 1898 (*PGG*, 12, 12.12.1899 suppl.).

Kuala Kangsar Monthly Reports, 6–1889 (*PGG*, 2, 613–14); 7–1889 (*PGG*, 2, 659–660); 10–1893 (*PGG*, 6, 983–4); 4–1894 (*PGG*, 7, 201–2); 9–1894 (*PGG*, 7, 580–1); 5–1896 (*PGG*, 9, 423–5); 10–1896 (*PGG*, 9, 773–4).

Kuala Selangor Annual Report, 1900 (SSGG, 14.6.1901 suppl.).

Larut and Krian Annual Reports, 1905 (*PGG*, 19, suppl. n.d.); 1909 (*PGG*, 23, suppl. n.d.).

Larut [Land Office] Annual Report, 1890 (*PGG*, 4, 338).

Larut [Land Office] Monthly Reports, 3–1891 (*PGG*, 4, 209–10); 5–1891 (*PGG*, 4, 368); 6–1891 (*PGG*, 4, 583).

Lefroy, G.A., 1888, Ijok and North Larut, *PGG*, 1, 143–8.

Lower Perak Annual Reports, 1906 (*PGG*, 20, suppl. n.d.); 1907 (*PGG*, 21, suppl. n.d.); 1908 (*PGG*, 22, suppl. n.d.).

Lower Perak Monthly Reports, 9–1891 (*PGG*, 4, 1002–5); 3–1892 (*PGG*,

5, 229); 5–1892 (*PGG*, 5, 493); 11–1892 (*PGG*, 6, 40–1); 12–1892
(*PGG*, 6, 92–4); 1–1893 (*PGG*, 6, 149–50); 8–1896 (*PGG*, 9, 683);
5–1897 (*PGG*, 10, 385); 9–1898 (*PGG*, 11, 763–5).

Malacca Annual Reports, 1881 (*SSGG*, 1882, 717–39); 1884 (*SSGG*, 1885,
941–64); 1887 (*SSGG*, 1888, 1285–96); 1892 (*SSAR*, 1892, 571–93);
1893 (*SSGG*, 27.1.1894 suppl.); 1894 (*SSGG*, 27.1.1894 suppl.).

Marriott, H., 1911a, *Report on the Census of the State of Johore 1911*,
Singapore.

——, 1911b, *Report on the Census of the Straits Settlements taken on 10th
March 1911*, Singapore.

Matang Annual Report, 1897 (*PGG*, 11, 157–63).

Matang Monthly Reports, 12–1892 (*PGG*, 6, 94–5); 5–1894 (*PGG*, 7,
439–42); 10–1894 (*PGG*, 8, 9–11); 12–1895 (*PGG*, 9, 41–2); 12–1897
(*PGG*, 11, 28).

Murton, H.J., 1878, 'Report on an expedition to Perak', *SSGG*, 1878,
101–10.

Nathan, J.E., 1922, *The Census of British Malaya 1921*, London.

Negri Sembilan Annual Reports, 1886 (NSSS 200/88); 1887 (*SSGG*,
1888, 1361–78); 1888 (*SSGG*, 1889, 1171–92); 1889 (*SSGG*, 1890, 1583–
99); 1891 (*SSAR*, 1891, 501–16); 1892 (*SSGG*, 30.6.1893, suppl.); 1896
(*FMSAR*, 1896, 49–60); 1897 (*FMSAR*, 1897, 44–56); 1907 (Kuala
Lumpur); 1908 (*Negri Sembilan government gazette*, 23.7.1909, suppl.).

Pahang Annual Reports, 1891 (*SSAR*, 1891, 522–4); 1892 (*SSGG*,
12.5.1893, suppl.); 1894 (*SSGG*, 9.8.1895, suppl.); 1896 (*FMSAR*, 1896,
61–73); 1897 (*FMSAR*, 1897, 56–76); 1898 (*FMSAR*, 1898, 57–77);
1900 (*FMSAR*, 1900, 73–92).

Pears, F., 1901, 'On the cultivation of rice as a catch crop', *Agr. Bull. Straits
FMS*, 1, 391–2.

Penang Annual Reports, 1873 (*SSGG*, 1875, 133–48); 1884 (*SSGG*, 1885,
721–40); 1887 (*SSGG*, 1888, 1255–84); 1891 (*SSGG*, 1892, 1815–33);
1897 (*SSAR*, 1897, 259–75).

Perak Annual Reports, 1886 (*SSGG*, 1887, 1187–223); 1887 (*SSGG*, 1888,
1143–73); 1891 (*PGG*, 5, 409–33); 1892 (*SSGG*, 2.5.1893, suppl.); 1895
(*PGG*, 9, 475–525); 1896 (*PGG*, 10, 603–63); 1898 (*PGG*, 12, 23.6.1899,
suppl.); 1899 (*PGG*, 13, 6.7.1900, suppl.); 1900 (*PGG*, 14, 5.7.1901,
suppl.); 1901 (*PGG*, 15, 21.11.1902, suppl.); 1902 (*PGG*, 16, 26.6.1903,
suppl.); 1904 (*PP*, Cd. 2777); 1905 (*PP*, Cd. 3186); 1907 (Kuala
Lumpur).

Perak Government Notices, 1889, No. 393, 'Discouragement of ladang
cultivation', *PGG*, 2, 839.

Perak, Land Department Annual Reports, 1890 (*PGG*, 4, 336–43); 1895
(*PGG*, 9, 235–40).

Perlis Annual Reports, 1909; 1910 (microfilms in University of Singapore
Library).

Pountney, A.M., 1911, *The Census of the Federated Malay States*, 1911,
London.

Raja Mahmud, 1920, 'Summary of padi returns, Federated Malay States and Straits Settlements and the Non-Federated Malay States for season 1919–1920', *Agr. Bull. Straits FMS*, 8, 154–5.

Selama Annual Reports, 1898 (*PGG*, 12, 22.12.1899, suppl.); 1900 (*PGG*, 14, 5.7.1901, suppl.).

Selama Monthly Reports, 4–1889 (*PGG*, 2, 428); 2–1890 (*PGG*, 3, 167); 3–1891 (*PGG*, 4, 213); 1–1894 (*PGG*, 7, 83); 6–1894 (*PGG*, 7, 395–6).

Selangor Annual Reports, 1883 (*SSGG*, 1884, 257–69); 1884 (*SSGG*, 1885, 997–1017); 1886 (*SSGG*, 1887, 565–90); 1888 (*SSGG*, 1889, 1045–83); 1889 (*SSGG*, 1890, 1505–57); 1890 (*SSGG*, 1891, 1313–73); 1891 (*SSAR*, 1891, 411–68); 1892 (*SSGG*, 14.7.1893, suppl.); 1893 (*SSGG*, 13.7.1894, suppl.); 1895 (*SSGG*, 10.6.1896, suppl.); 1896 (*FMSAR*, 1896, 37–48); 1898 (*FMSAR*, 1898, 32–44); 1899 (*FMSAR*, 1899, 24–41); 1900 (*SSAR*, 1900); 1901 (*PP*, Cd 1297); 1902 (*PP*, Cd 1819); 1905 (*PP*, Cd 3186).

Selangor, Lands Department Annual Report, 1889 (*SGG*, 1, 243–55).

Straits Settlements Annual Reports, 1855–6, 1859–60, 1860–1, 1861–2, 1862–3, 1863–4, 1876 (Singapore).

Straits Settlements *Blue Books* 1870–1910 (microfilm in National Library, Singapore).

Straits Settlements, Estimates of Revenue and Expenditure, 1893 (*SSGG*, 1892, 3219–81); 1897 (*SSGG*, 1896, 2199–269).

Sungei Ujong Annual Reports, 1890 (*SSGG*, 1891, 1375–400); 1892 (*SSAR*, 1892, 501–22).

Sungei Ujong and Jelebu Annual Report, 1893 (*SSGG*, 13.7.1894, suppl.).

Swettenham, F.A. 1875, 'Report of Her Britannic Majesty's Acting Assistant Resident at Salangore', Great Britain, *Accounts and Papers*, 1875, 53, 159–65. Other versions have separate pagination.

——, 1893, 'Memorandum by the British Resident, Perak, on correspondence concerning the cultivation of rice in the Protected Malay States', *PGG*, 6, 685–91.

——, 1894, Minute by the British Resident, Perak, in Maxwell, W.E., 1894, *Memorandum on the Introduction of a Land Code in the Native States of the Malay Peninsula,* Singapore (separately paged).

Tanjong Malim Monthly Report, 9–1897 (*PGG*, 10, 924).

Trengganu Annual Report, 1910, microfilm in University of Singapore Library, date and place of publication not stated.

Ulu Selangor Annual Report, 1900 (*SGG*, 14.6.1901, suppl.).

Ulu Selangor Monthly Report, 7–1890 (*SGG*, 1, 467).

Upper Perak Annual Reports, 1889 (*PGG*, 3, 229–31); 1891 (*PGG*, 5, 954–7).

Upper Perak Monthly Report, 8/9–1897 (*PGG*, 10, 920–1).

Wise, D.H., 1901 *Report on the System of Rice Cultivation practised in Pahang,* printed paper in Ag. B.R. Pahang to Res. Gen. F.M.S. 16.5.1901, KDO 208/01 (also in *Agr. Bull. Straits FMS* 1, 1, 13–19).

JOURNAL ARTICLES AND BOOKS
REFERRING TO MALAYA

Alwee, A. Wahab, 1967, *Rembau: a Study in Integration and Conflict in a Village in Negri Sembilan*, Centre for Asian Studies, University of West Australia.

Anderson, J., 1824, *Political and Commercial Considerations relative to the Malayan Peninsula and the British Settlements in the Straits of Malacca*, Penang (reprinted 1965, Singapore).

Annandale, N., 1900, 'The Siamese Malay States', *Scott. geog. Mag.*, 16, 505–23.

Annandale, N., and Robinson, H.C., 1903, 'Contributions to the ethnography of the Malay Peninsula, anthropological and zoological results of an expedition to Perak and the Siamese Malay States, 1901–1902', *Fasciculi Malayenses*, Anthrop. 1, 1–88, Liverpool.

As'ad Shukri Haji Muda, 1962, *Sejarah Kelantan*, Kota Baru.

Baker, J.A., 1940, 'A Kedah harvesting knife', *JMBRAS*, 18, 2, 43–5.

Balestier, J., 1848, 'View of the state of agriculture in the British possessions in the Straits of Malacca', *J. indian Archipel.*, 2, 139–50.

Bassett, D.K., 1964, 'British commercial and strategic interest in the Malay Peninsula during the late eighteenth century', in Bastin, J. and Roolvink, R. (eds.), *Malayan and Indonesian Studies*, Oxford, 122–40.

Baumgarten, F.L., 1849, 'Agriculture in Malacca', *J. indian Archipel.*, 3, 707–21.

Bellamy, G.C., 1895, 'The Sakeis of Selangor', *Selangor J.*, 3, 223–30.

Birch, J.W.W., (posth.) 1892, 'Retrospective notes, a glance at Selangor in '74', *Selangor J.*, 1, 9–12, 24–7.

Bird, I.L., 1883, *The Golden Chersonese and the Way Thither*, New York.

Blagden, C.O., 1892, 'Memorandum, on the aborigines of the Jasin district of Malacca, dated 1892', *JSBRAS*, 77, 177–80.

Blundell, E.A., 1848, 'Notices of the history and present conditions of Malacca', *J. indian Archipel.*, 2, 726–54.

*Bonney, R., 1971, *Kedah 1771–1821*, Kuala Lumpur.

Boxer, C.R., 1964, 'The Achinese attack on Malacca in 1629 as described in contemporary Portuguese sources', in Bastin, J. and Roolvink, R. (eds.), *Malayan and Indonesian Studies*, Oxford, 103–21.

*Braddell, R., 1937, 'Further notes upon A Study of Ancient Times in the Malay Peninsula', *JMBRAS*, 15, 1, 25–31.

———, 1939, 'An introduction to the study of ancient times in the Malay Peninsula and the Straits of Malacca', *JMBRAS*, 17, 1, 146–212.

———, 1941, 'An introduction to the study of ancient times in the Malay Peninsula', *JMBRAS*, 19, 1, 21–74.

Braddell, T., 1853, 'Notes of a trip to the interior from Malacca', *J. indian Archipel.*, 7, 73–104.

Brau de Saint-Pol Lias, 1883, *Pérak et les Orangs-Sakèys*, Paris.

Bremner, N.J. 1926, 'Report of Governor Balthaser Bort on Malacca 1678', *JMBRAS*, 5, 1–232.

Brown, C.C., (transl.), 1952, 'The Malay Annals (Sejarah Melayu)', *JMBRAS*, 25, 2 and 3 (reprinted 1970, Kuala Lumpur).

Browne, F.G., 1949, 'Storm forest in Kelantan', *Malay. Forester*, 12, 28–33.

*Burkill, I.H., 1917, 'The food-crops of the Malay Peninsula and some thoughts arising out of a review of them', *Proc. first agric. Conf. Malaya*, Kuala Lumpur, 138–53.

———, 1935, *A Dictionary of the Economic Products of the Malay Peninsula*, 2 vols., London.

Burridge, K.O.L., 1956, *A Report on Fieldwork in Batu Pahat, Johore*, (mimeo.), University of Malaya, Singapore.

Cameron, J., 1865, *Our Tropical Possessions in Malayan India*, London (reprinted 1965, Kuala Lumpur).

Chardon, R., 1940, 'A Malay tradition', *JMBRAS*, 18, 2, 108–48.

Clifford, H., 1897, 'A journey through the Malay states of Trengganu and Kelantan', *Geog. J.*, 9, 1, 1–37.

Collings, H.D., 1936, 'Report of an archaeological excavation in Kedah, Malay Peninsula', *Bull. Raffles Mus.*, ser. B, 1, 5–16.

Coope, A.E. (transl.), 1949, *The Story of the Voyage of Abdullah bin Abdul Kadir, Munshi*, Singapore.

Cowan, C.D. (ed.), 1951, 'Sir Frank Swettenham's Perak journals, 1874–1876', *JMBRAS*, 24, 4, 3–148.

Craig, J.J., 1933, 'Dry padi in Kelantan', *Malay. agr. J.*, 21, 664–6.

Cullin, E.G. and Zehnder, W.F., 1905, *Early History of Penang*, George Town.

Dale, W.L., 1959, 'The rainfall of Malaya', Part I, *J. trop. Geog.*, 13, 23–37.

———, 1960, 'The rainfall of Malaya', Part II, *J. trop. Geog.*, 14, 11–28.

D'Almeida, W.B., 1876, 'Geography of Perak and Salangore, and a brief sketch of some of the adjacent Malay states', *J. r. geog. Soc.*, 45, 358–80.

Daly, D.D., 1882, 'Surveys and explorations in the native states of the Malayan Peninsula', 1875–82, *Proc. r. geog. Soc.*, 7, 393–412.

Davison, W., 1890, 'Journal of a trip to Pahang etc. with H.E. the Governor', *JSBRAS*, 20, 83–90.

Deane, H.S., 1880, 'Report on a preliminary survey of the State of Perak', *SSGG*, 1880, 231–46.

Earl, G.W., 1861, *Topography and Itinerary of Province Wellesley*, George Town.

Favre, P., 1849a, 'A journey in Johore', *J. indian Archipel.*, 3, 50–64.

———, 1849b, 'A journey in the Minangkabau States of the Malay Peninsula', *J. indian Archipel.*, 3, 153–61.

Graham, W.A., 1908, *Kelantan a State of the Malay Peninsula*, Glasgow.

———, 1911, 'Kelantan, Trengganu, Kedah, Perlis', *Encycl. Britannica*, 11th edn., 17, 482–3.

Gray, C., (posth.) 1852, 'Journal of a route overland from Malacca to Pahang, across the Malayan Peninsula', *J. indian Archipel.*, 6, 369–75.

Great Britain, War Office, Intelligence Division, 1891, *Precis of Information concerning the Straits Settlements and the Native Malay States in the Malay Peninsula*, 2nd edn., London.

Gullick, J.M., 1951, 'The Negri Sembilan economy of the 1890s', *JMBRAS*, 24, 38–55.

———, 1955, 'Kuala Lumpur, 1880–95', *JMBRAS*, 28, 4, 5–131.

———, 1958, *Indigenous Political Systems of Western Malaya*, London.

Guthrie, A., et al., 1861, *British Possessions in the Straits of Malacca*, George Town. Unpublished version bears title, 'Statement presented to His Grace the Duke of Newcastle ... regarding British Possessions in the Straits of Malacca' (MS on microfilm in University of Singapore Library).

Hervey, D.F.A., 1881, 'The Endau and its tributaries', *JSBRAS*, 8, 93–124.

———, 1884, 'Rembau.', *JSBRAS*, 13, 241–58.

Hill, A.H. (transl.), 1955, 'The Hikayat Abdullah', *JMBRAS*, 28, 3, 5–345.

Hill, R.D., 1964, 'Note sur la culture du riz sec dans les états Malaisiens de Kelantan et de Trengganu', *Agron. trop.*, 19, 499–505.

———, 1966a, 'Rice cultivation systems in Malaya', *World Crops*, 18, 72–4.

———, 1966b, 'Dry rice cultivation in Peninsular Malaya', *Orient. Geogr.*, 10, 1, 10–14.

———, 1967, 'Agricultural land tenure in West Malaysia', *Malay. econ. Rev.*, 12, 1, 99–116.

———, and Arope, Ani b., 1969, 'Agriculture in Trengganu, Malaysia', *J. Singapore nat. Acad. Sci.*, 1, 3, 54–64.

*Ho, R., 1967, *Farmers of Central Malaya*, Canberra.

Hooker, M.B., 1968a, 'The interaction of legislation and customary law in a Malay state', *Am. J. comp. Law*, 16, 3, 415–30.

———, 1968b, 'A note on the Malayan legal digests', *JMBRAS*, 41, 1, 157–70.

Hornaday, W.T., 1879, 'Account of a naturalist's visit to the territory of Selangor', *JSBRAS*, 3, 124–31.

Husin Ali, S., 1964, *Social Stratification in Kampong Bagan*, Malayan branch Royal Asiatic Society monographs, 1, Kuala Lumpur.

*Jackson, J.C., 1968, *Planters and Speculators, Chinese and European Agricultural Enterprise in Malaya 1786–1921*, Kuala Lumpur.

Kelsall, H.J., 1894, 'Account of a trip up the Pahang, Tembeling and Tahan rivers, and an attempt to reach Gunong Tahan', *JSBRAS*, 25, 33–56, with a note by Ridley, H.N.

Kempe, J.E. and Winstedt, R.O., 1948, 'A Malay legal digest compiled for 'Abd al-Ghafur Muhaiyu'd-din Shah, Sultan of Pahang 1592–1614 A.D. with undated additions', *JMBRAS*, 21, 1, 1–67.

Khan, G. Muhammed, 1958, *History of Kedah*, Penang.

*Khoo Kay Kim, 1972, *The Western Malay States, 1850–1873, the Effects of Commercial Development on Malay Politics*, Kuala Lumpur.

Kitching, T., 1930, 'A Trengganu keri', *JMBRAS*, 8, 318 and Pl. 8.

Knaggs, W., 1875, 'A visit to Perak', *J. east. Asia*, 1, 1, 26–37.

Küchler, J., 1968, *Penang: Kulturlandschaftwandel, und Ethnischsoziale*

Struktur einer Insel Malaysias, Giessener Geographische Schriften, 13, Giessen.

Lake, H. [W.], 1894, 'Johore', *Geog. J.*, 3, 3, 281–301.

Lake, H.W. and Kelsall, H.J., 1894, 'A journey on the Sembrong river. From Kuala Indau to Batu Pahat', *JSBRAS*, 26, 1–33.

Lamb, A., 1960, 'Report on the excavation and reconstruction of Chandi Bukit Batu Pahat, Central Kedah', *Fed. Mus. J.*, 5, 1–108.

Leech, H.C.W., 1878, 'Ascent of Bujang Malacca', *JSBRAS*, 2, 225–7.

———, 1879a, 'About Kinta', *JSBRAS*, 4, 21–33.

———, 1879b, 'About Slim and Bernam', *JSBRAS*, 4, 34–45.

Leith, Sir G., 1804, *A Short Account of the Settlement, Produce, and Commerce of Prince of Wales Island in the Straits of Malacca*, London.

Leupe, P.A., 1936, 'The seige and capture of Malacca from the Portuguese', *JMBRAS*, 14, 1–178.

Lim Chong-yah, 1967, *Economic Development of Modern Malaya*, Kuala Lumpur.

Linehan, W., 1928, 'Notes on the remains of some brick structures in the Pekan district', *JMBRAS*, 6, 78–81.

———, 1936, 'History of Pahang', *JMBRAS*, 14, 2, 1–256.

———, 1947, 'The Prince of Chini', *JMBRAS*, 20, 2, 128–36.

———, 1951, 'Traces of a bronze age culture associated with iron age implements in the regions of Klang and the Tembeling, Malaya', *JMBRAS*, 24, 3, 1–59.

Logan, J.R., 1847, 'The Orang Binua of Johore', *J. indian Archipel.*, 1, 243–93.

———, 1848, 'Journal of a voyage to the eastern coast and islands of Johore', *J. indian Archipel.*, 2, 616–24.

———, 1849, 'Five days in Naning, with a walk to the foot of Gunong Datu in Rambau', *J. indian Archipel.*, 3, 24–41, 278–87, 402–12, 489–93.

———, 1851, 'Notes at Pinang, Kidah etc.', *J. indian Archipel.*, 5, 53–65.

———, 1887, 'Journal of an excursion from Singapore to Malacca and Pinang', *Miscellaneous Papers relating to Indo-China and the Indian Archipelago*, 2nd ser., vol. 1, 1–20, London.

Low, J., 1836, *A Dissertation on the Soil and Agriculture of the British Settlement of Penang or Prince of Wales Island in the Straits of Malacca; including Province Wellesley on the Malayan Peninsula*, Singapore (reprinted 1972, Singapore).

Löwenstein, Prince J., 1956, 'The origin of the Malayan metal age', *JMBRAS*, 29, 2, 5–70.

Macalister, N., 1803, *Historical Memoir relative to Prince of Wales Island in the Straits of Malacca*, London.

Macpherson, R., 1858, 'Narrative of a trip to Dok in the Muar Territory', *J. indian Archipel.*, new ser., 2, 295–300.

Marshall, C., 1954, 'Selangor what of the future?', *Malay. Forester*, 17, 50–63.

Maxwell, W.E., 1882a, 'A journey on foot to the Patani frontier in 1876', *JSBRAS*, 9, 1–67.

————, (transl.), 1882b, 'Misal Melaya (n.d.) in the Dutch in Perak', *JSBRAS*, 10, 245–68.

————, 1884, 'The law and customs of the Malays with reference to the tenure of land', *JSBRAS*, 13, 75–220.

————, 1894, *Memorandum on the Introduction of a Land Code in the Native States of the Malay Peninsula*, Singapore.

Maxwell, W.G. (transl.), 1911, 'Account of Malacca by Barretto de Resende', *JSBRAS*, 60, 1–24.

Medhurst, W.H., 1830, 'Journal of a voyage up the East Coast of the Malayan Peninsula', *Q. Chron. Trans. Lond. missionary Soc.*, 4, 145–56, 171–92.

Mills, J.V. (transl.), 1930, 'Eredia's *Description of Malaca* [*sic*] *Meridional India and Cathay*', *JMBRAS*, 8, 1–288 (original, 1613).

Mills, L.A., 1966, *British Malaya 1824–67*, Kuala Lumpur, originally publ. 1925, *JMBRAS*, 3, 2.

Moor, J.H. 1837, *Notices of the Indian Archipelago and Adjacent Countries*, Singapore.

Muhammed Ja'afar, 1897, 'Darihal Pkerja'an [*sic*] bersawah di Melaka', *JSBRAS*, 30, 285–304 (with a transl. into English by Blagden, C.O.).

Newbold, J.T. [T.J.], 1837a, 'Account of Rumbowe, one of the states in the interior of Malacca', append. in Moor, J.H. (ed.), *Notices of the Indian Archipelago and Adjacent Countries*, Singapore, 61–7.

————, 1837b, 'Johole and its former dependencies of Jompole [and] Gominchi', append. in Moor, J.H. (ed.), *Notices of the Indian Archipelago and Adjacent Countries*, Singapore, 67–71.

————, 1837c, 'Naning', in Moor, J.H. (ed.), *Notices of the Indian Archipelago and Adjacent Countries*, Singapore, 246–54.

*Newbold, T.J., 1837d, 'Sketch of the State of Muar', in Moor, J.H. (ed.), *Notices of the Indian Archipelago and Adjacent Countries*, Singapore, 73–6.

————, 1839, *Political and Statistical Account of the British Settlements in the Straits of Malacca*, 2 vols., London (reprinted 1971, Kuala Lumpur).

O'Brien, J.A., 1884, 'Jelebu', *JSBRAS*, 14, 337–43.

Ooi Jin-Bee, 1963, *Land, People and Economy in Malaya*, London.

Ord, Sir H. St. G., 1868, *Account of a Visit to the King of Siam at Whae-Whan on the East Coast of the Malayan Peninsula in August 1868*, Singapore.

Osborn, S., 1865, *Quedah*, Edinburgh and London.

Paterson, H.S., 1924, 'An early Malay inscription from Trengganu', *JMBRAS*, 2, 252–8.

Peacock, B.A.V., 1965, 'Recent archaelogical discoveries in Malaysia, 1964: Malaya', *JMBRAS*, 38, 1, 248–55.

————, 1966, 'Recent archaeological discoveries in Malaysia, 1965: Malaya', *JMBRAS*, 39, 1, 198–201.

Penney, F.G., 1881, 'Some notes upon agriculture in the Settlement of Penang', *SSGG*, 1881, 614–16.

Ridley, H.N., 1896, 'The forests of Selangor', *Selangor J.*, 4, 444–7.

Rigby, J. (ed.), 1908, 'The ninety-nine laws of Perak', in Wilkinson, R.J. (ed.), *Papers on Malay Subjects: Law*, Pt. 2, Kuala Lumpur.

Sadka, E., 1968, *The Protected Malay States 1874–1895*, Kuala Lumpur.

Sharom Ahmat, 1970, 'The structure of the economy of Kedah 1879–1905', *JMBRAS*, 43, 2, 1–24.

Sieveking, G. de G., 1954, 'Gua Cha and Malayan stone age', *Malay. hist. J.*, 1, 2, 111–24.

———, 1954–5a, 'Excavations at Gua Cha, Kelantan', *Fed. Mus. J.*, 1 and 2, 75–138.

Singapore and Straits Directory 1881, Singapore.

Singapore and Straits Directory 1901, 'Johore (including Muar)', 316–19.

Sircom, H.S., 1920, 'Original settlement of Pahang. Legend communicated by Haji Sam (of Minangkabau descent)', *J. FMS Mus.*, 9, 2, 150–1.

Skinner, C., 1964, 'A Kedah letter of 1839', in Bastin, J. and Roolvink, R. (eds.), *Malayan and Indonesian Studies*, London, 156–65.

Skinner, C.J., 1884, 'Statement shewing the result of the padi harvest in various districts of the Settlement of Penang', *SSGG*, 1884, 903.

Southwood, K.E., 1960, 'Lake Chini', *Malaya in Hist.*, 6, 1, 24–30.

Swettenham, F.A., 1880a, 'From Perak to Slim and down the Slim and Bernam rivers', *JSBRAS*, 6, 51–68a.

———, 1880b, 'Some account of the independent native states of the Malay Peninsula', Pt. 1, *JSBRAS*, 6, 161–202.

———, 1885, 'Journal kept during a journey across the Malay Peninsula', *JSBRAS*, 15, 1–38.

———, 1942, *Footprints in Malaya*, London.

Swinney, A.J.G., n.d., *The Pahang Corporation, Limited. Report on work done etc. on the Rumpen River during the year 1890*, London.

Thomson, J.T., 1849, 'General report on the Residency of Singapore, drawn up principally with a view of illustrating its agricultural statistics', *J. indian Archipel.*, 3, 618–28, 744–55.

———, 1851, 'Description of the eastern coast of Johore and Pahang, and adjacent islands', *J. indian Archipel.*, 5, 85–92.

Topping, M., 1850, 'Some account of Quedah', *J. indian Archipel.*, 4, 42–4.

Trapaud, E., 1788, *A Short Account of the Prince of Wales Island or Pulo Penang in the East Indies*, London.

Treggoning, K.G. (ed.), 1962, *Malaysian Historical Sources*, Singapore.

*———, 1965, *The British in Malaya: the first forty years 1786–1826*, Tucson.

Turnbull, C.M., 1966, 'Bibliography of writings in English on British Malaya, 1786–1867', in Mills, L.A., *British Malaya 1824–67*, 287–361, Kuala Lumpur.

*———, 1972, *The Straits Settlements 1826–67*, London.

Turney, C.H.A., 1894, 'From Kuala to Ulu Selangor in 1882', *Selangor J.*, 2, 3, 26–32.

Tweedie, M.W.F., 1936, 'Report on cave excavations carried out in Bukit

Chintamani near Bentong, Pahang', *Bull. Raffles Mus.*, ser. B, 11–25.

———, 1953, 'The Stone Age in Malaya', *JMBRAS*, 26, 2, 1–90.

Vaughan, J.D., 1857, 'Notes on the Malays of Penang and Province Wellesley', *J. indian Archipel.*, new ser., 2, 127–31.

'Viator' (pseud.), 1837, 'Trip to Johore river', in Moor, J.H. (ed.), *Notices of the Indian Archipelago and Adjacent Countries*, 264–8, Singapore.

Vincent, C., 1894, *Report on the Krian Irrigation Scheme*, Taiping.

Wales, H.G. Quaritch, 1940, 'Archaeological researches on ancient Indian colonisation in Malaya', *JMBRAS*, 18, 1, 1–85.

Wang Gungwu, 1960, 'An early Chinese visitor to Kelantan', *Malaya in Hist.*, 6, 1, 31–5.

Waterstradt, J., 1902, 'Kelantan and my trip to Gunong Tahan', *JSBRAS*, 37, 1–28.

Weld, Sir F.A., 1881, 'Travels in Malacca and Selangor, reprint of letter to Hon. Earl of Kimberley', Great Britain, *Accounts and Papers* 1882, 710–12.

Wheatley, P., 1954, 'Notes: land use in the vicinity of Singapore in the eighteen-thirties', *Malay. J. trop. Geog.*, 2, 63–6.

———, 1957, 'The seat of all felicities', *Hist. A.*, 3, 99–106.

———, 1964, 'Desultory remarks on the ancient history of the Malay Peninsula', in Bastin, J. and Roolvink, R. (eds.), *Malayan and Indonesian Studies*, 33–75, Oxford.

Wilkinson, R.J., 1908, 'Malay Law', in his *Papers on Malay Subjects*, vol. 1, 1.

Winstedt, R.O. 1920, 'History of Kedah', *JSBRAS*, 81, 29–35.

———, 1928, 'Kedah laws', *JMBRAS*, 6, 2, 1–44.

———, 1932, 'A history of Johore (1365–1895 A.D.)', *JMBRAS*, 10, 3, 1–167.

———, 1934, 'Negri Sembilan, the history, policy and beliefs of Nine States', *JMBRAS*, 12, 3.

———, 1953, 'An old Minangkabau legal digest from Perak', *JMBRAS*, 26, 1, 1–13.

Woore, T., 1832, *Penang or Prince of Wales Is.*, map 24 by 18 ins., London.

Wray, L., 1886, *Notes on Perak, with a Sketch of its Vegetable, Animal and Mineral Products*, London.

———, 1894, 'Cave-dwellers of Perak', *Perak Mus. Notes*, 2, 7–18.

Wright, A. and Reid, T.H., 1912, *The Malay Peninsula: a Record of Progress in the Middle East*, London.

Wyatt-Smith, J., 1964, 'A preliminary vegetation map of Malaya with descriptions of the vegetation types', *J. trop. Geog.*, 18, 200–13.

Zaharah bte Haji Mahmud, 1968, 'The development of the state of Kedah up to the end of the nineteenth century', *Proc. int. Conf. asian Hist., Kuala Lumpur 5–10 Aug. 1968*, (mimeo.), Kuala Lumpur.

JOURNAL ARTICLES AND BOOKS—GENERAL

Adas, M., 1974, *The Burma Delta*, Madison.

*Angladette, A., 1966, *Le Riz*, Paris.

Avineri, S., 1968, *The Social and Political Thought of Karl Marx*, Cambridge.

Barrau, J., 1965a, 'L'humide et le sec: an essay on the ethnobotanical adaptation to contrastive environments in the Indo-Pacific area', *J. polynesian Soc.*, 73, 3, 329–46.

*———, 1965b, 'Histoire et préhistoire horticoles de l'Océanie tropicale', *J. Soc. océanistes*, 21, 21, 55–78.

Benedict, P.K., 1942, 'Thai, Kadai and Indonesian: a new alignment in Southeastern Asia', *Am. Anthrop.*, 44 (new ser.) 576–601.

Beyer, H.O., 1947, *Philippine Saga: a Pictorial History of the Archipelago since Time began*, Manila.

*———, 1955, 'The origin and history of the Philippine rice terraces', *Proc. eighth pacif. sci. Congr.*, 1, 387–98.

Bishop, C.W., 1936, 'Origin and early diffusion of the traction plough', *Antiquity*, 10, 261–81.

*———, 1940, 'Beginnings of civilisation in Eastern Asia', *Antiquity*, 14, 301–16.

Boerema, J., 1931, *Regenval in Nederlandsch-Indië*, vol. 1, Batavia.

Boserup, E., 1965, *The Conditions of Agricultural Growth*, Chicago.

Bowring, Sir J., 1857, *The Kingdom and People of Siam*, 2 vols., London.

Brookfield, H.C., 1972, 'Intensification and disintensification in Pacific agriculture', *Pacif. Viewpoint*, 13, 1, 30–48.

Bruneau, M., 1968, 'Irrigation traditionelle dans le Nord de Thaïlande: l'example du bassin de Chiengmai', *Bull. assoc. géogrs fr.*, 362–3, 155–65.

*Burkill, I.H., 1951, 'The rise and decline of the greater yam in the service of man', *Adv. Sci.*, 7, 28, 443–8.

*———, 1952, 'Habits of man and the origins of the cultivated plants of the Old World', *Proc. Linnean Soc. Lond.*, 164, 12–42.

Burnell, A.C. and Tiele, P.A. (eds.), 1885, *The Voyage of John Huyghen van Linschoten to the East Indies*, 2 vols., London.

Callenfels, P.V. van Stein, 1936, 'The Melanesoid civilisations of Eastern Asia', *Bull. Raffles Mus.*, ser. B, 1, 41–51.

*de Candolle, A.L.P.P., 1884, *Origin of Cultivated Plants*, London.

Carter, A.C., 1904, *The Kingdom of Siam*, New York.

*Chang Kwang-chih, 1958, 'Some aspects of social structure and settlement patterns in Southeast Asia', *Bull. Inst. Ethnol. Acad. sin.*, 6, 67–78.

———, 1959, 'A working hypothesis for the early cultural history of South China', *Bull. Inst. Ethnol. Acad. sin.*, 7, 75–103.

———, 1963, *The Archaeology of Ancient China*, New Haven and London.

———, 1964, 'Prehistoric and early historic culture horizons and traditions in South China', *Curr. Anthrop.*, 5, 359, 368–75.

Chen Ta, 1923, *Chinese Migrations with Special Reference to Labor Conditions*, Washington.

Cheng Siok-Hwa, 1968, *The Rice Industry of Burma, 1852–1940*, Kuala Lumpur.

Cheng Te-K'un, 1969, *Archaeology in Sarawak*, Cambridge.

*Chevalier, A. and Roehrich, O., 1914, 'Sur l'origine botanique du riz cultivés', *Comptes rendus Séances Acad. Sci.*, 159, 560–2.

Cockrill, W.R., 1967, 'The water buffalo', *Sci. Am.*, 217, 6, 118–25.

Coedès, G., 1925, 'Documents sur l'histoire politique et religieuse de Laos Occidental', *Bull. École fr. extrême Orient*, 25, 1–200.

———, 1928, 'The excavations at P'ong Tuk and their importance for the ancient history of Siam', *J. Siam Soc.*, 21, 195–218.

———, 1937–66, *Inscriptions du Cambodge*, 8 vols, École fr. extrême Orient, colln. textes Indochine III.

———, 1964, *Les États Hindouisés d'Indochine et d'Indonésie*, Paris (new edn., also publ. as *The Indianized States of South-east Asia*, Honolulu, 1968).

———, 1966, *The Making of South East Asia*, London.

———, n.d., *Receuil des Inscriptions du Siam: Pt. 2, Inscriptions de Dvaravati, de Çrivijaya et de Laos*, 2nd edn. Bangkok.

Colani, M., 1930, 'Recherches sur le préhistorique Indochinois', *Bull. École fr. extrême Orient*, 30, 299–422.

———, 1935, *Mégalithes du Haut Laos*, vol. 2, Paris.

———, 1940, 'Origine et évolution du couteau de moissonneur', *Proc. third Congr. Prehist. Far East*, 194–9, Singapore.

Cortesão, A. (transl.), 1944, *The Suma Oriental of Tomé Pires*, 2 vols., London, (original, 1512–5).

Crawfurd, J., 1820, *History of the Indian Archipelago*, 3 vols., Edinburgh.

———, 1828, *Journal of an Embassy from the Governor-General of India to the Courts of Siam and Cochin China*, vol. 1, London (reprinted 1967, Kuala Lumpur).

Dagh-Register gehouden int Casteel Batavia vant Passerende daer ter Plaetse als over geheel Nederlandts-India Anno 1624–1682, 1887–1931, 31 vols., The Hague.

Dames, M.L. (transl.), 1921, *The Book of Duarte Barbosa*, vol. 2, London (original in Portuguese *c.* 1518).

de Comyn, T., 1969, *State of the Philippines in 1810*, Manila (original *Estado do las Islas Filipinas en 1810*, Madrid, 1820).

de la Loubère, 1693, *A New Historical Relation of the Kingdom of Siam*, London.

de Morga, A., 1867, *The Philippine Islands, Moluccas, Siam, Cambodia, Japan and China at the Close of the Sixteenth Century*, London (original *Sucesos de las Islas Filipinas*, Mexico, 1609).

De Morgan, J.J.M., 1886, *Exploration de la Presquîle Malaise Royaumes de Pérak et de Patani*, Rouen.

Encyclopaedia Britannica, 1910–1, 'Siam', 25, 2–10.

Far Eastern Geographical Establishment, 1917, *The New Atlas and Com-*

mercial Gazetteer of the Straits Settlements and Federated Malay States, Shanghai.

Finlayson, G., 1826, *The Mission to Siam, and Hué the Capital of Cochin China, in the Years 1821–2*, London.

*Fisher, C.A., 1966, *South-east Asia: a Social, Economic and Political Geography*, London and New York.

Forrest, T., 1792, *A Voyage from Calcutta to the Mergui Archipelago*, London and Edinburgh.

Foster, Sir William (ed.), 1930, *A New Account of the East Indies by Alexander Hamilton*, 2 vols., London, (originally publ. 1727 in Edinburgh).

*Franklin, S.H., 1965, Systems of production: systems of appropriation, *Pacif. Viewpoint*, 6, 2, 145–66.

Freeman-Grenville, G.S.P., 1963, *The Muslim and Christian Calendars*, London.

von Fürer-Haimendorf, C., 1938, 'Through the unexplored mountains of the Assam-Burma border', *Geog. J.*, 91, 201–19.

——, 1945, 'The problem of megalithic cultures in Middle India', *Man in India*, 25, 73–86.

Gervaise, N., 1688, *The Natural and Political History of the Kingdom of Siam*, (transl. O'Neill, H.S., Bangkok, 1928).

Goloubew, V., 1929, 'L'age du Bronze au Tonkin et dans le Nord-Annam', *Bull. École fr. extrême Orient*, 29, 1–46.

——, 1931, 'La province de Thanh-Hoà et sa céramique', *Rev. Arts asiat.*, 7, 2, 112–16.

——, 1932a, 'Excavations at Dong-Son (Province Thanh-Hoà, Annam)', *A. Bibl. indian Archaeol, 1930*, 11–14.

——, 1932b, 'Sur l'origine et la diffusion des tambours métalliques', *Praehist. Asiae orientalis*, 1, 137–150.

——, 1940, 'Le tambour métallique de Hoang-ha', *Bull. École fr. extrême Orient*, 40, 383–409.

Gorman, C.F., 1969, 'Hoabinhian: a pebble-tool complex with early plant association in Southeast Asia', *Science*, 163, 671–3.

——, 1971, 'The Hoabinhian and after: subsistence patterns in Southeast Asia during the late Pleistocene and early Recent periods', *World Archaeol.*, 2, 3, 300–20.

Grindrod, Mrs., 1895, *Siam: a Geographical Summary*, London.

Grist, D.H., 1959, *Rice*, London.

Groeneveldt, W.P., 1887, 'Notes on the Malay Archipelago and Malacca', *Miscellaneous Papers relating to Indo-China and the Indian Archipelago*, 2nd ser., vol. 1, 126–262, London.

Groslier, B.P., 1962, *Indochina, Art in the Melting Pot of Races*, London.

*Gustchin, G.-G., 1938, 'Le riz, origine et histoire de sa culture', *Riz et Riziculture*, 12, 61–96.

*Harris, D.R., 1967, 'New light on plant domestication and the origins of agriculture', *Geog. Rev.*, 57, 90–107.

*——, 1969, 'Agricultural systems, ecosystems and the origins of agri-

culture', in Ucko, P.J. and Dimbleby, G.W. (eds.), *The Domestication and Exploitation of Plants and Animals*, 3–15, London.

Harris, J. (compil.), 1764, *Navigantium atque Itinerantium Bibliotheca or a Complete Collection of Voyages and Travels*, vol. 1, London.

Harrison, B., 1954, *South East Asia: a Short History*, London.

Harrisson, B., 1964, 'Recent archaeological discoveries in Malaysia 1962–1963: Borneo', *JMBRAS*, 37, 2, 192–200.

Harrisson, T., 1963–4, '100,000 years of Stone Age culture in Borneo', *J. r. Soc. Arts*, 112, 174–91.

Harrisson, T. and O'Connor, S.J., 1969, *Excavations of the Prehistoric Iron Industries in West Borneo*, 2 vols, Ithaca.

Harvey, G.F., 1925, *History of Burma*, London.

Haudricourt, A.G. and Hédin, L., 1943, *L'Homme et les Plantes Cultivees*, Paris.

*Hawkes, J.G., 1969, 'The ecological background of plant domestication', in Ucko, P.J. and Dimbleby, G.W. (eds.), *The Domestication and Exploitation of Plants and Animals*, 17–29, London.

Heine-Geldern, R., 1935, 'The archaeology and art of Sumatra', in Loeb, E.M., *Sumatra, its History and People*, 305–31, Vienna.

———, 1937, 'L' art prébouddhique de la Chine et de l'Asie du Sud-Est et son influence en Océanie', *Rev. Arts asiat.*, 11, 177–206.

———, 1945, 'Prehistoric research in the Netherlands Indies', in Honig, P. and Verdoon, F. (eds.), *Science and Scientists in the Netherlands Indies*, 129–67, New York.

Higgins, B., 1959, *Economic Development; Principles, Problems and Policies*, New York.

Hill, R.D., 1965, 'Pastoralism in the Wairarapa', in Watters, R.F. (ed.), *Land and Society in New Zealand: Essays in Historical Geography*, 25–49, Wellington.

———, 1970, 'Peasant rice cultivation systems with some Malaysian examples', *Geog. polonica*, 19, 91–8.

———, 1971, 'Materials for historical geography and economic history of Southeast Asia in nineteenth century Malayan newspapers', *JMBRAS*, 44, 2, 151–98.

Hill, R.D. and Ühlig, H., 1970, 'Draft of a terminological framework for the geographical types of rice-cultivation', in *Modernization of the Pacific Region*, Inter-Congr. Meeting of the Standing Comm. on Geog., Pacif. Sci. Assoc., 1969, 71–6, Tokyo.

Ho, Ping-ti, 1969, 'Loess and the origin of Chinese agriculture', *Am. hist. Rev.*, 75, 1–36.

Hulsius, Levinus, 1601, *In die Orientalische Indien...*, Nurnberg.

Janse, O., 1931, 'Un groupe de bronzes anciens propres à l'Extrême-Asie méridionale', *Bull. mus. far east. Antiq.*, 3, 99–139.

———, 1936, 'Mission archéologique en Indochine', *Rev. Arts asiat.*, 10, 42–52.

Janse, O.R.T., 1951, *Archaeological Research in Indo-China*, vol. 2, Cambridge, Mass.

——, 1958, *Archaeological Research in Indo-China*, vol. 3, Bruges.

Janssen, M.L. (transl.), 1882, *Malaca L'Inde Meridionale*, Brussells, being Eredia, E.G. de, 1613, *Declaracam de Malaca...*, Lisbon.

Jones, J.W. (transl.), 1863, *The Travels of Ludovico di Varthema*, London (original in Italian, 1510).

Karlgren, B., 1942, 'The date of the early Dong-son culture', *Bull. Mus. far east. Antiq.*, 14, 1–28.

Keesing, F.M., 1962, *The Ethnohistory of Northern Luzon*, Stanford.

Kihara, H., 1959, 'Considerations on the origin of cultivated rice', *Seiken Ziho*, 10, 68–83.

Koenig, J.G., (posth.) 1894, 'Journal of a voyage from India to Siam and Malacca in 1779', *JSBRAS*, 26, 58–201; 27, 57–133.

Kolb, A., 1953, 'The migrations of the Polynesians and the cultivation of taro', *Eighth pacif. sci. Congr. Abstr. Papers*, 526–7.

Lach, D.F., 1965, *Asia in the Making of Europe*, vol. 1, Bks. 1 and 2, Chicago.

La Gironière, P.P., 1962, *Twenty Years in the Philippines*, Manila (first publ. New York, 1854).

Lamb, A., 1961, 'Kedah and Takuapa: some tentative historical conclusions', *Fed. Mus. J.*, 6, 69–88.

——, 1964, 'Takuapa: the probable site of a pre-Malaccan entrepôt in the Malay Peninsula', in Bastin, J. and Roolvink, R. (eds.), *Malayan and Indonesian Studies*, 76–86, Oxford.

Lefebvre, H., 1968, *The Sociology of Marx*, New York (originally publ. in French, 1966).

Little, R., 1848, 'An essay on coral reefs as the cause of Blakan Mati fever and of fevers in various parts of the East', *J. indian Archipel.*, 2, 449–94.

Loeb, E.M., 1935, *Sumatra, its History and People*, Vienna.

Lovat, Lady A., 1914, *The Life of Sir Frederick Weld*, London.

Low, J., 1829, 'Letter to Acting Secretary to the Government', 3.11.1829, *Burney Papers*, vol. 3, 1, 104, Bangkok 1910–14.

Lownes, M. and Bill, J., 1615, *The Estates, Empires and Principalities of the World*, London.

*Luce, G.H., 1940, 'Economic life of the early Burman', *J. Burma res. Soc.*, 30, 1, 283–335.

McCarthy, F.D., 1940, 'Comparison of the prehistory of Australia with that of Indo-China, the Malay Peninsula and the Netherlands East Indies', *Proc. third Congr. Prehist. Far East*, 30–50, Singapore.

McCarthy, J., 1888, 'Siam', *Proc. r. geog. Soc.*, 3, 117–34.

——, 1898, *Surveying and Exploring in Siam*, London.

——, 1902, *Surveying and Exploring in Siam*, London.

Majumdar, R.C., 1955, *Ancient Indian Colonization in Southeast Asia*, Baroda.

Malcom, H., 1839, *Travels in South-eastern Asia, embracing Hindustan, Malaya, Siam, and China, with Notices of Numerous Missionary Stations, and a Full Account of the Burman Empire, with Dissertations, Tables etc.*, 2nd edn., vol. 2, Boston.

Malleret, L., 1951, 'Les fouilles d'Oc-èo, rapport préliminaire', *Bull. École fr. extrême Orient*, 45, 75–88.

———, 1960, *L'Archéologie du Delta du Mékong, II, La Civilisation Matérielle d'Oc-Èo*, Publ. École fr. extrême Orient, 43, Paris.

———, 1962, *L'Archéologie du Delta du Mékong, III, La Culture du Founan*, Publ. École fr. extrême Orient, 43, Paris.

———, 1963, *L'Archéologie du Delta du Mékong, IV, Le Cisbassac*, Publ. École fr. extrême Orient, 43, Paris.

———, (ed.), 1968, *Un Manuscrit Inédit de Pierre Poivre: Les Mémoires d'un Voyageur*, Publ. École fr. extrême Orient, 65, Paris.

Man, H., 1868, *Supplement to Correspondence regarding the Comparative Merits of British and Native Administration in India*, Calcutta.

Marsden, W., 1811, *The History of Sumatra*, 3rd edn., London, (1st edn. 1783).

Maspéro, G., 1928, *Le Royaume de Champa*, Paris and Brussels.

Meilink-Roelofsz, M.A.P., 1962, *Asian Trade and European Influence in the Indonesian Archipelago between 1500 and about 1630*, The Hague.

Merrill, E.D., 1954, 'The botany of Cook's voyages', *Chron. Bot.*, 14, 5–6, 161–384.

Middleton, C.T., 1778–9?, *A New Complete System of Geography*, London.

Milburn, W., 1813, *Oriental Commerce: containing a Geographical Description of the Principal Places in the East Indies, China and Japan*, vol. 2, London.

Mills, J.V. (ed.), 1970, *Ma Huan, 'Ying-yai Sheng Lan'—the Overall Survey of the Ocean's Shores*, Cambridge.

Moreland, W.H. (ed.), 1934, *Peter Floris, his Voyage to the East Indies in the Globe 1611–1615*, London.

Nagai, J., 1959, *Japonica Rice: its Breeding and Culture*, Tokyo.

Neale, F.A., 1852, *Narrative of a Residence in Siam*, London.

Norman, H., 1895, *The Peoples and Politics of the Far East*, London.

Pallegoix, Monseignor, 1854, *Description du Royaume Thai ou Siam*, vol. 1, Paris.

Parmentier, H., 1918, 'Anciens tambours de bronze', *Bull. École fr. extrême Orient*, 8, 1–22.

Pelliot, P., 1903, 'Le Fou-nan', *Bull. École fr. extrême Orient*, 3, 248–303.

Phipps, J., 1823, *A Guide to the Commerce of Bengal*, Calcutta.

Purchas, S., 1625, *Hakluytus Posthumus or Purchas his Pilgrimes*, London, (also publ. Glasgow, 1905).

Raffles, T.S., 1817, *The History of Java*, vol. 1, London (reprinted 1965, Kuala Lumpur).

Ridley, H.N. 1911, 'An account of a botanical expedition to Lower Siam', *JSBRAS*, 59, 27–234.

Rumpf, G.E. (Rumphius), 1741–50, *Herbarium Amboinense*, vol. 5, Amsterdam (in Latin and Dutch).

*Sauer, C.O., 1952, *Agricultural Origins and Dispersals*, New York.

Schegel, G., 1903, 'Java: notions of the island from A.D. 414 till the beginning of the 13th century', *Toung Pao*, 4, 228–50.

*Sieveking, G. de G., 1954–5b, 'The distribution of wild species of rice', *Fed. Mus. J.*, 1 and 2, 140–3.

Smyth, H. Warington, 1898, *Five Years in Siam from 1891–1896*, 2 vols., London.

Solheim, W.G., 1964, 'Pottery and the Malayo-Polynesians', *Curr. Anthrop.*, 5, 360, 376–84.

———, 1970, 'Northern Thailand, Southeast Asia, and world prehistory', *Asian Perspectives*, 13, 145–62.

———, 1972a, 'An earlier agricultural revolution', *Sci. Am.*, 226, 4, 34–41.

———, 1972b, 'The "new look" of Southeast Asian prehistory', *J. Siam Soc.*, 60, 1, 1–20.

*Spencer, J.E., 1963, 'Migration of rice into Indonesia from mainland Asia, in Barrau', J. (ed.), *Plants and the Migrations of Pacific Peoples*, 83–9, Honolulu.

*Spencer, J.E. and Hale, G.A., 1961, 'The origin, nature and distribution of agricultural terracing', *Pacif. Viewpoint*, 2, 1, 1–40.

Stavorinus, J.S., 1798, *Voyage to the East Indies*, 3 vols., London.

Tachard G., 1686, *Voyage de Siam*, Paris.

Teeuw, A. and Wyatt, D.K. (eds.), 1970, *Hikayat Patani, the Story of Patani*, 2 vols., The Hague.

Temple, Sir Richard C. (ed.), 1905, *A Geographical Account of Countries round the Bay of Bengal, 1669 to 1679 by Thomas Bowrey*, Cambridge.

Tenison-Woods, J.E., n.d., *Geographical notes in Malaysia and Asia*, printed paper in Nixon collection, Kuala Lumpur.

Thomson, J.T., 1865a, *Some Glimpses into Life in the Far East*, 2nd edn., London.

———, 1865b, *Sequel to Some Glimpses into Life in the Far East*, London.

Triestman, J.M., 1970, 'Problems in contemporary Asian archaeology', *J. asian Stud.*, 29, 2, 263–371.

Turpin, F.H., 1771, *Histoire Civile et Naturelle du Royaume de Siam*, vol. 1, Paris.

Vajiranana National Library, 1915, *Records of the Relations between Siam and Foreign Countries in the 17th Century*, 2 vols., Bangkok.

van der Hoop, A.N.J.Th. à Th., 1932, *Megalithic Remains in South-Sumatra*, Zutphen.

———, 1934, 'Megalithic remains in Southern Sumatra', *A. Bibl. indian Archaeol.*, 7, 42–4.

van Heerkeren, H.R., 1958, 'The Bronze age of Indonesia', *Verh. K. Inst. Taal, Land, Volkenkunde*, 22.

van Leur, J.C., 1955, *Indonesian Trade and Society*, The Hague.

*Vavilov, N.I., 1926, *Studies on the origin of cultivated plants*, Inst. appl. bot. and pl. Breeding, Leningrad.

*———, 1951, 'The origin, variation, immunity and breeding of cultivated plants', *Chron. Bot.*, 13.

Vlekke, B.H.M., 1959, *Nusantara, a History of Indonesia*, The Hague.

Vogt., E.Z., 1968, 'Culture change', *International Encyclopedia of the*

Social Sciences, vol. 3, 554–8.

Wales, H.G. Quaritch, 1953, *Mountain of God*, London.

———, 1961, *The Making of Greater India*, London.

Watson, J.F., 1868, *Index to the Native and Scientific Names of Indian and other Eastern Economic Plants and Products*, London.

Watters, R.F., 1960, 'The nature of shifting cultivation, a review of recent research', *Pacif. Viewpoint*, 1, 1, 59–99.

Wavell, S., 1958, *The Lost World of the East*, London.

Wheatley, P., 1961, *The Golden Khersonese*, Kuala Lumpur.

———, 1965, 'Agricultural terracing: discursive scholia on recent papers on agricultural terracing and on related matters pertaining to northern Indochina and neighbouring areas', *Pacif. Viewpoint*, 6, 2, 123–44.

———, 1966, 'Refurbishing the nine cauldrons', a prefatory essay to Hermann, A., *An Historical Atlas of China* (reprinted Edinburgh), vi–xxix.

Wurtzburg, C.E., 1954, *Raffles of the Eastern Isles*, London.

NEWSPAPERS AND GAZETTES

Government Gazette, Prince of Wales Island, Singapore and Malacca, (official), George Town.

Jawi Peranakan, Singapore (in Malay, Jawi script).

Penang Register and Miscellany, George Town.

Perak Government Gazette, Kuala Lumpur.

Pinang Gazette, George Town.

Prince of Wales Island Government Gazette, George Town.

Singapore Chronicle and Commercial Register, Singapore.

Singapore Daily Times, Singapore.

Singapore Free Press, Singapore.

Singapore Free Press Weekly, Singapore.

Straits Settlements Government Gazette, Singapore.

Straits Times, Singapore.

Warta Kerajaan Negeri Sembilan.

Index